The New Teacher's Guide to Overcoming Common Challenges

This practical, hands-on guidebook offers support for your first years in the classroom by presenting strategies to overcome ten common challenges. Expertly curated by experienced educators, this book delivers quick access to timely advice, applicable across a range of educational settings. With contributions from National Board-Certified Teachers, National Teachers of the Year, and other educators involved in robust induction and mentoring programs, *The New Teacher's Guide to Overcoming Common Challenges* provides:

♦ Wise and practical tips from accomplished veterans and successful new teachers from across rural, suburban, and urban settings;
♦ Web access to an online teacher community and customizable resources created by the book's authors that can be quickly downloaded for immediate use in the classroom;
♦ Newly commissioned material that addresses the shift to remote learning brought about by the world pandemic.

Accessible and stimulating, this book is designed for a wide range of users, including PK-12 school districts who offer new teacher induction programming, traditional and alternative teacher preparation programs and teacher cadet programs, and individual in-service teachers. Don't face the challenges alone—learn from those who have been there!

Anna M. Quinzio-Zafran provides professional development for candidates and facilitators with the National Board Resource Center at Illinois State University and is a graduate faculty scholar in curriculum and instruction at Northern Illinois University.

Elizabeth A. Wilkins is professor of curriculum and instruction. She serves as the coordinator of the nationally recognized graduate career and professional development office for the Graduate School at Northern Illinois University.

The New Teacher's Guide to Overcoming Common Challenges

Curated Advice from Award-Winning Teachers

Edited by Anna M. Quinzio-Zafran and Elizabeth A. Wilkins

Routledge
Taylor & Francis Group

NEW YORK AND LONDON

First published 2021
by Routledge
52 Vanderbilt Avenue, New York, NY 10017

and by Routledge
2 Park Square, Milton Park, Abingdon, Oxon, OX14 4RN

Routledge is an imprint of the Taylor & Francis Group, an informa business

Library of Congress Cataloging-in-Publication Data
Names: Quinzio-Zafran, Anna M., editor. | Wilkins, Elizabeth A., editor.
Title: The new teacher's guide to overcoming common challenges : curated advice from award-winning teachers / edited by Anna M. Quinzio-Zafran and Elizabeth A. Wilkins.
Description: New York, NY : Routledge, 2021. | Includes bibliographical references.
Identifiers: LCCN 2020023944 (print) | LCCN 2020023945 (ebook) | ISBN 9780367612887 (hardback) | ISBN 9780367409791 (paperback) | ISBN 9781003105008 (ebook)
Subjects: LCSH: First year teachers--Handbooks, manuals, etc. | Teaching--Methodology--Handbooks, manuals, etc. | Teaching--Vocational guidance--Handbooks, manuals, etc.
Classification: LCC LB2844.1.N4 N485 2021 (print) | LCC LB2844.1.N4 (ebook) | DDC 371.102--dc23
LC record available at https://lccn.loc.gov/2020023944
LC ebook record available at https://lccn.loc.gov/2020023945

ISBN: 978-0-367-61288-7 (hbk)
ISBN: 978-0-367-40979-1 (pbk)
ISBN: 978-1-003-10500-8 (ebk)

Typeset in Palatino, Futura, and Rockwell
by KnowledgeWorks Global Ltd.

Visit the companion website: www.routledge.com/cw/Quinzio-Zafran

Dedication

This book is dedicated to our loved ones: Michael Zafran, Frances Wilkins, and Paul Gehrett.

■ Contents

Karen L. Kohler
Lydia Gerzel-Short

Teaming with the School Social Worker. 160
Nancy H. Betker

I'll Be There for You. 162
Heather Lyon

Five Key Strategies for Conducting Effective Parent–Teacher Conferences. 163
Pamela Kramer Ertel

Planning for Successful Parent–Teacher Conferences: A Navigation Guide 165
Leana R. Malinowsky

Conferencing with Parents: What Can We Do to Help Your Child
        Be Successful 167
Nedra L. Cossa

The Impact of a Phone Call 169
Alisa M. Ross

10 Student Assessment and Data Literacy 170
    Making Sense of Standardized Benchmark Assessments 170
    Daniel M. Frederking

    Assessment and Data Literacy. 172
    Amy Howerton

    Data Literacy for Teacher Teams 174
    Adam Larsen

    Don't Let Data Scare You Away! 175
    Harlee Morphis

    Lower Your Stress: Planning for Efficient and Effective Feedback
            to Students 176
    Monica Boehle

    The Power of Formative Assessments: Using Classroom Assessment
            Techniques (CATs) to Promote Learning. 178
    Altheria Caldera

    Good Enough? 179
    Julia Cuscaden

    The Sticky Note Formative Assessment: Three Uses 180
    Monica Boehle

    Eleven Practices to Consider When Grading 182
    Kelly Brooksher

    Now What? Making Instant Adjustments Based on Data. 184
    Joycelyn Forshay

    Portfolios: Progress Monitoring Over Time. 184
    Davon Clarke

◼ Preface

We started talking about developing a guide for new teachers in 2017. We listened to what our students in induction and mentoring were expressing as struggles for new teachers. We listened to other educators who worked with early career teachers. We listened to beginning teachers themselves, who shared their personal struggles as they moved from student teaching assignments to their first jobs. As we listened, we realized that we kept hearing about the same topics over and over again, so we asked probing questions to ascertain additional information concerning these challenges. After hearing the same concerns again and again, we knew that the time for listening was over, and that it was time to act.

We realized that the setting didn't matter. New teachers face common challenges whether they work in rural, suburban, or urban schools. We purposely developed the *New Teacher's Guide* around the ten most common challenges that educators experience. In addition to the *Guide* being compact and able to fit into a teacher's plan book, we designed this book to leverage a high tech, high touch approach in order to foster and build a community of practice around new teachers. Having the *Guide* gives readers access to participatory events like Twitter chats featuring the hashtag #newteachersupport, Instagram challenges, Facebook Q & A live events with authors, webinars that feature associated challenge topics, short podcasts, and social media infographics that act as reminders of important ideas in succinct and practical ways.

What makes the *Guide* unique is that it:

- ◆ Includes a variety of curated advice from practitioner voices (accomplished teachers and successful new teachers). Practitioners from rural, suburban, and urban settings share their practical tips based on real classroom/school experiences along with their wisdom in an effort to give back to and strengthen the profession.
- ◆ Contains web access to customizable resources created by the *Guide's* authors that can be quickly downloaded for immediate use in the classroom. www.routledge. com/cw/Quinzio-Zafran
- ◆ Provides traditional and alternative teacher preparation programs and teacher cadet programs an easy-to-read, supplemental, or primary resource that is affordable and directly relates to authentic practice, based on common challenges in today's classrooms.
- ◆ Affords PK-12 school districts who offer new teacher induction programming an accessible text to stimulate dialogue about practice and problem-solving common challenges.
- ◆ Addresses the shift to remote learning brought about by the world pandemic. We included a chapter to capture curated advice on how teachers can make that shift.

We hope that you will use this guide as inspiration to become part of the larger movement to support new teachers as they enter the profession. We encourage new teachers to share their concerns and celebrate their successes with others who want to shape the future of teaching. Become part of this community of practice by starting with ten common challenges.

Anna and Beth

Chapter 1

Teaching During a Pandemic

Cultivating Resiliency in Times of Crisis

Tonia Holmes-Sutton, EdD, NBCT
Nevada State Director for Teach Plus
NBPTS Board Director
Twitter: @tholmessutton
LinkedIn: www.linkedin.com/in/toniaholmessutton

It wasn't long after Governor Sisolak issued a Declaration of Emergency in the State of Nevada that the closure of all public, charter, and private schools was announced. It was Sunday, March 15, 2020. Nevadan teachers posted on social media about the school closures, wondering and worried about how they would lead and serve students and families in a crisis that the World Health Organization had declared a global pandemic. Novel coronavirus (COVID-19) was anticipated to be the worst pandemic virus since 1918, when an H1N1 virus infected nearly 500 million people worldwide.

As teachers networked and collaborated with one another to ensure that the needs of their students were met, they discovered that the systemic inequities that were ever present in the teaching and learning communities of the state's urban and rural districts were now exponentially magnified. Unable to return to the schools that served as safe havens to hundreds of thousands of students throughout the state, teachers learned that children and families weren't necessarily sheltered, *safely*, at home. With the closure of the schools came the closure of Nevada's casinos and all nonessential businesses – and the immediate loss of nearly 300,000 jobs, many of which employed students' families. Contending with incredible financial losses to their households, families were anxious about food insecurity and shelter, while also being concerned about becoming teaching partners to their children's teachers. Teacher leaders readied themselves to meet the unanticipated needs of students and families and orchestrated integrated community supports to provide essential resources to the state's 425,000 students.

Southern Nevada, home to nearly 75 percent of Nevada's residents, found teachers initiating community resource pages on social media to provide and deliver food to students and families that weren't near the school district's food distribution locations. Teacher leaders, some of whom served as Fellows in the Teach Plus Nevada Teaching Policy Fellowship, formed coalitions with families and community partners in successful advocacy for additional locations for food distribution in communities of high need. They also designed professional learning communities within and across school sites and grade levels to address the expectations of remote learning, lesson planning, and networking as well as to problem solve the challenges of student engagement. They also offered social-emotional support to one another in the most uncertain and stressful times of their teaching careers. Partnering with family members, who prior to COVID-19 may have entrusted academic responsibility to the schools, teachers held family meetings and one-on-one sessions with family members, via video platforms and cell phones, to help them become more adept at supporting their children's learning at home. Fueled by purposes and passions that had led them to education as a career, teacher leaders forged collegial relationships across state lines and engaged in national professional learning opportunities provided by leading education organizations, national and international educational coaches, and teaching colleagues with expertise in diverse content areas. They discovered that they were far more resilient than they had ever imagined they could be in the face of such adversity. And while caring for the needs of their own families, as well as that of their students, they engaged in systems advocacy and held policy discussions with members of the State Board of Education and the State and Deputy Superintendents of Public Instruction to reconceptualize teaching and learning in the digital divide.

Empowered by one another's courageous leadership and grace, they embraced leadership roles not officially assigned to them, and they designed and redesigned teaching and learning spaces that reimagined professional responsibility, professional learning, and professional designations. Teachers became the leaders that they desperately needed to address persistent challenges of equity and access with regard to technology, Internet, and learning opportunities, as well as to attend to students' physical, mental, and social–emotional well-being. They navigated social distancing to assist families in managing the stress and anxiety of students struggling to understand the rapidly changing circumstances of their daily lives. They "adopted" high school seniors whose hopes for proms, senior trips, and graduation ceremonies had been dashed. They led and served with a commitment to compassion.

Teachers recognized that the resiliency they'd cultivated during these unprecedented times would not return them to a "normal" they'd known, but it would prepare them for a newly constructed reality that demanded that educational equity and access be afforded to all students regardless of their status or station in society.

The pandemic has created many uncertainties and challenges. This may be our new "normal" for a while. As a new teacher, your commitment to working with students and families to meet their needs has never been more important. Be willing to reach out for support. Collaborate with colleagues. Look for ways to problem solve to address inequities and embrace opportunities to cultivate resiliency.

Remote Learning: Dismantle the World and Re-Create It

Clint Whitten
Seventh Grade English Teacher/Blacksburg Middle School
Montgomery County Public Schools, VA
Twitter: @TeacherWhitten

Remote teaching paired with a pandemic allows us to change the systemic problems in education. As Shirley Chisholm writes, "You don't make progress by standing on the sidelines, whimpering and complaining. You make progress by implementing ideas." Advice is ever-changing. However, the wisdom in listening to what you and your students need is never changing.

This is our chance to refresh what the root of education means, and to me, that is discovery. What can we discover about the world, ourselves, and about relationships during this new era of remote learning? Allow yourself to create an online curriculum with students' voices being the heart. What policies will you create together? We have the opportunity to think about what the system of education looks like if we redefine it.

During Emergency Remote Teaching, policies and structures change constantly. It is our job to be flexible, understanding, and vulnerable. Remember that human beings are behind both sides of remote learning. My Google classroom is now a place for television show suggestions, daily quotes, tips on how to build planes, and so on…all driven by students. I host weekly Zoom meetings because students need to see their teacher. I respond to student emails as soon as possible. We have to accept vulnerability and relationships now more than ever in education.

Remote learning is exhausting. Rely on your colleagues and share resources. I have simple goals for my students: Read and write about whatever they can access. Simple goals allow clear learning objectives. Remote learning exposes even greater equity issues. This type of learning disproportionally affects low-income families, particularly Black and Brown students. Therefore, you must provide tools specifically for those families. All students do not have the Internet, caregivers helping them work, or basic human needs. A paper packet will not help these students learn. Give them a book, a project (including the materials), or an independent study. Trust that you know your students.

This is not an academic crisis. This is a world health pandemic. Understand you and your students are human, and the concept of any remote learning must be student driven. Create a world wherein students are not given tests but are given chances to genuinely understand and explore the world.

But First ... Relationships

Shannon Rice
Special Education Teacher
Jefferson Central School District, Jefferson, NY
Twitter: @SRice498

When I began my journey into teaching, I never imagined that I would be trading YouTube videos of goats wearing pajamas with students to make them laugh. Teaching remotely due to a global pandemic has changed everything. I have decided to focus on what is most important: Relationships with my students.

As I made the shift to emergency learning, questions about standards, curriculum, and workload mounted. The way I prioritized was to focus on my students first. I have had to find new ways to communicate with my students and families on a daily basis. Emailing, phone calls, posting to online platforms, and sending greeting cards through the mail have all become regular practice. The social and emotional health of students is my priority. Teachers should identify what their priorities are, and focus on those elements first.

I check with every student regularly to see how they are doing. Do they need anything? How are they spending their time? Are they getting fresh air? What about managing emotions? These questions are much more important than reducing fractions, balancing chemical equations, or spelling words with the "-tch" pattern. I trade opinions about movies and TV shows. I ask about pets, siblings, and hobbies. Sometimes I just listen. I make sure my students know that I am still here for them, and that I care. Teachers need to ask questions, listen, and be "real" with their students.

My students know I'm not upset if they don't complete an assignment. I'm not mad that they email me at 10:00 pm instead of 10:00 am. I'm just happy they are communicating with me. Fostering relationships with students will pay greater dividends than any instructional technology or remote learning tool in our arsenal. These relationships will allow me to help my students emerge from this extraordinary experience and continue to grow as amazing young people. I'm putting relationships first.

A Shift in Our Perspective

Julie Padilla
Social Studies Teacher and Literacy Specialist
John V. Lindsay Wildcat Academy Charter School, Bronx, NY
www.linkedin.com/in/padilla-j-julie

While COVID-19 has caused us to experience a world of difference in our personal lives, we are also grappling with a shift in our own professional approaches. As educators, we are used to helping our students in person, giving them that smile that reassures them, and just being there for them. We need to take these same skills and translate them into support that can be felt through remote learning.

Teachers, we need to do away with whatever assumptions we have. Some of our students are coming from diverse backgrounds. The way our students are encountering the realities of this pandemic may be entirely different from what we know as individuals. We need to be continuously conscious of this. We also need to be realistic about our students and the goals we set for them. With this information, we can do our very best to provide that positive reinforcement they need. Letting our students know it is okay if they are having trouble, to continue to ask questions and make mistakes is essential. What we can do as their support system is what comes naturally to us as educators. We need to applaud our students' successes. We need to continue to acknowledge students for their growth. We need to celebrate our students and allow them to enjoy their time learning. Most importantly, at the end of the day we need to remember they are kids trying to navigate this world the best they can.

While these are tasks we are used to doing in the classroom, it can easily become something we forget while teaching remotely. Keeping these ideas at the forefront in our daily approach is vital and allows for remote learning to occur successfully.

Less Is More

Jennifer Jaros, NBCT
EL Teacher at Holmes and Hatch Schools
District 97, Oak Park, IL
Twitter: @JarosEsl

Unless remote learning is a part of the regular school curriculum, it will be used during less than ideal times. Remember: *Less is more*. I do not mean lowering expectations or quality of instruction, but the quantity of work needs to be differentiated. Social–emotional needs must be met before addressing academic learning. Even though I cannot physically share the same space and breathe the same air, I am still connected to my students and must nurture those bonds. This relationship may look and feel drastically different, but I am still their teacher and they are my beloved students.

As students are literally learning from home, the home life of each student must be considered. From the availability of technology, Internet, and basic supplies to parental supervision, physical/emotional safety, and parents' ability to assist with work due to work schedules, caretaking responsibilities, and language proficiency all play roles in the reality of remote learning for each student. I made parents aware of resources available through my district, including technology and Internet. In addition, I shared information on food and financial resources from the district as well as the larger community.

What I wish I had known at the beginning of remote learning:

- Remind parents that their best is more than enough.
- Collaborate with grade level, specials, and all resource/support teachers.

- ◆ Use virtual lessons as a way to teach academics and connect socially. This is healthy for both teachers and students.
- ◆ Remote teaching is not simply teaching through technology; it is a novel way of teaching, learning, and connecting.
- ◆ Grant yourself grace and space as you learn the new craft of remote teaching!

Delivering Quality Remote Instruction

David Perrin, EdD
Assistant Principal and Instructional Coach
Rochelle Township High School, Rochelle, IL
Twitter: @DavePerrin4

Like educators nearly everywhere, my colleagues and I have seen our instruction impacted by the COVID-19 pandemic and concomitant shift to remote learning. For new teachers, remote learning mirrors many of the challenges they already face. In my experience, the teachers, both new and veteran, who thrive during remote learning engage in three behaviors that allow them to continue to deliver quality instruction.

Successful remote learning teachers maintain and continue to build relationships with both students and colleagues. Teaching is a social activity, and the most impactful teachers are often the ones who work to understand their students' personal needs and interests. Remote learning makes relationship building more difficult, but it's important for teachers to find ways to connect personally with students during video chats, email, or other means. It's also important to provide a medium for students to interact with one another. Encouraging student engagement during remote learning can be a real challenge and building and maintaining strong relationships with students will help them feel invested and accountable.

They uphold standards but adjust expectations to provide grace and flexibility in how students demonstrate mastery. Remote learning exacerbates financial and social inequities, and it is vital to differentiate instruction and prepare materials for students both with and without technology. Remote learning also restricts curriculum. Teachers cannot possibly replicate every classroom experience for remote learning, so it is important to prioritize learning over compliance, minimize and create flexible assignments and due dates, and focus most on the standards that will promote students' success at their next level of education.

They embrace professional development and share liberally. Teachers who already utilized technology and elements of online learning or a flipped classroom are advantaged during a period of remote learning, and their students also experience a more seamless shift. Out of necessity during the pandemic, many other teachers experimented with new methods and technologies that may continue to prove valuable upon return to a traditional classroom environment. My district has used a district-wide "Teacher Resources" Google Classroom for several years, and during this period of remote learning it quickly became a clearing house for teachers to share e-learning instructional ideas with one another.

Tailor Your Remote Instruction to Meet Students' Needs

Sara Curran, EdD, NBCT
Fourth Grade Teacher
Community Unit School District 308, Oswego, IL

As I reflect on this unprecedented experience of remote learning, the most essential piece of advice I can give is to know your audience. To be successful, I have to be cognizant of students' home situations, amount of parental support, access to technology, achievement levels, and social–emotional needs. Promoting student reflection pieces, administering student surveys, and keeping detailed academic records are extremely important to address my students' needs in this remote environment. I would recommend collecting these pieces of student data promptly to provide beneficial communication and assignments for each student as well as to differentiate learning effectively. Flexibility and a student-centered approach are key!

When structuring curricula and assignments, I have also found it imperative to collaborate with my colleagues. Together, we have been able to provide students with varied experiences, accommodate for students' Individualized Education Programs (IEPs), and develop enrichment opportunities. We have also been able to combine ideas and assist each other with sifting through the barrage of available resources. We have considered various learning styles by incorporating video tutorials, differentiated levels of text, online games, read alouds of stories, and creative activities. If planning with colleagues is not possible, I would recommend joining social media groups with teachers of similar subjects. Ask for help! We are all in this together!

The lack of in-person contact makes it challenging to motivate and connect with students during remote learning. Hosting class meetings for younger students and small-group discussions for older students supports their social–emotional well-being and encourages valuable interactions in the remote learning environment. In addition, providing enticing reading topics, choices in activities, clear expectations, and constant feedback are vital to student motivation and academic success. I look for ways to connect with individual students whenever possible. A few simple words can go a long way!

Although remote learning definitely presents a new challenge, remember: We can do this!

Four Principles to Guide Remote Learning

Dr. David Carroll, NBCT
Maplebrook Elementary School/Madison Jr. High School
Naperville Community Unit School District 203, Naperville, IL

When faced with uncertainty in the spring of 2020, our school fell back on several tried-and-true principles to help us meet our students' needs. First, never assume that you know a student's motivation for learning. We found that many students did not have Internet access, their parents were working from home, or their siblings were sharing the same electronic resources. These factors prevented many students from participating fully in remote learning, though we falsely assumed they were uninterested in learning.

Second, communication is key. We found that many teachers were unknowingly scheduling overlapping meetings. Also, some teachers were contacting parents to report student nonengagement, while IEP case managers were recommending that students purposefully limit their remote work to only reading and math. Without communication, many teachers were wasting time tracking down students unnecessarily. In response, we established a shared document to communicate learning modifications and meeting schedules to all staff members.

Third, embrace differentiated learning. I used a variety of activities and assessment methods prior to remote learning, including experiential, interactive, and online-based activities. I had already established a routine of submitting electronic assignments each week, so students easily continued their online assignments as before.

Fourth, use your tools appropriately. Group meetings (like Zoom) should never be used as a lecture tool. Instead, they are an opportunity for students to interact and contribute. Formative games like Quizlet and Kahoot are great for recalling information, while PearDeck and FlipGrid allow for deeper analysis. Used properly, students can remain engaged, have fun, and continue their learning while at home.

Our Best Is Enough

Ms. Leana Malinowsky
Elementary Educator/Reading Specialist
Pvt. Nicholas Minue School, Carteret Public Schools, Carteret, NJ

Even with 12 years of teaching, making the shift to remote instruction has been one of the most challenging transitions I've experienced. The advice I would give to new teachers is the same advice I've been practicing. It's fine to feel upset or frustrated. Allowing myself the time to acknowledge my feelings provides me with energy to be my best when I teach each day.

I've also promised myself that I would take this situation as an opportunity to learn about various programs and platforms to help implement online instruction. Personally, exploring these areas would otherwise not have been on my "to-do" list; however, I am learning more than I ever expected with ideas to incorporate when returning to in-person learning. New teachers should also view this as an opportunity to explore new options, strategies, and ways to connect with students.

Differentiation, already important in my practice, has become even more critical. This unprecedented time has required me to reevaluate what instructional delivery looks like. I take each student's individual circumstances at home into consideration. I communicate with families frequently throughout the day what they need from me to be successful. New teachers should embrace their knowledge of technology and creativity while considering the needs of individual students and including personal experiences whenever possible.

I continue to explore ways I can teach students so that they relate to the material and feel a connection to the instruction while accessing topics I show them daily. Having to think outside the box for keeping learning authentically relevant through this experience has made me a stronger teacher and reminds me that students learn and grow more when content is meaningful to them. New teachers should embrace these opportunities to connect with students to grow as educators and become confident they are doing their best, and their best is enough.

What We Learned From the COVID-19 School Closings

Susan "Ernie" Rambo, PhD, NBCT
Programs Coordinator
Nevada National Board Professional Learning Institute, Las Vegas, NV
Linked In: https://www.linkedin.com/in/susanmrambo/
Facebook: Ernie Rambo
Twitter: @RamboTeacher
Instagram: ramboteacher
Websites:
http://www.nationalboardinstitute.com
http://www.ramboteacher.com/
https://www.ecet2sw.com/

Teachers in Las Vegas, Nevada, learned of their schools shutting down to prevent the spread of COVID-19 at the last minute, with no time to prepare students or to determine which students had technology or Internet access. There was no time for making pedagogical shifts, establishing Zoom accounts, or setting up Google classrooms. On a Sunday night, while preparing for the next week's lessons, teachers learned that all schools would be closed starting Monday and were informed to not engage in teaching or contacting their students until directed by their schools.

On the first day of closure, teachers created and joined virtual professional learning networks to share what they were learning about the shutdown. When could they start teaching? When would they see their students' faces again? Where could they see the packets that were being distributed to students? Was adequate food being handed out? How would teachers connect with their students? How would teachers connect with students lacking Internet access or without adequate experiences with technology to learn in an online environment? The immediate actions of the teachers, directed by the school district to wait for instructions rather than devise methods for remote instruction, demonstrated how educators are qualified and resourceful in finding ways to meet the needs of their students.

Three lessons we learned from the COVID-19 school closures:

♦ Developing strong connections with students and families provides a stronger foundation for adapting to unexpected situations.
♦ Teachers can and should determine their professional learning pathways.
♦ Teachers play a pivotal role in educating the community on how to address inequities that impact student learning.

Connections with students and their families help teachers determine the directions to take in planning instruction, assessing, and reflecting on student learning. Early in the school year, many teachers created multiple methods of communicating with their students' families. Families felt comfortable using these methods to communicate with teachers. Establishing and sustaining two-way communication with students and their families at the start of the school year created an environment of trust and teamwork that supported learning through the school closure.

Well-intended decisions by the local school board and district superintendent for providing remote instruction placed many educators in a space where professional learning was needed immediately and immensely. Teachers utilized the flexibility of time found in remote teaching by attending free webinars hosted by the National Board for Professional Teaching Standards, the Center for Teaching Quality, and the American Institutes for Research. Virtual panel discussions, Zoom meetings, Twitter chats, and Facebook groups, created by teachers, provided spaces for sharing remote teaching strategies and encouragement. For many teachers, this was the first time they chose professional learning engagements outside of what had been provided by their schools. Teachers need not limit their learning to what their school or district provides. What teachers learned during the COVID-19 school closures is that they can (and should) direct their professional learning based on an analysis of students' and teacher's needs.

Inequities in education access were magnified upon school closure. Students in affluent sections of the school district adapted to family learning environments more smoothly than students who depended on public libraries (also closed during this time) or fast food restaurants (such as McDonald's) for Internet access. Enrichment packets created by the school district were distributed at several locations throughout the county and were also available online, yet not all parents had transportation to reach the distribution centers. Families with the fewest technology assets were more likely to have to work outside of the home during the time that packets and food were distributed and could not supervise their children's learning during regular school hours. Teachers advocated for their students' needs by speaking out through media outlets and speaking up to the school board. Inequities can be misunderstood and go unnoticed by those who are not part of the education system. It is not enough for a teacher to teach effectively. Teachers need to address education policies and practices as part of their work. When they speak, it is not only to criticize the inequities, but also to propose solutions to guide policy makers. Teachers teach everyone—their students, students' families, and those who establish policies and protocols in education.

Teachers' conversations during the COVID-19 closures included words of frustration, of anger, of disbelief, but they also spoke of optimism, of empowerment, and of redirection. Teachers cannot patiently wait for changes to take place in our education system. As we move toward reopening our schools, all teachers need to lead with informing policy makers of what educators have learned from the school closures—how concerns for inequity and the social–emotional needs of our students must be addressed in order for learning to take place. By demonstrating their ability to shift with changes that will improve education for all students, teachers will be the agents for effective systemic improvement. New teachers can play a significant role in assisting their colleagues in the use of technology to support learning during these shifts.

Chapter 2

Classroom Setup and Management

A Principal's Advice: Invest in Your Future

Jesse Kraft
Principal
Lutie Lewis Coates Elementary School, Fairfax County Public Schools, VA

We talk about classroom management like it is a hot topic primarily for new teachers. Not true! In this job, you will encounter veteran teachers who never quite got these management skills down. They can be positive people who are adequate teachers. They may even give you good advice and mentorship. But watch them closely. With loose procedures, weak follow-through, and unclear expectations for student behavior, these teachers are playing a constant game of whack-a-mole in their classrooms. Misbehaviors pop up throughout the day, every day, and they pause their teaching just as often to deal with the ongoing issues. It must be exhausting!

Pushing yourself to become a master at classroom management is not just about creating a positive learning environment for students—it is an investment in yourself. You will teach academics better if behavior problems are minimized. You will feel successful at the end of the day if you are not drained from dealing with misbehaviors. You will have a longer, more fulfilling career if you can be the inspiring teacher you always wanted to be. That IS the goal, right?

Here is my advice for becoming a skilled classroom manager:

♦ **Determine your expectations and communicate them so students can understand.** Think through everything. Can students call out answers without raising their hands when you ask questions or is hand-raising necessary? What should transition times look and sound like? It all starts with this: Figuring out exactly what you want and explaining it effectively to your students.

♦ **Create your management system and teach it explicitly.** Reteach as needed. Should there be a multistep procedure for what a student does when s/he arrives in the classroom? What should a student do when s/he finishes an assignment early and you are working with a small group? Do you have a warning system for when the class is too loud? You will develop these procedures and more. Your various procedures come together to form a system for how students manage themselves in your classroom. Define it, display it, teach it.

♦ **Reinforce the right behaviors.** Use words, body language, and gestures to let your students know they are on the right track. Did they line up quickly and quietly?

Let them know. Did they show improvement today when cleaning up? Notice it, let your students know. Nothing motivates like success.

♦ **Be consistent.** This is the most important thing to know. All the aforementioned actions will fail without consistent follow-through. If you declare that certain misbehaviors will be met with consequences, but you relent when it happens, the students will notice. If you are great with reminding the class about their volume in one class but you let it go in a later class, they will conclude (correctly) that your expectations are conditional. Since consistency is so crucial to your success, I recommend that any system you create in your class be as simple as possible. Simple processes are easier for you to manage.

♦ **Build personal relationships with each student.** When students feel that you care about them, they listen. You do not have to be a push-over in your efforts to build respectful relationships. Students want the safety of knowing that someone is in charge. When that authority figure shows them love, they conclude (again, correctly) that they are valued. When this happens, they respect and adhere to the system and work to meet the expectations. If they break a rule and experience consequences, they can recover. They realize that you care, your punishment was not personal, and you want them to succeed.

You can use the classroom management plan download to articulate your expectations to plan and self-reflect on your progress.

As you work on your management skills, remember what is at stake. If you can create and manage a positive and productive classroom environment, the stability and safety of the room bring out the best in your students. You also benefit because you spend your day focused on teaching.

Bottom line: Invest the time into developing and honing your classroom management plan. During your first years of teaching, by facilitating a well-managed classroom, you will have more time to unpack your curricula, find your place on your team, survive the evaluation process, establish parent communication, develop grading practices, and hone your instructional delivery. You will go through countless trial-and-error processes in all these areas. It will be easy to divert your focus from reflecting on and constantly refining classroom management practices. Do not let that happen! These skills will make or break you, so invest the time into mastering your management. You have a long career ahead of you—you may as well make it a rewarding one.

When It Comes to Classroom Management, Less Is More

Jana Hunzicker, Associate Professor
Bradley University, Peoria, IL

When I was in second grade, our classroom was home to an elf. Yes, an elf. Mr. Quiet was only eight inches tall, but he exerted a great deal of influence. On the first day of school, we found him perched on the chalkboard ledge, and each day he relocated to a new position.

Our teacher explained that Mr. Quiet liked students who talked with quiet voices. She told us that when he sat close to us, he was pleased with our behavior. A week later, with Mr. Quiet reclined on a bookshelf near my desk, I did not make a peep all day.

Of course, Mr. Quiet was just an inexpensive Christmas decoration. Even a bunch of seven-year-olds could see that he was just a toy, yet much like with Santa Claus, we hoped that maybe he was real. Through Mr. Quiet, our teacher found a way to encourage good behavior so that fewer consequences for misbehavior were needed. She understood that when it comes to classroom management, less is more.

To effectively manage a classroom, you do not need an eight-inch elf, but you do need three to five classroom rules, a list of progressive consequences, and examples of rewards for good behavior. You must also see yourself as an authority figure. But a well-managed classroom does not end there. Just as my teacher used Mr. Quiet, you will need a variety of strategies to motivate and coach students toward good behavior so that you can give fewer consequences.

The behavior management cycle (Canter, 2010) is one effective strategy for coaching students toward appropriate classroom behavior. First, give clear directions describing exactly what you want students to do. Then, have them practice. As soon as students begin, use behavioral narration to describe students who are doing exactly what you asked. For example, "Jamal is getting supplies for his group without talking; Group 3 is getting out their notebooks. Nice!" Such comments provide positive reinforcement for the students who are following your directions and prompt those who are not with an indirect reminder.

Behavioral narration will work for all but the most challenging students. These students will need individualized, more subtle cues. For example, if Hamed is telling a joke and misses your attempt at behavioral narration, try proximity. Don't say a word. Just walk over and stand nearby as you continue to supervise the rest of the class. Chances are Hamed will take the hint and save his joke for later. Another subtle-but-effective cue is "the look." Try this one from across the room. Just lower your chin, catch the offending student's eye, and hold her gaze. Her misbehavior is likely to stop without a word. For added emphasis, you can use "the voice." For example, when a student in Group 3 raises his arm to throw a paper wad across the room, simply say his first name using a firm voice. When he lowers his arm and gives you a sheepish grin, you can direct him to the recycling bin.

Only after using behavioral narration and subtle cues should you consider giving consequences. When you do, remember that less is more. Unless a student does something so dangerous or disrespectful that it warrants an immediate call to the office, begin with the lightest consequence on your list, like a warning or one minute after class. Progress to more serious consequences only if the misbehavior continues.

Although giving consequences is necessary for maintaining a well-managed classroom, it can temporarily make matters worse. Some students may talk back or escalate the misbehavior to impress their peers or to see what you will do. When you are tempted to give another consequence, don't forget that less is more. Try the broken record technique instead. When a student demands to know why she has been given a consequence, don't take the bait. Instead, simply keep repeating your direction—like a broken record: "Shelly, I expect to see you after class today." Once the student realizes that you will not be drawn into an argument, she is likely to relent.

Effective teachers find ways to encourage appropriate classroom behavior so that fewer consequences are needed. Even without an eight-inch elf like Mr. Quiet, behavioral narration and subtle cues are classroom management strategies you can use immediately. (You can download Mr. Quiet's Management Tips.) Classroom interactions are more enjoyable for everyone when you emphasize coaching over consequences. Because when it comes to classroom management, less is more.

Reference

Canter, L. (2010). *Assertive discipline: Positive behavior management for today's classroom* (4th ed.). Bloomington, IN: Solution Tree Press.

Creating an Effective Plan for Positive Behavior Management

Shannon Rice
Special Education Teacher
Jefferson Central School District, Jefferson, NY
Twitter: @SRice498

Part of designing the learning experience is planning for effective classroom management. The teacher's plan sets the tone for the rest of the school year. Management is often thought of as a list of rules and consequences. This format is reactive and often ineffective. Instead, consider teaching behavioral expectations proactively as a set of skills that students need to learn. Teachers don't punish students for not having a set of academic skills. Instead, we assess, teach, practice, assess, and reteach as needed to help a student progress. The skills of positive behavior should be approached in the same manner. A basic set of steps that are easily adaptable can set you on the path to creating a positive behavior management system.

1. Set between three and six clear expectations that will be universal for your class. These will apply no matter the location, the type of learning students are engaged in, or who the adult is. These are general guidelines, such as "Respect," "Safety," "Hard Work," and "Honesty." This will become the common language used when addressing behavioral expectations with students. Keep these ideas broad and basic.
2. Make a list of the different learning environments or situations that will regularly occur in your classroom. These could include entering the classroom, small group work, independent work, laboratory stations, or whole class activities. Choose situations that happen most frequently (daily or several times weekly). Create a chart listing your expectations down the left side, and your situations across the top. This downloadable chart is called a behavior matrix, and is now the heart of your classroom management plan.

3. For each situation, fill in your matrix with your expectations. For example, what will "Respect" look like during small group time? What about during independent work? Record concrete, observable items for each box. Include ideas such as returning materials to the appropriate location at the end of tasks, language to use when responding to peers in discussion, or how to handle common situations. All language should be positive (no "do nots").

   Many teachers will choose to create parts of the matrix with their students as a beginning-of-school activity. This is useful for building shared ownership of the learning environment. If you choose to do this, you should still complete a matrix yourself prior to working with your students so that you know what information should be included.

4. Plan to teach your students the desired behaviors. This can be done through brainstorming together, acting out or role-playing situations, or having students make posters depicting positive behaviors. Don't skimp on this part. Too often teachers, particularly as students get older, expect students to "already know" what is expected or assume that they should only need to be told once. Avoid simply providing a handout about behavioral expectations with other beginning-of-course paperwork. Teaching desired behavior is as necessary as teaching any academic skill.

5. Plan for practice and review. It is important for students to practice the behaviors you want to see, especially at the beginning of the year. Just like an academic skill, students need to practice and receive constructive feedback on their performance in order to improve. Ensure the behavior matrix is posted in an accessible location and referenced frequently.

6. Provide ongoing feedback to individual students. Feedback is critical, both for students who are demonstrating desired behaviors, and for those who need correction. Students who are demonstrating positive behaviors need reassurance and encouragement to continue. When providing corrections, do so in a way that is constructive, preserves individual dignity, and maintains a growth mindset. Address students individually, not in front of their peers. Help them understand the long-term benefits of these skills. Set individual goals and differentiate as needed.

7. Assess individual student progress with your behavior matrix and provide continued feedback throughout the year. A return to instruction and practice may be necessary, particularly during times of the year that are stressful, such as the holiday season or after a break. Documentation of assessment can also be helpful when discussing challenges with parents or with colleagues.

8. Have a reward system. Students of all ages should be acknowledged for their positive choices. Rewards do not have to be large or costly, often something as small as a smile, high five, or a sticker is all the acknowledgment a student needs. Give students the opportunity to determine how they would like to earn rewards based on your matrix. Providing ownership can motivate students to set high standards for themselves.

Classroom management of student behavior requires thoughtful planning and instruction but is well worth the investment. When students understand what is expected of them and receive regular feedback, they have a stake in the process. The result is a classroom that can focus on the importance of continued learning without distraction from widespread problem behaviors.

Make It Safe and Positive

Sarah Brown
First Grade Teacher
Fisher Grade School, Mahomet, IL

I never thought I could teach first grade. I was so scared of managing 20 primary students who are very different from the third graders that I was used to in student teaching. When I started out, I stuck to one thing that a previous teacher taught me: Build a relationship with each of your students. I learned that year how important it was to get to know my students beyond their test scores. Without a caring relationship between the teacher and student, I've found it is extremely difficult to develop any level of trust. Although I have adjusted my classroom management every year I have taught, I always keep our class community strong. During my third year of teaching, I had a student who was very challenging. I felt like a first-year teacher all over again, just trying my best to manage his behavior. I knew that what I was doing in class wasn't working like the years before. I had to stop myself and think about how I could maintain a positive learning space for this specific student. It was obvious that he didn't feel safe or comfortable, and I had to take the time to fix this. Every day was a new adventure with him, but before he left for summer that year, he looked up at me and said, "Miss Brown, I'm really going to miss you." He showed me again how a relationship with students can make all the difference.

Making Relationships Stick

Allison Krasnow
Eighth Grade Math Teacher
Berkeley Unified School District/Willard Middle School, Berkeley, CA
Twitter: @allison_krasnow
Blog: www.picrust.wordpress.com

Building positive relationships with all students is one of the most powerful things you can do as an educator. When students feel seen, listened to, and have a trusting relationship with you, classroom management gets easier while students' motivation and engagement increase. In my eighth grade classroom, I use customized stickers as one of my classroom management strategies. While I have multiple ways of praising students who are doing well and redirecting those who aren't, I find that my stickers are a powerful way to silently communicate with my students.

Why use stickers for silent communication with students? It's a way of giving feedback and encouragement without interrupting the flow of your lesson. Finding ways to allow all 30 of my students to feel seen and heard daily is a time management challenge. While students are working in groups, or independently, I can come over, stick a sticker on someone's hand, and walk away. While the student reads the message, I am already able to check in with another student.

When a student is off task, it's common to call out the student's name, asking him or her to stop doing something. Too often, these same students hear their names called out over and over, for things they are doing wrong. I work very hard to never say aloud, in front of the whole class, the name of a student who is off task. I believe that as much as possible, we should say students' names in front of the class for positive things. All students want attention. However, some only know how to get it through negative behaviors. By redirecting some negative behaviors silently, students often stop these behaviors because they aren't getting any public attention for them. I do a lot to support those students to reengage and am quite strict with my expectations and consequences. The following are the key components for how I use customized stickers as part of my classroom management strategy:

♦ I know that students need space when they are upset about grades or not doing well on an assignment from class. I am always there to support and help them, yet I recognize that teens are often not ready for assistance in that moment.

♦ I try to stay very aware of status issues in my classroom. I especially like to use the positive stickers for students who need positive recognition and who may not be getting it publicly or from their peers. More often, I use positive stickers for students who have struggled and persevered or for those who started class irritated at something and turned things around.

♦ I always hand out stickers by silently walking over to a student (or a group of students), sticking one on the outside of their hand and walking away. It may be followed by a squeeze of the shoulder or making eye contact as I walk away. Later, I may pull the student aside for a private conversation. However, in the moment, whether I am beaming with pride or really frustrated with off-task behavior, my demeanor is the same and I simply place the sticker on their hand.

♦ Students love them! THEY COME AFTER CLASS AND BEG FOR MORE, even seniors in high school! I try to keep them on their toes, never knowing what other phrases I have stashed away in my sticker drawer. I use them sparingly, and NEVER give them when someone asks for one. Receiving a sticker is always a surprise.

I created my stickers on the website VistaPrint. You can easily find coupons online. Download the directions.

Flexible Design for Optimal Learning

Cynthia Dawn Martelli, EdD, Associate Professor
Florida Gulf Coast University, Fort Myers, FL

> One cannot have a community of learners without having a positive instructional climate. Instructors help to create this climate by everything that they do, from the way they respond to student questions to the arrangement of the classroom chairs.
>
> —Alexa Darby, n.d.

A learning space is an essential aspect of a student's education experience. Flexible design takes a classroom from the traditional setting with individual desks and chairs to a less conventional design arrangement. Kayla Delzer (2015) describes this trend as a "Starbucks" environment. Once, while visiting her local Starbucks, she noticed people chose different seating options. Delzer herself always gravitated to the more comfortable seating, as others selected traditional tables and chairs. She liked having a choice in her seating and decided to bring this variety to her classroom. This more flexible arrangement gives students the freedom to choose the environment where they learn best. For example, if students work best sitting on a rug with a clipboard, then they would choose that option over another provided in the classroom. This would be very similar to the atmosphere in a Starbucks. Not all students learn in the same way. Having a choice where to sit and in what type of chair can make a difference (Grubbs, 2019).

Benefits of Flexible Design: The Five Cs

Your students will require environments that encourage discovery and deeper learning. Flexible design is fundamental to creating an environment of optimal learning for your students and consists of several benefits:

♦ **Choice:** Choosing where to work and with whom enables your students to have some control over their learning environment. By offering choice, you encourage them to consider their learning needs and preferences.

♦ **Collaboration:** When students change seats to work with a new group, you create conditions that encourage collaboration with peers. This classroom design offers the opportunity for students to pair up, work in small groups, or discuss as a whole class. By creating these various classroom environments, you then facilitate more collaboration and communication, which can enhance creativity and critical thinking.

♦ **Community:** Getting to know each other is key during flexible design. Your students are encouraged to share space, supplies, and perspectives when working with each other in different locations within the classroom and with a variety of design elements. Your students' learning environments should reflect those of the real world.

♦ **Commitment to Learning:** Learning environments can have a direct impact on your students' achievement. They can take an active role in their educational journey when provided with a choice as small as where they prefer to complete an assignment. You give them a sense of ownership that encourages them to be more invested in their own education.

♦ **Classroom Management:** A hidden benefit of flexible design can be stronger classroom management. You will need to develop clear rules and expectations with students as well as be consistent in their practice. Students who understand the daily routine will be empowered by the opportunity to have choices and are more likely to take responsibility for their learning.

Flexible design is more than simply having a variety of different, fun (e.g., beanbags, swivel, furry, and saucer) seats and spaces to meet in the classroom. It is about utilizing student voice, creating buy-in, heightening collaborative learning, and prioritizing students' needs concerning the environment in which they work. "Students know how they learn best. Give them credit for the knowledge they bring to the classroom and make them partners in the creation of a positive instructional climate" (Darby, n.d.). Flexible design can result in a more active, engaging, enthusiastic room of students learning. Download the steps to creating a flexible design in your classroom that will support your students' needs and interests.

References

Darby, A. (n.d.). Understanding universal design in the classroom. National Education Association. Retrieved from http://www.nea.org/home/34693.htm

Delzer, K. (2015, October 1). Why the 21st century classroom may remind you of Starbucks. *EdSurge*. Retrieved from https://www.edsurge.com

Grubbs, J. (2019, April 24). Finding a comfy place to learn. *The Fort Morgan Times*. Retrieved from https://www.fortmorgantimes.com

Building an Atmosphere for Trust: Doing Science

George Dewey, NBCT
Physics Teacher
Fairfax County Public Schools, Fairfax, VA

If I have learned anything from my students after several decades in the classroom, creating an ambience of trust is essential to our mission as teachers. Most recently, I have been teaching 10–12th grade students in a physics program that includes a class of ESOL (English for

Speakers of Other Languages) students—ten different countries, seven different languages—in a large northern Virginia public high school. Building an atmosphere of trust in the classroom is imperative for student success.

For starters, the **room arrangement** places students facing each other in assigned seats at long laboratory tables in eight teams of four. This conveys two important messages: (1) the expectation for purposeful communication and dialogue between students and (2) the course begins and ends in the laboratory. As Michael Shermer infers, science is a verb not a noun.

For me, and I suspect for most teachers, the "Happy New Year" greeting comes in September (August), rather than in January. Consequently, the most important day of the year is the **first day** of school because it sets the tone for the entire year. Therefore, since I want my students to know they will be performing the role of a scientist all year, we begin with a discovery activity on the very first day.

Establishment of trusting relationships must come first, though. Our school is scheduled around 90-minute blocks, so the initial 35–40 minutes of the first class are spent **visiting each** of my 28–32 students. I ask them to help me pronounce their names correctly, followed by a couple of short questions about their current math level and what they found easiest and hardest in their previous science courses. This helps me to better understand how to differentiate for these students. As I do these mini-interviews, the rest of the students are busy filling out a two-sided page with their course schedule and answers to questions like, "What do you enjoy doing when you have free time?" Or, "Describe the person who has meant the most to you in your life." I use this information to get to know the outside interests of my students.

The **science activity** that follows can be either a black box or mystery tube where students predict the arrangement of objects inside (Miller, 2014). Recently, investigating the physics of toys has been fun as well as challenging for the students. Students are asked to describe the physics principles that they think make the toy do what it does based on their observations. In all cases, students work in pairs with their elbow partner, diagramming their predictions on 24×30-inch whiteboards. Once all boards are displayed around the room, then the partners describe and share those predictions with the class. In this way, scientific ideas are explored, insights shared, and a respectful and trusting atmosphere is established between listeners and teams of presenters. This introduces the students to how they will, in teams of 2–4, similarly present lab data or problem solutions throughout the course.

Day two begins with **class rules**. Given a scenario like, "You are directing an important meeting with 25 of your friends. In a short time, your boss expects you to come to agreement on an issue of choice and report your committee's conclusion." With no discussion, each individual student is to write on a sticky note the most important rule she or he would tell the committee to follow to accomplish their goal as expeditiously as possible. The sticky notes are then posted anonymously on a sideboard in the room.

Only after they post do I explain why I asked them to do this. I then copy each comment on a page (see download), under what seems logical headings, for us to project and discuss the next day. When consensus is reached on major rules, I lead a discussion to come up with no more than three class rules, which become our rules for the year (see download). Each quarter we review their rules, though all I need to do when adolescent energy becomes too extreme, is remind them that these are their class rules, not mine. While each class has its own personality, when emotions or learning struggles overwhelm the best intentions of students, this sense of student agency has worked to help them compensate for their conflicted feelings or academic roadblocks.

Another benefit occurs in **testing situations**. Although some teachers unwisely choose testing time to grade papers/homework or use elaborate physical barriers to discourage cheating, I have found two simple steps work best: (1) all phones are stored in backpacks for the testing period and (2) I circulate continually during the test period, keeping vigil on each student at all times, plus giving personal assistance answering questions or giving hints, if needed.

These are a few of the effective ways I have used to build an atmosphere for trust in which each student can feel cared about and cared for. Students more easily accept the challenges involved when performing an experiment as a scientist does, exploring and predicting without knowing the answer in advance. Most labs are discovery rather than confirmatory in nature. This can become a powerful life lesson as well.

Reference

Miller, S. (2014). Modeling the nature of science with the mystery tube. *The Physics Teacher*, *52*(9), 548–551. doi:10.1119/1.4902200.

Building a Strong Classroom Community

Laura Roeker
University of Wisconsin–Madison, Madison, WI

Perhaps one of the most challenging aspects of being a new teacher is knowing how to build a strong classroom community. Taking the time to build positive relationships with and among students mitigates many of the classroom management issues that teachers often face. Here are some ways to build a strong classroom community:

- ◆ Start the year by telling students how excited you are to be working with them because you believe they will be the kind of students who will aspire to your classroom mission of leadership, kindness, and respect. Remind your students of this often throughout the year.
- ◆ Begin every day with a Morning Meeting (Kriete & Davis, 2014). It is a way for students to start their day on a positive note and practice crucial social–emotional skills they need for an engaging classroom culture.
- ◆ Play team-building games and emphasize kindness and positive support. For example, when playing a group juggle game, discuss what you expect out of students if someone drops a ball. You could encourage them to clap, then say, "It's okay, you'll get it next time," or pat the person on the back.

- Notice and consistently reinforce positive behavior you see. For instance, "I notice that Lenora is sitting quietly and ready to begin. Way to go, Lenora," or "Gabrielle and Xu managed their materials carefully during lab."
- Stand at the door and greet students as they enter your classroom. If age-appropriate, ask them to choose a high five, fist bump, handshake, or wave to start their day. Tell them how glad you are to see them at school today.
- Use appropriate humor with your students. Be light-hearted and have fun with them.
- Share vulnerabilities with your students to build trust. Acknowledge your personal obstacles by sharing stories of how you have had difficult times learning something new or struggled to get along with someone. Take these opportunities to describe how you used social–emotional skills to navigate those situations.
- Read books that matter. Select and read books about characters with complex lives that students can identify with or feel validated by. Expose them to materials that help them better understand the diverse world around them. Literature is a fantastic way to build empathy for others, discuss difficult topics, and develop social skills. Download the associated teacher resource for book ideas.
- Teach students kindness. You must teach students to be kind in all things that they do; for example, make eye contact and smile at each other when working in pairs or small groups, acknowledge classroom contributions with peers in age-appropriate ways, invite someone to sit by them at lunch. You must constantly be on the lookout for opportunities to reinforce kindness and redirect unkind behaviors.
- Contact all families within the first two weeks of school by phone and tell them how glad you are to be working with their child, if you have a self-contained classroom. For those who work with multiple sections of students, devise a plan for family outreach. Share one positive contribution the student made to your classroom. Continue to contact family members throughout the year when their child is successful, and make sure to tell the students when you do so.
- Connect positively with difficult students every day. Have them assist you in the classroom, find ways to show them that you genuinely care, and affirm them when they do something well. Often the students who have the hardest time at school need the most love and attention. Make your classroom a homeplace for these students (Love, 2019).
- Hold all students to high expectations. Be firm when you need to be. Be consistent for all students. Be fair in discipline and consequences.
- Close every class giving students a chance to reflect on the positive moments of the day.
- Think of ways to get your students' attention in a positive or neutral way rather than being punitive. Consider using proximity, a look, distraction, or having a student move to a new location instead of yelling at a student to stop a behavior.
- Clearly express your expectations. Before walking in the hallway, attending an assembly, starting a project, going on a field trip—anything—tell students clearly what you expect of them. When you see students meeting your expectations, offer approval.

References

Kriete, R., & Davis, C. (2014). *The morning meeting book* (3rd ed.). Turner Falls, MA: Northeast Foundation for Children.

Love, B. L. (2019). *We want to do more than survive: Abolitionist teaching and the pursuit of educational freedom.* Boston, MA: Beacon Press.

The Evolution of the Perfect Classroom Setup

Chelsea Marelle
Special Education Teacher
Simpson Elementary/Gwinnett County Schools, Atlanta, GA

The start of the school year can be overwhelming for new teachers, and you will probably spend hours after all the professional development meetings perfecting your classroom before the first day of school. I had the same urgency my first year of teaching. I spent hours setting up my classroom only to rearrange everything a million times. I learned quickly that a classroom setup in not meant to be concrete. Instead, it is a work in progress throughout the year that is flexible and always evolving to match the growth of your students. For example, I set up a beautiful reading corner full of books on CD, flexible seating, and pillows to welcome my first class. After school, I was so upset to find the pillows and books thrown around the space. It was in that moment that I realized I had to explicitly teach the expected procedures and expectations for using the different areas of our classroom. I removed the furniture and left only books for the next day. Then I sat my class down to talk about how disappointed I was in the mess left. Together, we came up with appropriate procedures and used role-play and repetition to learn them. When the students could independently perform the procedures, and I felt they were ready, I brought the furniture back as a reinforcer for taking care of our classroom materials.

Using SPACE Wisely

Lois A. Groth, PhD, Associate Professor
George Mason University, Fairfax, VA

Think back to your favorite classroom from your student days. Envision yourself standing at the door and peering inside. Remember how it felt to get a glimpse of all that space. Now you are the teacher responsible for creating the learning environment. When setting up learning environments, it is all about use of SPACE:

S is for Student Centered

Teaching is really about the students, not about the teacher. When setting up the space, think through the ways the classroom environment reflects a student-centered philosophy. How much of the space do "teacher things" take up and how much is left for the students? Teachers who minimize their own footprint in the classroom allow more space for students. The décor in the classroom needs to be purposeful for student learning. "Decorations" should be kept to a minimum—there will not be space for them.

P is for Perspective

Perspective pertains to point of view. Try to view the classroom space from your students' perspective. Sit in the student desks, on the floor at the meeting place, and at the tables. Where are your eyes drawn? What are the distractions? Be sure the things students must be able to see (e.g., boards) are visible from all vantage points in the space. Once students arrive, get down at their eye level and observe the flow in your space. Adjust the environment and/or routines to avoid traffic jams. Ask students for their input and suggestions about changes needed.

A is for Atmosphere

Just as it did when you were a student, standing at the door of the classroom and peering inside is a useful strategy for getting a sense of the atmosphere of the classroom space. Ideally, the space is inviting, making students want to enter and spend time there. Striking the balance between too much and too little is often a personal preference. Have someone else take a look at your space. Ask them how it makes them feel. It can be challenging to modify the "institutional" look and feel of the space. Fluorescent lighting often feels cold. Consider alternative forms of light such as table lamps, floor lamps, and/or twinkle lights (if permitted) around bulletin boards. You want the classroom space to be welcoming.

C is for Community

Community is developed through relationships. To build connections, we have to be able to meet face-to-face and eye-to-eye. This may be a meeting space where everyone can sit or stand in a circle, or it may mean a desk arrangement that allows everyone to see each other's faces. Community building is a shared process. Is there a place in the room where the students will be able to put their own stamp on the community? How will visitors to the classroom begin to understand the community just by looking at the space?

E is for Easily Organized

The key to keeping classroom space easily organized is to put the students in charge. This means that everything should have a place. Mark and label where materials go in ways that the students will be able to follow. If they are emerging readers, use pictures/icons. Build time into classroom routines to allow students to put things back where they belong. Keeping the space neat and organized builds community and makes the atmosphere more inviting. Making students responsible for keeping the space organized builds responsibility.

Effective classroom setup and management can be overwhelming. Download the Using SPACE Wisely Classroom Setup Checklist to help you use your SPACE wisely.

Fostering Classrooms as Safe Spaces

Candice Chiavola
English Teacher/Model Teacher
New York City Department of Education, Hackensack, NJ

As I enter my twelfth year as a high school English teacher, I continue to think about what makes me most proud in the work I do with my students. While I look forward to their academic success, what satisfies me most is when students let me know that our classroom is a safe space for them, defined as "a nurturing and emotionally supportive environment" (Vuckovic, Floyd, & Riley, 2019, p. 173).

It is important for students to feel welcome and comfortable being themselves in our classes. Some of my favorite teaching moments are when students let their peers and me see their most vulnerable selves, and often this is just when students are being unapologetically themselves. Their guards come down. They forget that they're in school, in a room full of people they don't know that well. So, I thought about what makes students feel comfortable in that way. Here are the principles that ground a safe classroom:

- **Be yourself.** Let students know what kind of person you are—likes, interests, and even flaws. Students are more comfortable being themselves when you are, too. I find myself answering students' questions with *I don't know, but I'll think about it and get back to you.* I'm not *the* authority on anything. I might be *an* authority, but that's different. But I'm myself—corny jokes, cat obsessions, and all.
- **Remind students that the classroom belongs to everyone.** It's not the teacher's space. It's *our* space, and everyone can move about it as necessary (within reason). I encourage students to quietly get up and take the pass if they need to use the restroom or throw their trash out when needed. This demonstrates that students are responsible and trustworthy. There's something unnatural about a space that's *too* regulated.
- **Be curious about your students.** On the second day of school, I have students complete surveys that ask for not only basic information but also fun questions that help me understand who they are. I also use this survey to learn what name or nickname(s) they use, what languages they speak, what pronoun(s) they prefer, and what they hope to get out of the class. Then I try to remember those names and pronouns.
- **Make your thinking and choices visible.** Students trust their teachers when they understand why they have made specific choices regarding work you are doing. Often, students ask *why are we doing this?* I don't get offended. I answer that valid question. Students trust teachers who are honest about their intentions/goals and are more likely to get on board with whatever they propose to try in class.
- **Provide space for student choice.** Sometimes, if a book hasn't gone over well, or students seem to be struggling with a particular activity, I ask them why and what we could've done instead. Or, since I have some freedom in the curriculum, I ask the students, through informal polls or online surveys, what they'd like to read,

either specific titles or genres. Students are more invested in the work and feel more included when their opinion(s) play a role.

♦ **Listen to your students' concerns.** Teachers don't always know best. The older I get, the more disconnected I feel from my students' lives or the pop culture they like. So, when something isn't working, or they aren't getting it because it's more removed than you thought, *listen*. Adjust. Don't get offended. Use their suggestions to grow and improve. Let your students know their voices matter.

♦ **Allow space for dissent.** Especially in these charged political times, this can feel overwhelming. At the start of a new school year, I make clear to students that this is a space in which we can have discussions and disagree, but disagreement must always be respectful. Not everyone has had the same experiences. I often begin the year watching Chimamanda Ngozi Adichie's TED Talk, *The Danger of a Single Story*, to set the tone that we should avoid stereotyping and sweeping generalizations when we talk about race, gender, sexuality, religion, or life in general. As teachers, it's our responsibility to address insensitive or misguided comments without shutting students down. This might be the most difficult, but important, thing we do. I try to address problematic comments in the moment, so other students who may feel attacked feel they have an advocate. I find myself saying something like, "I think it's important to be careful that we don't generalize." Or "We should remember that some of the people in this room haven't had the same experience you have."

Teaching is not without its difficulties, and the emotional labor can be taxing. When teachers make efforts to foster safe classrooms, students will be happier and more diligent, and teachers will have opportunities for pedagogical and emotional growth. You can download the accompanying graphic organizer, Fostering Safe Classrooms, to plan methods and approaches in creating and cultivating classrooms that are safe for all students.

Reference

Vuckovic, M., Floyd, B., & Riley, J. (2019). The first year colloquium: Creating a safe space for students to flourish. *Journal of the Scholarship of Teaching and Learning, 19*(2), 172–186. doi:10.14434/josotl.v19i1.23517.

Substitute Folder Essentials

Christine Beardslee
Reading Interventionist
Private Nicholas Minue Elementary School, Carteret, NJ

This guide is set up to help you create a quality substitute folder. The following recommendations are tried and true and have assisted many substitutes throughout my 20-year career. Being detail oriented and organized will ensure the safety of your students and that your substitute has the tools needed to have a successful day with your class.

Here is what your folder should include:

- Class list and seating chart: This should be in the very front of your folder. It is crucial for taking attendance and tracking students during a fire drill or lockdown.
- Your detailed lesson plan: List your activities for each period or subject area, along with specific directions on the work you are assigning and how it is to be completed.
- Classroom work and materials: Provide all classroom work and materials labeled with specific directions on how you would like the work completed. Is the work to be completed as a whole group? In pairs? Independently?
- Homework: Would you like your homework from the previous day collected and corrected? Would you like the substitute to notate who did not return their homework?
- Teacher schedule: Be sure to include a map of the building and any duties you may have such as bus duty, hall duty, or lunch duty. If your class assembles in a general location such as on the playground or in the cafeteria, be sure to include this information for your substitute.
- Class schedule: Make sure it is detailed and explains any specific daily routines, especially student dismissal procedures.
- Specials: If your students have any specials such as Music, Art, Technology, and World Language, this should be in your lesson plan as well as the location of the classroom, so the substitute knows where to drop off and pick up the students.
- Additional services: If you have any students who are pulled out for additional services such as Speech, Basic Skills/Intervention, Physical Therapy, Occupational Therapy, and/or Counseling, notate it in your lesson plan. Include the specialist's name and the time frame the student will be working with him/her.
- Student allergies/medications: If you have students with specific allergies such as nuts, milk, or gluten, this also needs to be documented. Does the student have an EpiPen or medications in the nurse's office? Should an emergency occur, this information needs to be disclosed. Students may need their medication administered the same time every day, so consistency is key.
- Your classroom management plan: How do you monitor student behavior? How do you expect the substitute to handle student misbehavior? Is there a seasoned grade-level colleague they can go to for support or send the student to? If the situation is of a serious nature, how should the substitute handle it?
- Helpers: Provide the names of three helpful students who know your routines and procedures, where to find particular items in your classroom, and how to get around the school building such as the cafeteria, nurse, or main office.
- Potential student conflicts: You will want to let the substitute know if you have any challenging students who need to be watched intently as well as any students who should not be near each other. Giving the substitute a heads up will help him/her take preventative measures so no problems arise.
- Contact list: Provide a list of important contacts and their phone extensions in your folder as well as post them near your classroom phone. Your list should include the school's secretary, nurse, guidance counselor, principal, vice principal, and an experienced grade-level colleague.
- Lockdown/Fire drill procedures: Include your school's detailed plan for fire drills and lockdowns, along with a map, class schedule, and parent contact list, should an evacuation occur.

- List of student birthdays: If any of your students are celebrating a birthday, be sure to give the substitute a heads up. If you typically give out something to commemorate student birthdays, leave the item for the teacher to distribute so the child does not feel left out.
- Bathroom policy: How many students do you allow out at a time? Do they sign a ledger? Take a bathroom pass?
- Feedback form: Leave a spot within your folder to allow your substitute teacher to provide appropriate feedback on how the day went. Have them identify what went well and any problems that occurred during the day.
- Classroom changes: Be sure your folder is always accurate and up to date should there be changes to your schedule or class roster.

By including all this information in your substitute folder, you are ensuring the safety of your students, making sure your classroom runs as smoothly as possible, and setting students up for a productive day of learning. Download the checklist so you can prepare your substitute folder.

Chapter 3

Culturally Responsive Teaching

Unpacking the Mysticism: Culturally Responsive Teaching as Deliberate Practice

Saroja R. Warner, PhD, NBCT, Senior State Technical Assistance Director
WestEd

I recently rediscovered an article from the newspaper of a school where I taught, in which seniors chose to spotlight teachers who "made a difference," and there I was, one of six. The title was "It's a Kind of Magic." The author, a former student of mine, wrote about his experiences in my class, ending with "in 20 years, when most of us think back on teachers who have impacted us the most, Ms. Warner will certainly be at the top of the list."

I have always thought of myself as a culturally responsive teacher. Reading the article and reflecting on my practice got me wondering if the sentiments conveyed in the article are attributable to that practice. Do these sentiments ring true more than a decade later? What do they remember about my teaching? And, whatever I got right then, was it magic or much more deliberate than that?

Thanks to social media, I reconnected with over two dozen of my former students to explore these questions. They are a diverse group: Racially, ethnically, and linguistically, in relation to gender, sexual orientation, socioeconomic background, and ability. After speaking with them, some of whom are well into their thirties and married with children, and reflecting on my practice over the years, I came to appreciate that culturally responsive practice is actually not magic. It is deliberate and intentional. There are no quick tips or tricks to offer for enacting culturally responsive teaching, because it is a journey. But I learned a lot from my former students that continues to resonate today, many years later.

Enthusiasm is contagious. I consistently heard from my former students that they remembered me first and foremost as someone who "knew her stuff" and got them excited about learning it. Every great teacher invests time and resources in growing their content knowledge. Culturally responsive teachers consistently find ways to connect content to students' lives, their histories, and cultures. But the x-factor pedagogically, perhaps the magic of it all, is bringing the energy and enthusiasm every day to your classroom. Most of us teach what we are passionate about. My students remembered how excited I was about what I was teaching, and it made them excited, too. Every lesson you plan, be sure that you not only connect the curriculum to students' experiences and interests, but that you let your enthusiasm shine boldly.

Teach more than just the content. Although I taught high school social studies, I deliberately and intentionally incorporated ways to develop students' critical thinking and social and emotional skills in my lessons. It was heartwarming, to say the least, to hear my former students reflect on the life lessons and skills they developed back then.

One former student, who today is a senior leader in a global industry, said, "I didn't see it then, but appreciate now all the skills you taught us. Not about U.S. history per se, rather skills I relied heavily on during college and day-to-day in my job. The group activities in your class and the skills we learned, like managing across difference and working as a team, were foundational. Over the years I've tapped on those skills and have grown them to be able to succeed in my work today."

Another said, "It was so different in your class because you pushed us to question. I was used to believing whatever teachers and books told me, and you disrupted that whole way of being for me. I admit it was uncomfortable at first. But I get it now. You taught us how to critique and challenge the status quo. That just because things are the way they are doesn't mean they have to stay that way. That has been powerful for me in my life."

In addition to critical thinking skills, other skills they called out and attribute to their happiness and success today are self-awareness, confidence, resilience, managing conflict, willingness to take risks, and awareness and appreciation of cultural diversity. Developing these types of skills is essential in the work of culturally responsive teaching.

Relationships Matter. I don't think it's a coincidence that everyone I spoke to described interactions with me as "humanistic." One said, "I remembered feeling scared of you and your class because I heard you were a really hard teacher. But I soon realized that it wasn't that you were mean or hard, you just expected a lot out of us."

Yes, culturally responsive teachers believe all students can learn, and hold high expectations for each student. But the x-factor again, as I heard from my students, was the humanity I brought to our interactions. They all shared remembrances of facing adversity; some as seemingly insignificant now as figuring out which peer groups to join and others as heavy as dealing with their parents' divorce or the death of a family member. They shared stories about conversations we had that helped them through those challenging experiences. They all talked about how important it was for them to have teachers (for that matter, adults they respected) who *listened* to them. They valued the opportunities created for them to be heard. And for my Black and Brown students, feeling like there was always a safe space for their voice; they would be heard and recognized for contributions to the discussion.

This is fundamental best practice as a culturally responsive teacher, it all hangs on the strength of the relationships you develop with your students. You must trust them. And they will trust you. Show them you care, that you love them and are invested in them being their best selves. They will learn compassion and empathy when you do, and they will remember you.

Culturally responsive teaching is not magic. It starts with learning what it means, in both practice and mindset, and committing to reflective practice and growth. I encourage you to download and use the accompanying tool I developed to support teacher reflective practice and professional learning and development. Shout out to New America for the paper from which this tool was developed.

Building Classroom Culture on a Foundation of Equity

Rocio del Castillo, EdD, Assistant Superintendent
Huntley Community School District 158, Huntley, IL

Julia Stearns Cloat, EdD, Coordinator
Kaneland Unit School District 302, Kaneland, IL

As a first step toward building a classroom in which lessons are culturally responsive, it is important to consider the distinction between treating your students equally and treating them equitably.

- Treating students *equally* means that all students receive the same treatment regardless of their needs.
- Treating students *equitably* means that all students receive what they need, when they need it.

As you establish culture in your new classroom, keep in mind that treating students *equally* can only be *equitable* if all students begin at the same starting point and can achieve success with the exact same opportunities, access, and resources. Since it is extremely unlikely that your students will come to your classroom at the same starting point, work to establish a culture of *equity* in which every student has access to the educational resources and rigor they need at the right moment in their education regardless of race, gender, ethnicity, language, disability, sexual orientation, family background, and/or family income. As a new teacher, you can build culturally responsive teaching on a foundation of educational equity with a few key strategies.

Assess Personal Biases

The reality is that we all have personal biases. As educators, we must acknowledge the institutional inequities that exist and then take a hard look at our own personal biases. When personal biases go unchecked, they can factor into the decisions we make about students. To prevent that from happening, you should recognize and reflect on the biases that exist within yourself.

For example, a teacher may hold the cultural bias that all Asian students are good at math. To address the bias, she should begin by acknowledging when her inner voice is saying things about her Asian students that are not supported by the actual performance of individual students. Once she has acknowledged the bias, she will need to continue to reflect on it and keep it in check, so it does not influence her decisions. She may ask herself, "Am I holding my Asian students to a higher standard or placing them in higher math groups without evidence?" or "Do I recognize when my Asian students are struggling with a math concept or problem and get them the help they need?"

Keeping personal biases in check is an ongoing process, so we have provided the document "Assessing Personal Bias," which you can download, as a visual reminder of the difference this mental exercise can make for you and your students. Print the document and hang it in your classroom as a reminder to yourself to not let personal biases go unchallenged.

Get to Know Students

Getting to know your students and the factors that make up your students' personal and family lives will help you to make lessons more culturally responsive, build relationships with students, and keep personal biases from influencing decisions. Getting to know your students can be as easy as finding the time to talk with them and to demonstrate a genuine interest in them. Not all students will want to talk in front of their peers, so set aside time to talk to students one-on-one or in small groups to find out about their families, interests, and cultures. Show your students that you are interested in learning about them and that they bring value to your classroom community. Once you know your students better, it will be easier to take factors such as their socioeconomic status, family makeup, and culture(s) into consideration. This will also enhance your relationships with your students and provide opportunities to make the learning experiences more personalized to better meet their needs.

Use Culturally Responsive Materials and Assessments

When you know your students and are aware of your biases, you select materials and assessments that are culturally responsive. The materials you choose should reflect the cultures of your students and expose them to different cultures. Also, assess your students using authentic assessment tools (e.g., observations, rubrics, conferring, and performance tasks) that are culturally and linguistically responsive. These tools assess your students' performance and progress more than traditional classroom assessments do. For example, use a text that reflects each student's background when conducting a running record. Or instead of a paper and pencil test, use observations of lab work to assess the scientific understandings of emergent bilingual students.

Elevate the Student's Culture and Languages

Often educators hold the idea that emergent bilinguals lack the resources to be successful in school (Menken, 2017). Take a moment to consider how you represent culture and language in your classroom. What holidays do you celebrate? Are the posters on your walls representative of your students? Do the books that you use reflect the same languages and cultures of your students? If not, you may be missing opportunities to enrich your students' lives through the languages, cultures, and collective experiences of them and their families. With just a little effort, you can take advantage of the diverse backgrounds and experiences that your students bring with them as they walk through the door of your classroom every day.

Start simply by learning where your students and their families are from. Then begin to honor their cultures and experiences by reading books that they see themselves in, celebrating the holidays that they and their families celebrate, and learning a few words of their language. As your relationships with your students and their families develop, you can further elevate their culture and individual experiences by involving their families.

Involve Families

The concept of family engagement is not universal. There is a cultural component to family engagement that makes it essential for teachers to make the expectations for engagement clear to families. Getting to know your students' families and encouraging their involvement in your classroom will benefit both you and your students by:

♦ Helping you to know and understand your students better
♦ Supporting your students' bicultural and multicultural identity development
♦ Making your students' families feel more comfortable at school
♦ Making it more likely your students' families become partners with the school.

It is impossible to say exactly how to go about engaging families—too much depends on the cultural makeup of your class. In order to determine how best to involve families, you will need to connect and communicate with them in ways that build relationships. However, here are some suggestions that will be a start toward finding ways to connect with your students' families to help them feel welcome, while raising the cultural awareness in your school and classroom.

♦ Invite your students' families for show-and-tell, mystery reader, storytelling, and so on.
♦ Teach content that reflects the collective experience expertise of your students' families.
♦ Use classroom assignments as a reflection of your students' beliefs, being careful to first examine the cultural assumptions and stereotypes that may hinder interconnectedness.

As you work toward building a classroom that is culturally responsive, keep in mind that the difference between treating students *equitably* and treating them *equally* is powerful. The opportunities we provide students reflect the value that we place on fairness, justice, and equity. In order to change the inequities created as a result of societal and institutional racism, put the needs of underrepresented students and their families first.

Reference

Menken, K. (2017). *Leadership in dual language bilingual education*. Washington, DC: National Dual Language Research Forum.

Inspiring Students Means Embracing Culturally Responsive Teaching

Lindsay Smith, NBCT
Fourth Grade, Oak Park District 97, Oak Park, IL

Anton Miglietta, NBCT
Instituto Justice and Leadership Academy, Pilsen, Chicago

> *How do we inspire all our students to become literate, skilled, knowledgeable, critically active, and proud lifelong learners?*

Culturally Relevant Teaching (CRT) is our most significant response to that question. Why? Because students' own cultures, histories, communities, interests, and realities really matter in learning. How do we know? Because *history* documents it, *brain-based research* explains it, *National Board for Professional Teaching Standards* expects it, *Common Core* standardizes it, the *Danielson Framework* evaluates it, *Golden Apple* awards it, countless *scholars* prove it, *students* and *parents* demand it, and our own *classroom practices* assure us of it.

What does CRT look like in each of our classrooms, especially as white teachers not from our students' communities? In Lindsay's fourth grade classroom, situated in a suburb just outside Chicago, where racist school-based incidents have occurred, CRT means adapting to students' needs and interests while teaching anti-racist perspectives and historical accuracy. Her students are collaborating with a Zimbabwean archaeologist to write and illustrate an informational coloring book about Great Zimbabwe. Their research began by studying three ancient African societies to celebrate the vast accomplishments of precolonial Africans. The students were especially curious about Great Zimbabwe's advancements in agriculture, building, and metal-working, so they decided to revise the unit to take a deeper dive. Her class reached out to archaeologist Dr. Ashton Sinamai after expressing disappointment in Eurocentric-based resources on Great Zimbabwe. The book they create will be used as a learning tool for years to come!

In Anton's high school history class, situated between two of Chicago's historic Latinx communities, Pilsen and Little Village, CRT means responding to students' requests to take civic action against the Chicago History Museum (CHM) after students realized on a recent field trip that no Latinx history of Chicago was exhibited there. Instead of moving to the next planned unit, Anton asked his students, all of whom are Latinx, what they wanted to do about CHM's omission. Students sought to write/send letters, create social media posts with colorful protest posters, and demand a meeting with museum leaders. This became the new unit—and students succeeded! They not only hosted a media-covered meeting at the CHM (search: *IJLA high school students and Chicago History Museum*, CBS2 News Chicago, *Chicago Sun-Times*, Univision, and others), they pushed CHM to apologize. As a result, CHM has agreed to host a major Latinx exhibit that involves students and community elders in the exhibit's curatorial processes and in promoting a citywide all-call for ideas. Anton's students built a successful campaign that continues to bear fruit with research field trips, hosting Latinx scholars in class, serving as panelists at Therese Quinn's book release, *About Museums, Culture and Justice to Explore in Your Classroom*, and by collaborating with groups such as the Latinx Caucus of the Chicago Teachers Union. One student leader, Samira, received an invitation to apply for Princeton University's Prize in Race Relations. Their work can be followed at LatinxHistoryNow! on Facebook.

To us, the most significant push for CRT has reverberated from communities of color. Native Americans have resisted Spanish missionaries, then American boarding schools, since the 1600s. African Americans have always struggled for literacy while enslaved, then for equal access to schools both before and after the Civil War. Black teachers working with Carter G. Woodson in the 1920s combatted public school miseducation by teaching from CRT perspectives in Bronzeville, Chicago. In the 1960s, Mississippi Freedom Schools and Black Panther Party liberation schools opened. Chicana/o students led the East L.A. Blow-outs in 1968 to demand cultural relevance. By the late 1990s, ethnic studies programs were initiated in Arizona and elsewhere. In the 2000s, numerous struggles ensued over preserving ethnic studies, combatting culturally biased testing, and resisting English-only schooling, just to name a few. Throughout these movements, revolutionary-minded educators such as Woodson, Paulo Friere, Grace Lee Boggs, Henry Giroux, Gloria Ladson-Billings, Miles Horton, Linda Darling-Hammond, the Rethinking Schools collective, and countless others have paved the road we walk today.

The field of education fully supports CRT as well. Common Core State Standards (National Governors Association, 2010) prompt students to "integrate and evaluate multiple sources of information presented in diverse formats and media...in order to address a question or solve a problem" (CCSS.ELA-Literacy.RH.11-12.7). The Danielson Framework emphasizes that a distinguished teacher "systematically acquires knowledge from several sources about individual students' varied approaches to learning, knowledge and skills, special needs, and interests and cultural heritages" (Danielson, 2013, p. 13). The Golden Apple Foundation asks its nominated teachers to describe how they design and implement culturally responsive instruction in their classroom. Brain-based learning inspired this headline in Edutopia from 2010: "Science Shows Making Lessons Relevant Really Matters" (Bernard, 2010). National Board Certification for Teachers, the most demanding professional certification program in teaching, also supports CRT. In the first of its Five Core Propositions, the National Board for Professional Teaching Standards (NBPTS, 2016) asserts that "accomplished teachers understand how students develop and learn. They consult and incorporate a variety of learning and development theories into their practice, while remaining attuned to their students' individual contexts, cultures, abilities, and circumstances" (p. 24).

Embracing CRT, especially when teaching marginalized students, means examining yourself and what you teach. This is especially true for white and/or middle class-raised teachers. You will likely need to peel away more layers of dominant social constructs that ignore or explain away societies' inequities. This means viewing U.S. history and current realities through the eyes of marginalized communities. Students deserve curriculum rooted in affirming content, in which their cultures' accomplishments, movements, struggles, and heroes are celebrated, and systemic root causes of present-day issues are interrogated. Think about CRT as the difference between empowerment and oppression, because no curriculum is neutral. So, which will you choose?

References

Bernard, S. (2010, December 1). Science shows making lessons relevant really matters: Personal relevance is as vital to the learning brain as it is to the person learning. *Edutopia*. Retrieved from https://www.edutopia.org/

Danielson, C. (2013). *The framework for teaching evaluation instrument*. Princeton, NJ: Danielson Group.

National Board for Professional Teaching Standards. (2016). *Exceptional needs standards* (2nd ed.). Arlington, VA: Author.

National Governors Association Center for Best Practices, Council of Chief State School Officers. (2010). *Common core state standards for English language arts in history/social studies*. Washington, DC: Author.

Culturally Responsive Environment

Stephanie Kiley
Special Education Teacher
Devereux Glenholme School, Prospect, CT

Developing a culturally responsive environment conducive to learning should be a school-wide priority beginning with the teachers and administrators. Educators need to facilitate an environment where the educational, cultural, and emotional needs of students are met, and also develop a program where students can succeed outside of the school setting.

In my current high school classroom, I am responsible for teaching individuals from Nigeria, Japan, Bermuda, the Grand Cayman Islands, as well as multiple different states in America. Discussing differences in identity in the classroom influences our experiences and shapes how individuals view the world, themselves, and others. Valuing diversity is crucial for all students to feel comfortable to learn. As a culturally responsive special educator, I have implemented several methods of addressing factors of culture in behavior interventions in my classroom. I express interest in all of my students' ethnic backgrounds, while also fostering an inclusive classroom environment with various activities. I also encourage students to share about their backgrounds as a means to arm the entire class with knowledge about different traditions, cultures, and values.

When it comes to creating instruction for a student who is from a culturally and linguistically diverse background, values play an important role in behavior and education. Teachers and parents need to collaborate and communicate when putting expectations into effect so that students have a clear understanding of what they are expected to do both at home and at school. No matter where individuals come from, they bring their backgrounds with them.

Embracing the Essence of Your Students

Alisa M. Ross, EdD, Assistant Professor
Southern University and A&M College, Baton Rouge, LA

When students enter our classroom, they should feel the respect we have not only for the profession but also for them. Each student brings a sense of uniqueness to the classroom, from the language they speak to their ethnic background. Our duty is to make our students feel welcome, safe, and motivated to learn. Classrooms should be student-centered. Furthermore, teachers should provide opportunities for students to own and have choice in their learning.

In order for teachers to embrace Culturally Responsive Teaching (CRT), they must be willing to learn about their student's background. In other words, while getting to know your students during the first week(s) of school, provide opportunities for them to share their culture with the class. Next, find ways to allow your students to incorporate their cultural heritage into the classroom and curriculum. Once you demonstrate to your students that you genuinely care about their culture, experiences, and accomplishments, and can understand their perspective, your students will be more receptive to the content you're trying to teach them.

Communication is key in all relationships. Teachers have to collaborate with their peers during Professional Learning Communities in order to develop effective interdisciplinary lessons as well as create individualized learning plans for their students. In addition, teachers have to communicate with parents to discuss their students' academic strengths and areas for improvement. When teachers engage in dialogue with their students, they discover new information.

A few years ago, the school district where I was employed required secondary-level teachers to foster CRT in our classrooms. This was the result of a devastating event that occurred in our city prior to the start of the school year. An African-American male was killed by a Caucasian police officer. As one could imagine, the tension was thick in the city. The target school district was concerned due to the ethnic backgrounds of its students and teachers.

The teachers were not given a blueprint on how to embrace each student's culture. Instead, we were told what we were to accomplish by the end of the school year. Upon learning of my new teaching assignment, I held a conversation with my students. I asked them to share what concerns they faced as African-American and Salvadorian students attending a Title I, inner-city high school. The negative stereotypes and public criticism my students faced were depressing. Together, we decided to tell our own story.

The first step was to create a questionnaire that addressed areas of concern among the students. Next, they interviewed other students, teachers, and administrators to gather their viewpoint of the school. Third, we analyzed the data and created charts and graphs to illustrate their findings. The last component of the project was a video my students created to summarize the research question and the solution.

My students took ownership of the project because it was THEIR story. My Salvadorian student surveyed other English as Second Language students. The finished product captured the experiences, viewpoints, and desires of the high school students. It was our goal to become agents of change!

How to Use the Associated Document

The resource is divided into two sections. The first section provides seven instructional strategies teachers could implement in their classrooms to facilitate student-centered instruction that fosters CRT. The second section contains five self-reflection questions. It is highly recommended that the questions be answered after each unit you teach, in preparation for the forthcoming unit of instruction.

Anti-Racist Teaching and Justice

Clint Whitten
Seventh Grade English Teacher
Blacksburg Middle School, Montgomery County Public Schools, VA
Twitter: @TeacherWhitten

As a white teacher, I write this article for new teachers interested in culturally responsive instruction, particularly with attention to race. My goal is simple: I want schools and new teachers to be true advocates for racially marginalized youth and to create educational experiences that develop concern for justice for all youth. I first describe Robin DiAngelo's book *White Fragility: Why It's So Hard for White People to Talk About Racism* (2018) and its usefulness in diversifying the curriculum. I then offer strategies for how you might incorporate these resources into your classrooms. I also suggest how new teachers, particularly white educators, might navigate these conversations on race with both students and other teachers. I conclude with a push for anti-racist teaching and a call for justice in the schools.

Halfway through my first year of teaching, I started to shift my focus on my curriculum. I realized through analyzing my whitewashed curriculum that educational institutions mimic racial inequalities. The canon and common texts do not reflect all student populations. I started my journey of engaging in discussions on race by listening to and reading more from Black and Brown authors, such as Toni Morrison, Maya Angelou, Angie Thomas, Jason Reynolds, Rupi Kaur, Benjamin Alire Sáenz, and Amy Tan. I began a Project LIT book club chapter at my school that focuses on providing diverse, relevant text to students. Yet I began to realize that racism in schools is not mended with diversity and inclusiveness.

Furthermore, we white educators need to be engaged with race work. "The work of confronting racism has historically been left to people of color .... Racism hurts us all" (Schwartz, 2019). In my second year of teaching, I sponsored the Black Student Alliance at my middle school due to student interest. I listened, was a resource, and provided outside resources because students of color need safe spaces in schools.

Apart from beginning organizations and shifting the curriculum away from white voices, I've also engaged in discussions around race in the classroom, with faculty, and on Twitter. When engaging in conversations on race, white educators need to own our humility. Ask questions to mentor teachers and administrators, such as "Will the administration support me when discussing this topic? Or should I send out an email or letter home before showing this resource?" Is the discomfort coming from the students or the adults? Students matter. This work is teachers' work, too. This past year, I led a faculty book club on *White Fragility*. During the conversations, we looked for applications of anti-racist work in our classrooms, school, and community. These, and other resources, are available in my download.

The book club ideas that were generated included:

♦ Teach about micro/macro-aggressions, racial bias, stereotypes, and so on.
♦ Acknowledge your privilege, but do not hide behind it or give it power.
♦ Understand the trauma and the emotional weight that many students of color experience.
♦ Representation in curriculum matters.
♦ Step off your platform and let a new voice step up.
♦ Cite Black and Brown people.
  • Dr. Rudine Sims Bishop wrote "Mirrors, Windows, and Sliding Glass Doors."
  • Kimberlé Williams Crenshaw coined "Intersectionality."
♦ Complete a bias test: https://implicit.harvard.edu/implicit/
♦ Utilize free, downloadable resources from Teaching Tolerance, Rethinking Schools, Zinn Education Project such as Teaching People's History.

Discussion ideas about social justice generated through online professional development, coworkers, and reading:

♦ The Raised Fist is a symbol of trying to gain freedom.
  • Did the Confederate flag ever stand for a group of people who weren't already free and in power?
♦ Which social groups have been historically targeted for hate crimes?
♦ Consider where Black and Brown children are living, working, and thriving in your community. Ask questions: Is there a discrepancy?
♦ Who is being disciplined more?
♦ Who is benefiting from this story?
♦ Is there racial bias happening?
♦ Are you denouncing white supremacy in all forms?
♦ How many Black and Brown faculty are at your school? How many Black and Brown voices are your students hearing about? How are you protecting them?

In addition to diversifying the curriculum and forming a book club, new teachers can engage in discussions on Twitter to help navigate complicated spaces of K-12 classrooms. Twitter chats about race and education are hosted by Valeria Brown at #CleartheAir, Jarred Amato at #ProjectLItChat and Julia Torres, Tricia Ebarvia, Lorena Germán, and Dr. Kim Parker at

#DisruptTexts. New teachers can also follow Black and Brown educators including Shana White, Dr. Christopher Edmin, and Kelly Wickham Hurst. Learn about becoming anti-racist.

Toni Morrison writes, "And my feeling is that white people have a very, very serious problem, and they should start thinking about what they can do about it. Take me out of it" (Morrison 2016). White educators should not be white saviors. Black and Brown students do not need saving from white people. Listen and learn from the historically marginalized voices. Through shifting curriculum voices, providing spaces for Black and Brown youth, and engaging in conversations around race, culturally responsive teaching truly becomes centered.

References

DiAngelo, R. (2018). *White fragility: Why it's so hard for White people to talk about racism*. Boston, MA: Beacon Press.

Morrison, T. (2016, May 22). Toni Morrison interview on "Jazz" (1993) [Video file]. Retrieved from https://www.youtube.com/watch?v=CGeNJewyo4o

Schwartz, H. L. (2019, April 12). When I said "white," I meant "white:" Why white Pittsburghers should care about racism and what to do about it. *Public Source*. Retrieved from https://www.publicsource.org/

Relationships Between Teacher and Students

Joshua D. Case
Science Teacher
Iselin Middle School, Woodbridge Township, NJ

Think back to a time when you were on the other side of the room, when you were that young student in class. You probably remember some of your teachers, right? Which teachers do you remember the most? They were most likely the ones who had a positive impact on your learning and social–emotional being. The relationships between students and teachers are professional and sincere. When you come to your classroom as a teacher, you should feel as though your students are your own children.

When students have strong bonds with their teachers, they are less likely to act out and more likely to be productive and responsible in class. The benefits of responsible and regulated relationships between students and teachers are numerous. Within the classroom, students tend to behave appropriately around teachers they trust and like. This promotes effective instruction and classroom management. In the greater school community, students who feel heard and understood by the faculty have more pride in themselves and their peers. School spirit, student involvement, and the home lives of students all improve through effective student–teacher relationships. Teachers benefit as well, having higher morale and seeing positive instructional results through teaching students with whom they have positive relationships.

Setting the Stage for Culturally Responsive Teaching from Day One: Learning from Your Students

Marisol Diaz, PhD, Visiting Assistant Professor
Skidmore College, Saratoga Springs, NY

There is, in fact, no teaching without learning.

—Paulo Freire

I have always wanted to be a teacher. From my earliest childhood memories, I remember playing *escuelita* (little school) with my younger brother and sister as well as neighbors from our apartments. We played for hours on a regular basis. Our *escuelita* ran for several years, and to this day, we all remain very close friends and have fond memories of our favorite game.

Although at the time *escuelita* was only a game we played, I learned some of my most valuable lessons about what it meant to teach. One day while playing *escuelita* and sitting with my brother, who has Down Syndrome, I wondered to myself about his cognitive capabilities and his ability to learn. I was 10 years old at the time and very curious about what he could and could not do. Through much experimenting with various lessons, I found that if I connected the lesson with something he liked or knew well (in his case anything related to food or Power Rangers), he would learn the concept I was trying to teach faster and more accurately. I learned that this was true for all my *escuelita* students, and that getting to know them facilitated the process of teaching.

Understanding that I had to get to know my students in order to teach them effectively was one of the most valuable things I learned from *escuelita*. Although this seems like an easy and straightforward statement, its implementation and depth are much more complicated. For example, what does it mean to really teach something, and what must a teacher learn? Have teachers not learned enough in school? What else is there to learn? After all, isn't the job of a teacher to teach?

Fast-forward several years, and I was an elementary teacher at a large Title I school that enrolled nearly 1,300 students. Somehow I felt that my formal education had not prepared me enough on the importance of how a teacher begins the school year and the impact this may have for the rest of the academic year. I knew that I wanted to make my students feel welcomed from day one, and I also knew I needed to get to know them in order to be effective at teaching.

The day before the first day of school, I came up with an idea that could initiate this process and ensure that I communicated to my students that who they were was important and central to me. While this activity was a great icebreaker for the first day of class, it was also an invaluable pedagogical tool that laid a foundation for getting to know students, which is an important aspect of culturally relevant teaching. I want to caution that this project is not an end-all or check-off activity for culturally responsive teaching. On the contrary, it is a practical beginning step (one of many) toward getting to know students.

The name of the project is simply titled "Me." As the students arrive on the first day of school, at their desks is a sheet of paper with questions, a round paper cut-up of a blank face and two little hands (pattern available as download). When students are done filling out the questions, they draw themselves in the blank face and color their hands. I then join all the pieces together to create a mini version of each student. I place everyone's creation on a wall hand-by-hand and then use this as a place to publish student's writing during the year.

I read each child's answers very carefully and make notes to inform the type of lessons I can create that reflect students' background knowledge. I have found that doing this "Me" project is a quick way to gather valuable information from my students. Throughout the year, I gather more information about them and send a more extensive version of the "Me" project home for students to complete with their family.

It has been my experience that when a student struggles with a particular concept, referring back to their "Me" project helps me think of ways to connect new material with things that are familiar to them. It also informs my teaching style and approach. This project challenges me to be creative and find ways for all my students to connect to the content I am teaching. Learning about my students has been key to my teaching and their successful academic achievement.

Reference

Freire, P. (1970). *Pedagogy of the oppressed* (M. Bergman Ramos, Trans.). New York, NY: Herder & Herder.

Incorporating Global Perspectives in the Pre-K–12 Classroom

Peggy Shannon-Baker, PhD, Assistant Professor
Georgia Southern University, Statesboro, GA
Twitter: PShannonBaker

Although we teach locally, we live in a global society. How can you incorporate global awareness into your classroom when you are already so busy? This article provides some practical short-term and long(er)-term strategies for you to incorporate global perspectives.

What Is Global Education?

Global education emphasizes the interconnections between cultures, people, and countries. It addresses our awareness of cross-cultural issues around the world and how our local experiences connect to the larger global society. Global education starts with learning about other cultures, developing an appreciation for them, recognizing interconnections between cultures, and incorporating them into our teaching practices (Merryfield, 1997).

Why Are Global Perspectives Important?

You may have students who are or whose family members are recent immigrants. You and your students will also most likely engage with people of different cultures, whether online, at work, or during playtime. Bringing in global perspectives in the classroom better prepares your students (and you!) for these cross-cultural interactions.

How Can I Incorporate Global Perspectives in the Classroom Now?

Here are some short-term strategies that are ideal for the summer before the school year starts or any time during the school year.

- ◆ Learn about the local community, families, and students. Take the time to go out into the community to see what cultures are represented. Attend local events and celebrations to learn about the community. What small businesses are there? What cultural or religious organizations are there?
- ◆ Identify local community members, organizations, and/or parents with international ties (e.g., born or worked abroad). Ask them to come in to share about their culture or experiences.
- ◆ Identify the cultural origins of the author, characters, and setting when teaching fiction. When using nonfiction text in math, social studies, and science, consider the cultural underpinnings of people you study. Get into the habit of providing this quick and easy background information to highlight places around the world that are connected to the content you are teaching. You can likely find this information in the author's biography or by doing a quick online search.
- ◆ Research and include a short introduction to the history of the content you are teaching. There is likely an international connection, such as who developed a type of mathematical thinking or the influences for a particular author.
- ◆ Infuse culturally diverse materials and stories into your lessons. This can start from day one by searching for materials that reflect the diversity of students in your class and in relation to the larger world. Use social media like Pinterest, Twitter, and Instagram to follow organizations that share these resources, and learn about new materials to incorporate. Do this through identifying interdisciplinary themes that have impacted multiple countries (Merryfield, 1998).

How Can I Incorporate Global Perspectives in the Classroom This Year?

Here are some long(er)-term strategies. These might require a month or more to develop, but could have a longer impact.

- ◆ Inventory books, examples, sources, and other curricular materials currently used in class or that the students have access to at school (e.g., in the library or online). By identifying what you and the students have access to, you can assess what is available and what other countries or cultures could be added to those materials. Download the resource for this article for a set of questions to ask as you complete this inventory. Partner with other teachers, teacher leaders, or a librarian to complete the inventory. Share the findings with your grade level or content team, school administration, or external administrators. If funding is not available for your school to add to these resources, reach out to local organizations or start a crowd-sourcing funding campaign for support.

♦ Partner with a local organization that works abroad. This could be a local nonprofit, religious organization, or university. If they work in schools abroad, consider setting up a pen-pal system between the classes to connect the students. Find out if they have scholarships or other support for teachers to go abroad, if you are interested. Going abroad can be a great way to learn about the culture, and also bring back information, pictures, and artifacts to share with your class.

♦ Teach students how to locate global and culturally diverse sources. Develop an assignment that includes researching the global perspectives or history on a topic. Incorporate scaffolded lessons on how to identify good sources of information (Merryfield, 1998).

References

Merryfield, M. M. (1997). A framework for teacher education in global perspectives. In M. M. Merryfield, E. Jarchow, & S. Pickert (Eds.), *Preparing teachers to teach global perspectives: A handbook for teacher educators* (pp. 1–24). Thousand Oaks, CA: Corwin Press.

Merryfield, M. M. (1998). Pedagogy for global perspectives in education: Studies of teachers' thinking and practice. *Theory & Research in Social Education, 26*(3), 342–379.

Culturally Responsive Teaching: Working with Families

Alexis Jones, PhD, Assistant Professor
Eastern Illinois University, Charleston, IL

These parents just don't value education.
Why don't they learn English to support their children?
As the teacher, I know more about school and the curriculum.

Have any of you heard these comments in the teacher's lounge yet? Thought them yourself? Sadly, these are familiar myths that arise when teachers struggle to work with diverse populations (Ferlazzo, 2011; Valencia & Black, 2002). When frustrated with low parent–teacher conference attendance, difficulty getting a family member to sign a permission slip, or poor student behavior, teachers may turn to *deficit thinking*, a mindset that blames the victim as opposed to looking at the more complex reasons for school problems. Deficit thinking can result in students feeling that they are the problem, and that they do not belong in your classroom. And, since schools are more than just places to teach content, you need to be sure that your students learn that all cultures and values are valid and accepted.

Much has been written about best practices in school–family engagement (Abdi, 2016; Ferlazzo, 2011). In summary, the following table explains what you should be doing:

Focus less on...	Focus more on...
One-way communication (e.g., notes home)	Two-way communication (e.g., phone calls, messaging apps, home visits) http://www.pthvp.org
What parents and families can do *for* the school	What parents, families, and schools can do together *in* the school
Talking to families about their children	Asking families about their children
Discussion about why families do not come to school more	Professional discussions about identity, privilege, and diversity

What Can You Do?

If you find yourself annoyed that only 16 of your 25 families signed up for parent–teacher conferences, and then only ten of them actually attended, you may think, "Wow, *my* parents never missed a meeting with my teacher. What is wrong with families these days?" Or a colleague might shake her head and say, "These families just do not care about school the way we used to."

One way to address deficit-laden thoughts and comments like these is to reframe them. A helpful sentence starter might be, "I wonder…"

> I wonder if they are nervous about what I will say about their child. Not everyone has positive experiences at school.
>
> I wonder if something came up at home that got in the way. Do they have transportation to school? Childcare? Maybe there is something our school can do to make it easier for families to get here.

Use the Family Contact download to keep a log of your contacts with students' families.

An excellent resource for teachers wanting to learn more about culturally responsive teaching is the website Teaching Tolerance: www.tolerance.org. The resources on their website are free to educators (including administrators and counselors) and include lesson plans, educator grants, and professional development in the form of workshops, webinars, and podcasts. For example, a quick search of their Family & Community Engagement webinars produced results for serving English Learners' families as well as engaging students and families in democracy. Let us do what we can to work *with* families as opposed to working *on* families.

References

Abdi, N. (2016, December 30). How to improve education for immigrant students by ending deficit thinking [Web log post]. Retrieved from https://cehdvision2020.umn.edu/blog/improve-education-immigrant-students-ending-deficit-thinking/

Ferlazzo, L. (2011). Involvement or engagement? *Educational Leadership, 68*(8), 10–14. Retrieved from http://www.ascd.org/publications/educational-leadership/may11/vol68/num08/Involvement-or-Engagement%C2%A2.aspx

Valencia, R. R., & Black, M. S. (2002). "Mexican Americans don't value education!"—On the basis of the myth, mythmaking, and debunking. *Journal of Latinos and Education*, 1(2), 81–103.

An Inclusive, Student-Centered Environment

Collin Edouard
Music Teacher
KIPP STAR and Friends Seminary, Lake Worth, FL

As a new teacher, consider the nuanced differences among your students, such as their ethnicity, socioeconomic status, family cultural traditions, primary language spoken, or gender identity. Acknowledging and being sensitive to these categories of individuality is important because this is how your students identify within your classroom.

The first chance you have to make a positive impression on your students is when you learn how to pronounce their names. You might come across less Euro-centric names, in which the phonemes are not as familiar to you. However, the effort you put into saying your students' names correctly will make them feel seen and included in your classroom. Moreover, learning their names and using them frequently during classroom conversation is good practice.

Being culturally sensitive in your classroom might require you to team up with administration and/or colleagues to find the most inclusive vernacular during discourse in your classroom. Interpreting your school's mission statement in the context of your classroom setting is an excellent way to start thinking about the environment you and your students will share throughout the year. Being an educator means new topics and discussions about things like gender identity will come up that might have been foreign to you as a student. With that being said, it might be beneficial to learn everyone's pronouns as a class, as it will not only help you as you learn the most efficient ways to support your students, but it will also help establish a safe environment among classmates. Being culturally sensitive isn't necessarily ignoring what makes us all different; it's about embracing and celebrating those differences and finding ways to collaborate and learn from one another to bridge the chasm of cultural and societal misconceptions.

The materials and resources you choose to share in your curriculum speak volumes to your students about your values and convictions. Therefore, it is imperative that you choose material from a variety of scholars, philosophers, composers, writers, and so on. Using a diverse group of scholars to share with your students will allow you as the learner to consume many perspectives on specific subject areas. Moreover, using scholars from backgrounds represented in your classroom will allow students to participate and share their thoughts as it pertains to their culture and experiences.

In addition to acknowledging the cultural and economic differences in your classroom, this practice helps you become aware of the power dynamics between you and your students (especially students who are minorities), who will be interpreting how you address them with a double consciousness. The term "double consciousness", first coined by W. E. B. Du Bois (1968) in his autoethnographic work *The Souls of Black Folk*, addresses the internal conflict those in subordinate groups experience in an oppressive society. Similarly, your students may interpret the manner in which you interact with them differently than you do.

As you begin your journey working with students, remember that you are also learning with them. Information during lessons should be regarded as a collaboration of thought regardless of grade level. The approach of "the keeper of knowledge" may have a tendency to stifle discovery for you and your students. If a student asks a question to which you do not know the answer, find comfort in saying, "I don't know. How can we find out?" Reflect on quotes from scholars such as Paulo Freire speaking about how we think and learn in the process of collaboration:

> I cannot think for others or without others, nor can others think for me. Even if the people's thinking is superstitious or naive, it is only as they rethink their assumptions in action that they can change. Producing and acting upon their own ideas—not consuming those of others. (Freire, 1970/2014, p. 108)

Do not take away the magic of discovery from your students by applying your own thoughts and convictions upon them, because you will be inadvertently coaching them on your hidden curriculum.

Your classroom should feel safe and inclusive with a focus on student-centered learning. You may download the resource, "Action Steps to Build an Inclusive Student-Centered Classroom." Being an educator requires practice, patience, and reflection, so look at lessons that might not have worked the way you intended as opportunities to grow. The relationships you build with your students will be the most rewarding part of being an educator, and the path to building those positive relationships begins with cultural responsiveness in your teaching.

References

Du Bois, W. E. B. (1968). *The souls of Black folk: Essays and sketches*. Chicago, A. G. McClurg, 1903. New York: Johnson Reprint Corp.

Freire, P. (1970/2014). *Pedagogy of the oppressed* (M. Bergman Ramos, Trans.; 30th anniversary ed.). New York, NY: Bloomsbury Academic.

POWER Teaching: Using CRT to Change the World

Suzanna Nelson, MEd
Seventh Grade ELA Teacher
Clark County School District, Las Vegas, NV
Instagram: @thethriftyteacherlady

Nelson Mandela once said, "Education is the most powerful weapon which you can use to change the world." In modern education, accepting and appreciating the culture of all students is critical in order to make those powerful connections that lead to successful learning.

Culturally Responsive Teaching (CRT) is a pedagogy that recognizes the significance of including students' cultural references in all aspects of learning (Ladson-Billings, 1994). It is not enough to simply include diverse literature in the curriculum. CRT is less about what you teach and more about how you teach it.

How does one become a culturally responsive teacher? By becoming a POWER teacher. By **P**urposefully planning instruction, providing **O**pportunities for all, **W**elcoming diversity, **E**quipping for independence, and **R**esponsive practices.

POWER Teaching
Purposeful Instruction

Class time is precious. Being purposeful with instruction is key to establishing and maintaining high standards for all students. How can you expect your students to be prepared and succeed if you walk into the classroom unprepared? How can you expect your students to be proficient during high stakes testing when they have not been exposed to a variety of complex texts? Purposeful instruction is essential. But what does it mean to purposefully plan?

+ Complete all lesson plans in advance
+ Read and annotate all texts yourself before giving to students
+ Seek out a variety of complex texts, regardless of your subject matter
+ Plan your lesson around the standards, instead of planning the standards around your lesson
+ Use data-driven instruction

Opportunities for ALL

Every student, regardless of background, language, or ability, should be given the opportunity to learn. One size definitely does not fit all when it comes to teaching. While some students thrive by working independently, some need extra support. Some students excel when it comes to group work, but others become a little too overbearing. It's your responsibility to create a classroom environment that provides opportunities for all of your students.

+ Plan engaging instruction
+ Utilize intentional grouping
+ Provide opportunities for structured discourse regularly throughout instruction
+ Share detailed directions (both verbal and written)
+ Implement chunked instruction
+ Display visuals to aid learning
+ Expose students to complex texts while providing scaffolding

Welcome Diversity

Saying that diversity is welcomed in the classroom is easy but demonstrating it is entirely different. Consider the following:

+ Establish a strong relationship with families
+ Include inclusive texts in curriculum regularly

♦ Set high expectations for classroom respect
♦ Think and talk about race, culture, socioeconomic status, and gender
♦ Model appropriate classroom behavior

Equip for Independence

The goal of all educators should be to prepare students for independence. One effective way to do this is by establishing and maintaining high standards. Scaffolding is extremely important for achieving this, but remember that too much unwarranted scaffolding can be unhelpful. It just interferes with independence. All instructions should be in the Zone of Proximal Development (ZPD). The ZPD is the difference between what a learner can do without help and what he or she can do with help. Create an environment where your students feel safe enough to take risks. How can your students become independent if they are afraid to fail? You can do several things to help students gain needed independence:

♦ Create an open environment
♦ Ask open-ended questions
♦ Promote a positive mindset
♦ Let students form their own opinions
♦ Assist students with goal setting and follow through

Responsive Practices

Classrooms are full of diversity and culture. It is incredibly important to respond to and appreciate diversity in your classroom on a regular basis. As a teacher, it is your responsibility to lead by example and provide students with the most diverse and accepting classroom possible. You can do that in several ways:

♦ Identify your own biases
♦ Promote positive social interactions
♦ Design student-centered instruction
♦ Capitalize on culturally sensitive situations you can use as opportunities to learn

With all of the requirements expected of modern educators, the thought of adding on one more thing can seem daunting. But you don't need to think of CRT in that way. Rather, think of it as a set of best practices that complement and enrich the curriculum you already have. You're not simply providing students with diverse materials; you're intentionally planning, providing opportunities, welcoming diversity, equipping students for independence, and responding appropriately that leads to student success.

It may not happen overnight, but with continued effort and consistent use of the strategies, you too can become a POWER teacher. Download and use the "Are You a POWER Teacher?" checklist to gain your teacher strength. Use this power to create the change you wish to see in the world.

Reference

Ladson-Billings, G. (1994). *The dreamkeepers: Successful teachers of African American children.* San Francisco, CA: Jossey-Bass.

Chapter 4

Curriculum and Instruction

Intentional Instruction

Dustin Wright
Principal
Franklin Middle School, Fairfax, VA

If I took the time to sort through my old files, I am sure that I could find an assignment I completed as a freshman in college where I had to define what "great classroom instruction" looks like. Over time, that initial definition has changed and evolved into a set of characteristics that can be applied in any instructional setting and at any time of the day … even in the hallway! With the right mindset and beliefs, all teachers can demonstrate these characteristics to support the success of their students.

High-quality classroom instruction is:

♦ **Authentic:** How is it relevant to your students? How does it connect to the world around them? How will they leverage this knowledge or skill in the future?

♦ **Urgent and Just-in-Time:** You have all the time you need, but nothing more. Every minute counts, and you don't have a day to lose. You will never know if the lesson that didn't get your best effort could have been the day that unlocked a magical breakthrough with one of your students. Don't ever miss out on a chance to make a connection.

♦ **Intentional:** The instructional choices you make should have a purpose. You should be able to clearly define the reason(s) you make a decision. Always be able to articulate how you got there and where you are going next.

All three of these characteristics of high-quality instruction are important, but let's spend a little time discussing intentional instruction from your perspective.

As you work with highly skilled educators during your career, if you take time to observe their actions and decisions, big and small, you will notice intentional instruction everywhere you look. They will display intent in the choices they make about curriculum and content as they design their instructional delivery. You'll also see intent through the interventions and reteaching they implement with individuals and small groups. But you'll also see intentional actions in the way they teach students to line up in the hallway, in the sequence of students that they ask to respond to a prompt, and even in the minor adjustments the teacher makes to the papers on a student's desk as they circulate through the classroom. Every decision is made for a reason, and it is informed by where you have come from and where you want to go next.

As a new teacher, can you deliver intentional instruction starting on the first day of school? Absolutely! Starting your career with this mindset will set you up for success in the future. Being intentional with all aspects of your instruction takes some practice (see download), so here are some things to get you started:

Develop Your Ability Over Time

Intentional instructional practices are on a continuum. Your instructional delivery won't look the same as your veteran teammate's, and that's okay! It doesn't matter where you are right now, as long as you are moving in the right direction. Your ability to define your intent for yourself and others will develop over time. The important thing is to continue to challenge yourself to be intentional.

Set Reasonable Goals for Yourself

Start simple. Start small. But, if nothing else, just start. Don't start with an entire unit. Don't even start with a single lesson. Start with a few minutes of a lesson or a few small interactions with students. Begin with the content of that lesson. Why did you choose it? How can your students connect to it? Then, challenge yourself to articulate why you asked them the reflective questions you selected or how you decided to move to the next part of the lesson when you did. As you become more comfortable, push yourself to answer some of these questions following a lesson, and then, over time, try to answer them before you deliver instruction.

Ask Yourself Curricular Questions

How is this connected to something you have already done? How will this support something you are going to do in the future? Don't limit yourself to only asking these two questions about curriculum. Your answers can help guide you as you consider instructional sequence, pace, delivery, differentiation, intervention, and much more.

Because of your dedication and commitment, great things will happen in your classroom this year. You are going to work hard, and you are going to make decisions that are in the best interests of your students. As you continually grow as an educator, combine these strengths with intentional instructional choices. The ability to maximize the impact of every interaction in your classroom will lead to high levels of success for you and, most importantly, for your students.

Tackling the Year's-Worth of Standards

Kelli Hamilton, EdD
Seventh Grade Language Arts Teacher
D428 DeKalb, IL 60115

Starting a new teaching job is overwhelming and stressful. You want the students to like and respect you, but you also want them to learn something. You've spent years preparing for this moment. The walls are decorated, and you've recorded all the holidays and important dates in your planner. Now it is time to tackle what is probably the most overwhelming part of your job: Turning a list of national standards and district objectives into seamless and comprehensible classroom activities. The key to tackling this stressful job is breaking the task into manageable chunks.

Begin by familiarizing yourself with the list of standards that you are expected to teach. Most districts will align their curriculum with a national set of standards such as the Common Core State Standards. Your district likely has a document that outlines the most important standards and/or the order in which you should address those standards. Your district may even include a pacing guide that will clarify the order and the amount of time that you are expected to spend on each standard. Look over these documents carefully to get a feeling for how the curriculum will flow over the school year.

Once you have looked them over, choose one of those standards to be your first focus. Read the standard carefully and think about how many and what types of skills are embedded within it. For example, the Common Core Language Arts Standard RL 7.2 reads, "Determine a theme or central idea of a text and analyze its development over the course of the text; provide an objective summary of the text" (National Governors Association Center for Best Practices, Council of Chief State School Officers, 2010). Although this is only one standard, there are multiple embedded skills. As a teacher, you may want to break apart this standard and teach each skill separately. However you decide to organize the embedded skills, consider what the students might do to demonstrate that they have mastered the content.

Decide what you want your students to be able to do before you begin planning individual lessons. For example, in the middle school language arts standard listed above, students need to provide an objective summary of a text. Notice how it doesn't specify whether the assessment should be verbal or written. It is up to you, then, to decide how to assess this part of the standard. When you begin your planning by thinking about what the students will need to do in the end, it helps you focus your instruction.

Now that you have chosen a standard to begin with and determined what the students will do to show mastery, think about what you might want to know from the students before you begin instruction. You might want to know what sort of prerequisite skills your students have. Or, you might be interested in what type of background knowledge they already possess. Using the same standard above as an example, I might want to first know if my students know what a theme is. Do they know what I mean by "objective summary"? By thoughtfully crafting a pretest or some sort of pre-assessment, you can gather information that will guide your instruction.

When you know what you want your students to be able to do and what they already know, you can plan instruction that is tailored to their needs and focused on helping them master a specific standard. If you are teaching students an entirely new skill, a good rule of thumb is that they will need at least three exposures to the new skill before you give them the final assessment. Make a list of at least three different tasks or activities that you could have your students do to practice meeting the standard. Keep in mind that these don't have to be consecutive. As a language arts teacher, I want my students to practice certain skills multiple times throughout the year. One exposure might be in September, another in December, and the last might be in April. However, a math teacher might want his students to practice a prerequisite skill multiple times in one week in order to develop confidence before tackling a more complex skill.

It may seem like you have put in a great deal of time without actually getting down to the business of planning, but what you have created is an instructional roadmap. Using this roadmap will make it easier for you to be sure that you teach everything your district expects, and help you feel more confident that every student has mastered each standard. Utilize the download, Long Term Planning Guide, to help you prepare.

Reference

National Governors Association Center for Best Practices, Council of Chief State School Officers (2010). *Common core State standards for English language arts in history/social studies.* Washington, DC: Authors.

Optimize Your Classroom by Using Blended Learning

Soyini Chism
Physical Education Teacher
Joliet Township High School, Joliet, IL

Be aware. Today's students are mortally connected to their devices. They were born into a globally connected, always-on world. The Internet, smartphones, smart televisions, streaming *everything*, and social media have fundamentally impacted every fiber of their existence. Internet Technologies (IT) can bring the world into your classroom and contribute to student-centered learning. You must find a way to blend students' technology skills with your curricular expectations. So, cater to the technological proficiencies of your students by including ITs that support their skills. In my classroom, I use a teaching model called blended learning (BL).

What Is Blended Learning?

BL is an educational approach that combines the face-to-face traditional classroom with an e-learning platform. E-learning utilizes ITs to access curricular resources and is usually delivered completely online. BL allows teachers to personalize learning and differentiate instruction by giving students some degree of autonomy. BL uses synchronous (communicating in real time) and asynchronous (time-delayed communication) modalities to deliver instruction. Students have more control over learning. It helps foster their critical thinking by being flexible, active, and constructivist in nature.

Blended Learning Models

To guide the implementation of an effective blend for your students, Christensen, Horn, and Staker (2013) categorize the BL landscape into four models: Rotation, flex, á la carte, and enriched-virtual.

The *Rotation Model* allows students to rotate among learning modalities on a prescribed schedule. At least one modality includes online learning. The rotation model includes four related iterations.

Station Rotation	Students rotate through learning modalities while in a classroom.
Lab Rotation	Students complete online modalities in a computer lab outside of the classroom.
Flipped Classroom	Lesson content is presented offsite via computer prior to the class meeting, then students use classroom time to complete related tasks with teacher assistance.
Individual Rotation	Students determine the rotation based on individual needs.

The *Flex Model* is Information Communication Technology-heavy, very fluid, and gives students a high degree of autonomy. Teachers provide support and instruction on a flexible, as-needed basis, while students work through course curriculum and content.

The *Á La Carte Model* allows students to take online courses that supplement their face-to-face courses.

In the *Enriched-Virtual Model*, a majority of content is completed remotely. Students attend a brick-and-mortar location for face-to-face instruction as needed.

Practical Applications of BL

You can implement the BL instructional model in both core and participation courses. Here are examples you might use in biology or physical education with secondary students. Both examples follow the Flex model for students attending classes with a teacher twice a week.

Biology: The Structure of a Cell

Traditional Instruction
Day 1: You introduce the structure of a cell by projecting a diagram on the smart board and briefly discuss each part. Students are grouped and tasked with defining each part (cell membrane, cytoplasm, and nucleus).

   Day 2: Students report to class and open their Google Classroom accounts to find instructions for the class period. Students use their devices (school-issued laptops, Chromebooks, cell phones, etc.) to discover the function of each part. Students are encouraged to work in small groups and are required to submit a brief summary of their findings.

E-Learning
Assignment 1: Students are assigned to watch a video about the structure and function of a cell. The video, found on Ed Puzzle, is embedded with questions that must be answered while viewing.

   Assignment 2: Students use Flip Grid to define and explain the structure of a cell.

   Assignment 3: Students use Virtual Labs to complete a quiz about the structure of a cell.

Physical Education: Health-Related Fitness Components and the Nike Training Fitness App

Traditional Instruction

Day 1: You introduce students to the Nike Training Club (NTC) app. You use a smart TV to mirror the setup and functionality of the app from your cell phone. The students follow along with their cell phones. You then revisit two health-related fitness components, cardiovascular endurance and muscular strength, and briefly discuss their application during fitness training.

Day 2: Using the Remind app, the students were prompted the night before to select and download an NTC workout that focuses on either cardiovascular fitness or muscular strength and be ready to perform the workout as soon as class begins the next day. As students enter class on day two, they immediately begin their workouts either individually or in small groups.

E-Learning

Performance task 1: Students will use the NTC app to select a workout that focuses on flexibility. The workout must be at least 30 minutes in length.

Performance task 2: Students must engage in a cardiovascular endurance workout that will generate 5000 steps or more over 2 days.

Performance task 3: Students must research and select a fitness app that targets all five health-related fitness components and be ready to share with the class during the next required attendance day.

How might you use BL with your students? See the download for ideas and resources you can access.

Reference

Christensen, C. M., Horn, M. B., & Staker, H. (2013). *Is k–12 blended learning disruptive? An introduction to the theory of hybrids* [White paper]. Retrieved from Clayton Christensen Institute for Disruptive Innovation website: https://www.inacol.org/wp-content/uploads/2015/02/is-k-12-blended-learning-disruptive.pdf

Celebrate Victories

Alex Stampher
CSUMB Student Teacher
Rancho San Juan High School/Salinas Union High School District, Marina, CA

Though I am a student teacher pursuing my preliminary credential in California, I previously taught at a small trade college. There, I learned to teach the curriculum in a vacuum.

I was provided a textbook, my predecessor's syllabus, and began teaching two days later. I scrambled day by day. The students must have sensed the general lack of direction.

Now, I have the opposite experience. There is support on all sides. I am placed at a brand-new high school full of dedicated, collaborative teachers. Our district provides time for all new teachers to meet with the curriculum specialist. Despite the support, learning about the curriculum, standards, and planning is still overwhelming.

When meeting the standards seems daunting, I try to keep the big picture in mind while still celebrating small victories. A good teacher knows how best to guide students to the end goal of each semester, quarter, unit, and lesson. A joyful teacher celebrates the small victories along the way.

Currently, it's the beginning of the school year. My English students will soon be providing a written argument about the extent to which culture influences identity. This task is challenging and abstract, but yesterday, a struggling student took the first step. His first assignment was to write a succinct memoir about himself. He took extra time to process the task and was nonverbal when encouraged to brainstorm with another student. In the end, however, he was successful. He wrote "I get through hard times every time."

Five Effective Tech Tools for Learning

Gary J. Miller, EdD, Assistant Professor
The University of Texas at Tyler, Tyler, TX

Bill Gates (1997) remarked, "Technology is just a tool. In terms of getting the kids working together and motivating them, the teacher is the most important thing." You are the essential building block to learning, and there is no disputing the importance you play in student success. It is also undeniable that integrating technology in the classroom helps students develop skills and knowledge essential for tomorrow's workforce. As a dynamic, interactive tool for exploring ideas, technology encourages a collaborative environment for creating, communicating, and learning. Your role is to find ways to leverage available technologies, along with traditional subject-based pedagogies, in order to enhance student achievement and strike a balance in an information-rich classroom.

In many instances acquiring knowledge is a social activity, particularly when learner-centered lessons are designed to engage a room full of energetic students. As a result, the synthesis of ideas and sharing of information frequently happens through discussions facilitated by some form of technology integrated into the classroom. Given the interactive nature of many technologies, these digital tools can play a meaningful role in your students' cognitive and social development. As a learning tool, technology can provide a variety of opportunities for student input and engagement focusing on individual needs and interests.

Your students have spent their entire lives surrounded by information. With that in mind, here is a list of five tech tools for the classroom that can effectively communicate their learning. These free innovative apps can inspire your students' creativity and increase engagement through a variety of social interactions.

- ◆ Poll Everywhere (http://polleverywhere.com)
  - • Ask questions for live classroom interactions
  - • Collect student responses, seeing instant results
  - • Compatible with Google Slides, PowerPoint, and Keynote
- ◆ Evernote (https://evernote.com)
  - • Store student and teacher work using its drag-and-drop or web clipper tool feature
  - • Sync uploaded materials across multiple devices for easy access, including photos, audio files, scanned documents, and written assignments
  - • Invite students to collaborate on group projects
- ◆ Pinterest (https://www.pinterest.com)
  - • Provide a summer reading list
  - • Share examples of exemplary classroom projects
  - • Exchange articles and commentary from leading news sources
- ◆ Flipgrid (https://flipgrid.com/)
  - • Create meeting places for students to discuss posted topics
  - • Inspire learning through shared book talks
  - • Engage and share ideas through the educator community
- ◆ Padlet (https://padlet.com)
  - • Create online bulletin boards for upcoming assignments
  - • Display information on any subject, including important images, links, and videos
  - • Design a place for students to post information and share ideas

Reference

Gates, B. (1997, October 12). For the record. *Independent on Sunday*, p.23. Retrieved from https://link.gale.com/apps/doc/A66943977/STND?u=albu78484&sid=STND&xid=2f0451d4

How to Plan for Optimal Engagement

Brendan McCormick, EdD
Eighth Grade Language Arts Teacher
Kaneland CUSD 302, Maple Park, IL
Facebook: Brendan McCormick
Instagram: brendanjmccormick
LinkedIn: Brendan McCormick, EdD

Engagement is the most effective teaching practice you can develop in your classroom to foster student learning. It is central to your role as a teacher. Your ultimate goal should be encouraging consistent optimal engagement for as many students as possible. Optimal engagement is achieved when students experience high levels of enjoyment, challenge, and interest simultaneously within the context of a learning activity (Shernoff, 2013). Your challenge is to make engagement individualized. What highly engages one student may, in fact, disengage another. Engagement also varies throughout a student's day, depending on social and environmental factors.

Engaging students effectively and consistently becomes easier with experience and reflection. However, it is possible for you to plan lessons so that learning activities appeal to multiple engagement contexts. By layering these contexts in different combinations over the course of a lesson, optimal engagement becomes more likely for more students. These contexts form a checklist to ensure that one lesson contains multiple engagement approaches, and that lessons over a period of time draw from a variety of pedagogical choices.

The following academic contexts have been shown to enhance engagement when you promote high levels of positive emotions, challenge, and interest:

Establish Positive Social Interaction Between Students

Engagement is often fostered through peer interaction, and many students look forward to school simply because they get to be with their friends. Given that enjoyment is a necessary component of engagement, you should embrace the social aspects of school rather than separate them from learning activities. The key is to intentionally plan for various types of social interaction (e.g., cooperative learning, teacher-chosen partners, student-chosen partners, and ability and differentiated grouping). Make sure that you pair interaction with appropriately challenging activities.

Promote Positive Relatedness

No one has more influence over the climate in your classroom than you. Students expect their teachers to promote positivity and relatedness. Quite simply, it is important for students to like their teachers and enjoy being in their classrooms. This means not only forming positive relationships with students on an individual level, but also modeling respect and empathy for everyone since these attributes trickle down to students' behavior toward one another. You can accomplish this through various interactive methods such as whole-class discussions or inquiry, or through leading simulation, role playing, or gamification.

Foster Authenticity and Interest

You must ensure that schoolwork is not only challenging and enjoyable but meaningful for students if it is to inspire their highest levels of focus. This means that students must perceive assignments to be worthwhile, interesting, relevant, and not just busywork. The clearest path toward this goal is allowing students to connect their interests, talents, and hobbies to their assignments. On a social level, you can create assignments that have immediate connections to school life, real-world issues, or occupations.

Appeal to Students' Creativity

It is imperative that you expect students to be creative in your classroom, regardless of what subject you teach. Creativity is often associated with hands-on work or arts and crafts. These types of assignments foster enjoyment for many students. However, at its root, creativity requires students to produce something to demonstrate their learning. Innovation has a place in the classroom. Such assignments challenge students to reach higher levels of critical thinking by asking them to demonstrate a deeper understanding of content and skills in their own way.

Increase Student Autonomy

Students are more likely to be engaged if they are given choice and control over the direction their schoolwork takes. You would do well to build options into schoolwork, such as what form or medium the work takes, where students are allowed to work within the classroom, whether they work by themselves or with others, and which side to take in an argument. You should even extend autonomy into the creation of classroom rules and procedures.

Anticipate Disengagement

Thorough lesson planning requires anticipating that some students may not be as engaged as others. Student disengagement can and will occur for many reasons beyond your immediate influence. Disengagement is most likely when students are not interested in the content being covered, or when expectations are either too difficult or too easy. Disengagement presents itself in the form of negative emotions such as boredom, apathy, stress, or anxiety, which are telltale signs that a lesson has simply not been effective. If you can predict which aspects of your lesson may not be as engaging, you can either revise the lesson as a whole or strategize ways to intervene or differentiate for particular disengaged students.

Download the Optimal Engagement Checklist to assist you in planning strategies for specific lessons.

Reference

Shernoff, D. J. (2013). *Optimal learning environments to promote student engagement*. New York, NY: Springer.

More Doing, Less Explaining

Zach Hall
Choir Teacher
Oregon High School, Oregon, IL

In the beginning of my first year of teaching, I noticed that the pacing of my class felt sluggish. I did not understand why many members of the class were disengaged, and I was concerned that we were not accomplishing much. I shared my problem with a colleague, who then offered to come in and observe my class. I was a little uncomfortable about it, but I accepted the offer. When we met to reflect, he asked me to estimate how much of the time

I spent explaining to the class versus the amount of time that I gave my students to engage in meaningful activities. I was prepared for my estimate to be a little inaccurate, but I was shocked to find out how much time I actually spent talking. I was horrified that my poor students had to listen to me over-explain for close to half the class period. In future lessons, I made a deliberate effort to explain in fewer words and in less time. As a result, I found that the whole class engaged more with each lesson, and we accomplished much more together. Whenever I notice that I am losing the attention of my students, I monitor how much time I spend explaining, and it helps immensely.

Providing Choice and Voice for Your Students

Katelyn Giordano
Barrington Middle School, Prairie Campus Language Arts Teacher
Barrington School District 220, Barrington, IL

As educators, our job goes far beyond teaching our students content area skills. In our classrooms, we are preparing our students for their futures, for the people they are becoming.

The best way we can prepare our students is to empower them. In doing this, we capitalize on their natural curiosity and desire to explore, while encouraging them along their individual paths.

Providing Choice

No matter what grade level or subject you teach, empowering students starts with you providing opportunities for choice and valuing student voices. Within your curriculum, there are countless ways to do this. It could be as simple as allowing students to choose the topic they are researching or the method by which they will demonstrate their understanding. But it could go as far as personalized paths that incorporate self-pacing and student-directed learning groups.

When looking for opportunities to personalize your content, there are three areas to consider. Each of these areas is outlined in the downloadable Guide to Providing Student Choice.

Choice in Product
The first area is product, which is a natural way to begin. Invite your students to choose the way they will demonstrate their learning, or the product of their growth. Share the learning target or objective you've been working toward, and then give them the choice to show what they know. Your students will capitalize on their strengths. This type typically exists at the end of a unit and acts as a summative assessment for students.

Choice in Process or Pacing
Personalizing the process or pacing of a unit is a bit more robust, and to be quite honest, requires a lot of front-loading on your part as the teacher.

Keep one extremely important thing in mind when giving students choices in the process or pacing: Scaffolding. Without proper scaffolding and tools to help your students manage their time, they won't be successful. To do this, you must understand the difference between control and structure. Control is dictating what everyone is doing, how they are doing it, and when it is getting done every second of every day. Structure, on the other hand, is providing tools, deadlines, and clear expectations that are to be followed.

The available structures for providing choice in process are wide ranging, but the one that works best is really up to you and in how you implement it. You have to be comfortable with your choice of structure because that is the only way it will be successful! A few ideas or options of this type are outlined in the Guide to Providing Student Choice.

Choice Within Content

To many, this might be the most intimidating option when it comes to student choice. It is important to remember that your content exceeds the specific curriculum or units you are provided. In language arts, for example, the content is reading and writing. And those two things, at their foundation, are personal endeavors. As humans, we read mostly because we enjoy it, and we write because we have something to say.

When you personalize the content for your students, it doesn't mean you scale back the rigor or allow them to graduate your class without mastering any skills. It does mean that you give them a voice in how they will experience and own the learning of those skills. When you provide choice in content, you allow them to learn about topics or ideas *within your content area* that still accomplish your desired objectives. You can find some strategies for providing choice in the content area on the Guide to Providing Student Choice.

Whatever the method, giving our students freedom to make choices is vital to their development and success. A valuable side effect is the boost it provides their intrinsic motivation.

Our students are human just like we are, and as such, they are motivated by the things they like. When we infuse opportunities to investigate their interests, we make our content relevant and support students' autonomy. We allow them to see themselves in our curriculum, which is absolutely vital to its success. The desire to do the work increases because your students truly care about what they are doing. After all, it was their choice.

Authentically Valuing Student Voices

The work of choice begins with authenticity. Learning about authentic learning experiences is one thing—and these types of experiences are valuable—but what is even more important is our own authenticity in the classroom. If we provide surface-level opportunities for autonomy and voice, our impact will remain shallow. But if these opportunities are genuine and come from a place of legitimacy, the effect will go so much farther.

Equally as important is the notion of student voice. As people, our students have a strong desire to feel valued and accepted. This cannot be overlooked or underestimated. And yet, our curricula often do not leave room for our students' voices. Truthfully, our curricula can offer such strict regulations that it negates and diminishes student voice completely. It is our duty and our privilege to stop this. We must foster relationships within our classrooms and build a classroom culture that cherishes the many voices within it.

Ultra-Notes: Reflective Analysis for the Active Teacher

Aaron Sitze, MSEd, NBCT
Social Entrepreneurship Instructor
Oregon Community Unit School District 220, Oregon, IL
Twitter: @AaronSitze

I have this image of a circus performer, masterfully contorted, balancing spinning plates on each of her limber joints—plates on her elbow, heel, nose, plates in each hand—and I think, "Yeah, that's about what first-year teaching is like."

The truth is, we teachers spin a lot of plates. We handle lesson plans, IEP/504 accommodations, parent contacts, team meetings, school-wide initiatives, and state mandates. As a new teacher, you will spend the bulk of your time simply keeping the plates from crashing down. However, the reality is this: Within those crazy first few months, there are moments of greatness—a lesson that delivers an impact so big that the students are buzzing when they leave the room, pacing so tight that the ringing bell feels like a cinematic conclusion—moments where you truly understand why teaching is the greatest profession on Earth.

And in the back of your mind, you hear a voice saying, "This is great! You gotta remember to do this again next year!" But then, another new email arrives, the plates start to wobble, and you turn your attention away. In all likelihood, you will not remember to do it again next year. The conundrum for a new teacher, therefore, is how to be an effective *reflective practitioner*, one who takes the essential time to self-evaluate and iterate pedagogy based on daily feedback, while simultaneously being an effective *active practitioner*, one whose time is (over)filled with grading, planning, and responding.

My solution to this conundrum was Ultra-Notes. On the surface, I needed a way to remember what I did each day of the week—what the objective was, how I opened and closed the lesson, what materials I used. But underneath it all, I also needed a way to remember "how it went"—if there were dead minutes at the end or if I rushed to pull it all together, if there were "moments of greatness." However, I did not have the time or energy to devote to daily journaling.

So, I had the students help me. The Ultra-Notes process works this way: Each day, I assign a different student to take Ultra-Notes. For that day, the student separates her/himself from active participation in the lesson, perhaps sitting at the teacher's desk, with an Ultra-Notes form. (Document is available for download.) Prior to class, they jot down the date and the daily objective that is posted on the board. From bell to bell, they create a narrative of the day: "Mr. Sitze told a story about being afraid of monsters as a kid. Class discussed their worst fears and the best and worst way to solve them. Started Chapter 5 as a group. Stopped to discuss whether the characters were reacting in a positive or negative way to their fears." On and on. Besides this, they also collect handouts and write down any required notes.

More important, however, is what they do afterwards. On the back of the Ultra-Notes page, they write a reflection—elements that were interesting, additional questions sparked from the lesson—as well as a "Grade the Lesson" evaluation, where they can make suggestions about how it could have gone better.

The results of Ultra-Notes?

♦ **RECORD-KEEPING:** Ultra-Notes give you a day-by-day record of lessons: The good, the bad, and the ugly. When kept in a three-ring binder, this becomes a physical curriculum to which you can refer down the road.

♦ **REFLECTION:** When I have time and space, I can leaf through the unit's lessons, remembering what I did, and from a student's point of view, if it was effective.

♦ **RESPONSIBILITY:** Students taking Ultra-Notes have an important job to do, and they should be treated like colleagues that day. As the other students are working, you can ask the scribe, "Do you think it's going well? Are they getting it?" For that day, they, too, feel like teachers.

♦ **RETURNING STUDENTS:** "I was gone for ___ days. What did we do?" This question, usually one that requires a complex answer, now has a simple one: "Check the Ultra-Notes."

Of course, elementary school teachers cannot rely on this method, though the spirit can remain the same: One option might be to have a "confessional style" booth in the room where a student could video-record her reaction to the lesson, similar to a reality-TV setup. This might not get the same degree of detail a high school student might create, but it would still a) effectively keep a record of the day, b) give the student a sense of responsibility and ownership, and c) act as a randomized formative assessment (for example, if the student can, or cannot, retell the essence of the lesson) that itself is useful information.

In the end, Ultra-Notes are not an answer so much as the recognition of an important question. As a new teacher, how will you plan to be both *active* and *reflective*, to keep the multitude of plates spinning while also cultivating the student experiences that make your job so great?

Defeating Apathy, Building Motivation

Dr. David Carroll, NBCT
Maplebrook Elementary School/Madison Junior High School
Naperville Community Unit School District 203, Naperville, IL

Student apathy can be one of the most frustrating aspects of teaching. As a new educator, I accepted that some students just were not meant to excel in my subject. Surely, apathy was inevitable. And I was wrong.

You might say that some people naturally gravitate toward or away from what you teach. Maybe you believe that students are born with talent for your subject. But motivation is not a fixed commodity given at birth beyond your control. If it was, there would be no purpose to practice new skills or apply new knowledge, and we would have no need for inspirational teachers.

Hopefully, you believe that every student can be motivated to learn what you are teaching. The growth-mindset (Molden & Dweck, 2006) suggests that practicing, failing, and seeking feedback are all necessary ingredients for motivated learning. On the other hand, students with a fixed mindset tend to be apathetic toward new ideas or skills, and they tend to fear failure.

You can create a growth-mindset classroom by following two core principles. First, establish an optimal learning environment by embracing responsibility and respect with every routine. Practice your class routines over and over until they require no prompting from you, including transitions, whole-group listening, and small-group discussions. Second, make a connection between your students' past experiences and their future opportunities.

Learning Environment

No matter what subject you teach, learning cannot happen if students are unorganized, disrespectful, or if they feel unsafe. Help your students prioritize their work in your classroom by setting up a Priority Triangle. The Priority Triangle establishes responsibility and respect as the foundation of your class, at the bottom of your triangle. Nothing is more important. Many of the ingredients necessary for a healthy learning environment (trust, academic risk-taking, perseverance, and mutual respect) are rooted in the supportive interactions between you and your students (Sparks, 2019). Engaging lessons leverage that trust with content that affects students personally. If you find yourself presenting material the same way to two different individuals or groups, you are not leveraging your knowledge of students efficiently.

Your content is the next priority on the pyramid. As a teacher, you must be willing to stop teaching the content if responsibility and respect break down. As needed, you will practice your routines until they are once again automatic. Only then can content learning continue.

Having fun is the last priority. Fun can be replaced with other age-appropriate goals, but the idea is that the enjoyment of accomplishment can come only after the content is mastered and students have reflected. Do not let students put fun or enjoyment ahead of learning content. The Priority Triangle is available in the download for you to customize to your age group or content area. Post it prominently so that you can refer to it frequently, especially during the first few weeks of school.

Past Experience and Future Opportunities

Apathy is rooted in a disconnect between the skills and knowledge you are teaching and your students' vision for applying them in the future. Your students will be motivated when they see a purpose or application in the content you are presenting. It is up to you to bridge their past experiences to future opportunities, and there are several easy ways to do so!

♦ **Contextualize Learning.**
   The best teachers provide a context in which students can apply their knowledge. Mathematical story problems are an easy example of contextualizing concepts into authentic problems. Keep in mind, story problems can be suited to fit any content area. The most effective story problems relate closely to the uniqueness of the students in your class. Students in younger grades may apply basic concepts through role playing, simulations, and games. While advanced high school students may be problem solving complex literary, scientific, or historical phenomena in the context of current geopolitical events. Your contextualized instruction uses students' experiences to fit hypothetical scenarios into their own world.

♦ **Employ Storytelling.**
Storytelling is one of the most effective means for providing context to instruction (Roney, 1996). The stories may be about your own experience or about the experience of an important contributor to your subject area. Stories provide a means for students to bridge the abstract (your experiences) to reality (their experiences). Well-conceived stories reward students' curiosity with powerful lessons. More importantly, they help build your students' "library" of experiences so they can better contextualize new knowledge. Use the "dinner table test" to gauge your stories. If your students are talking about your class or retelling your stories at the dinner table, then you have taught an enduring lesson that extends beyond the school bell.

♦ **Make Connections Through Analogies.**
Students gain knowledge by attaching new ideas to old ones (Bruner, 1977). Without that connection, it is very difficult to build new knowledge. Great teachers help motivate apathetic students by drawing analogies. There is a craft in finding similarities between dissimilar concepts or objects. The most unusual, silly, or creative analogies are often the ones students remember the longest.

You became a teacher to make a difference! An unmotivated student is exactly the kind of student who needs you—a caring teacher who can paint a picture of the future! Students will respond to your careful consideration of their interests and experiences.

References

Bruner, J. S. (1977). *The process of education: A landmark in educational theory.* Cambridge, MA: Harvard University Press.

Molden, D. C., & Dweck, C. S. (2006). Finding "meaning" in psychology: A lay theories approach to self-regulation, social perception, and social development. *American Psychologist, 61*(3), 192–203. doi:10.1037/0003-066X.61.3.192.

Roney, R. C. (1996). Storytelling in the classroom: Some theoretical thoughts. *Storytelling World, 9,* 7–9.

Sparks, S. D. (2019, March 12). Why teacher–student relationships matter: New findings shed light on best approaches. *Education Week, 38*(25). Retrieved from http://www.edweek.org/

Blast Off with Formative Assessments

Lydia Gerzel-Short, EdD, Assistant Professor
Northern Illinois University, DeKalb, IL

Karen L. Kohler, EdD, Lecturer
Texas A&M University – San Antonio, San Antonio, TX

Classroom-based assessments provide beneficial information for students and teachers (Stiggins, 2007). Specifically, formative assessments allow students time to think, reflect, and share knowledge with peers (Tomlinson, 2007). Formative assessments give teachers a glimpse into *how* instruction meets the diverse learning needs of students. Teachers of any grade can engage students in learning by employing these five formative assessments.

Mini Whiteboards

One of the easiest types of formative assessment uses dry-erase markers and mini whiteboards. The assessment is instant and provides students with immediate feedback. Mini whiteboards are also great for a variety of learners who need opportunities for kinesthetic or visual learning (Dodge, 2009). Consider using mini whiteboards for individual or group assessments when:

♦ Writing letters, numbers, or words.
♦ Explaining algebraic expressions.
♦ Presenting the effects of historical events on today's society.
♦ Listing components of a chemical reaction.

Linking Word Webs

As a powerful formative assessment tool, word webs that include linking words (e.g., is like/is unlike, causes, represents) create critical thinking opportunities for students (Gerzel-Short, Miller, & Mills, 2018). Using linking word webs before, during, and after instruction helps students create learning pathways. Teachers might consider using linking word webs individually or in small-group assessments because they provide a visual connection to instruction and student understanding. Teach students how to create linking word webs by:

♦ Adding linking terms.
♦ Drawing arrows between concepts or ideas.
♦ Sketching lines within a web category or to bigger ideas.
♦ Including concrete images to abstract concepts or terms to aid in recall.

Picture It

Graphic organizers assist students in visually organizing and making connections to information (Singleton & Filce, 2015). Picture It is an example of a formative assessment that promotes higher-order thinking by encouraging students to draw, label, and explain their understanding of a topic. For example, provide a paper copy of a film strip or an electronic graphic organizer (e.g., http://www.storyboardthat.com) so that students can make connections. Implement Picture It when:

♦ Illustrating the life cycle of plants, animals, or insects.
♦ Drafting past events from various historical figures' perspectives.
♦ Summarizing the sequence of events in an expository or narrative text.
♦ Creating a comic strip explaining the Pythagorean theorem.

Turn, Talk, Ignite!

Students benefit from numerous opportunities to respond to instruction (Gerzel-Short et al., 2018). Turn, Talk, Ignite provides a forum for scaffolded interactions between small- and whole-group instructions. The Ignite component gives students time to express in drawing/writing the dyad discussion. Establishing dyad norms (e.g., how to maintain eye contact, how to stay focused on discussions, how to take turns) is an essential first step when incorporating Turn, Talk, Ignite in the classroom. Integrate Turn, Talk, Ignite when:

- ◆ Discussing a read-aloud.
- ◆ Teaching new vocabulary terms/academic language.
- ◆ Formulating opinions regarding current events.
- ◆ Elaborating on math solutions or results of science labs.

Blast-Off!

Use Blast-Off to provide a glimpse into how your students understand instruction. Exit slips give students opportunities to reflect on personal learning through drawing/writing responses (Marzano, 2012). Blast-Off (in the download) provides students with a means to determine their level of understanding. Create reflective opportunities for drawing and writing by:

- ◆ Incorporating time at the end of a lesson.
- ◆ Assigning exit slips as an entrance ticket for the following day.
- ◆ Adding other concepts to exit slips (e.g., cause/effect, summarizing a lesson in a few sentences).
- ◆ Asking students to write questions they still have about the lesson.

Formative assessment is a vital aspect of instruction because it creates opportunities for reflection and individualized learning. You can launch your instruction when you include these strategies.

References

Dodge, J. (2009). *25 quick formative assessments for a differentiated classroom: Easy, low-prep assessments that help you pinpoint students' needs and reach all learners.* New York, NY: Scholastic.

Gerzel-Short, L., Miller, R., & Mills, J. R. (2018, April). The explicit connection: Vocabulary and secondary students with LD. *LD Forum*, 2–6. Retrieved from https://council-for-learning-disabilities.org/wp-content/uploads/2018/04/LDF_2018_Apr-FINAL-040518.pdf

Marzano, R. J. (2012). The many uses of exit slips. *Educational Leadership*, 70(2), 80–81.

Singleton, S. M., & Filce, H. G. (2015). Graphic organizers for secondary students with learning disabilities. *Teaching Exceptional Children*, 48(2), 110–117. doi:10.1177/0040059915605799.

Stiggins, R. (2007). Assessment through the student's eyes. *Educational Leadership*, 64(8), 22–26.

Tomlinson, C. A. (2007). Learning to love assessment. *Educational Leadership*, 65(4), 8–13.

Start Positive, Professional Conversations with Your Questions

Dr. Mary C. Clement, Professor of Teacher Education
Berry College, Mount Berry, GA

As a new teacher, you may be hesitant to ask questions. Why? No one wants to look unprepared or even "dumb" for asking a question. However, your questions can jumpstart very professional conversations that support relationship building. The keys to asking questions include who, what, when, and where. Additionally, phrasing a question in a very diplomatic way improves the likelihood of a conversation, rather than a terse answer.

Who to Ask?

During new teacher orientation, find out "who's who." You may be assigned a mentor who can answer many of your questions privately. There may be a department chair or lead grade-level teacher who will provide answers to your content-specific questions. Building-level teacher leaders may be available to lead your new teacher meetings, or they may have office hours for new hires. Administrators are busy people, but sometimes they are your best resource. A well-placed question to a principal can get you noticed in a good way.

What Do I Ask?

Ask things that are not covered during your new teacher orientation meetings and/or in the handbook or on the website. The last thing that a veteran teacher or administrator wants to say over and over is, "That information is on our website (or in our handbook, or on the handout in front of you)." After reading everything, decide on your big questions. Keep a running list with a comment beside each one about when and where to ask each question. Remember the old adage, "Don't cross that bridge until you get to it." Daydreaming about snow days and asking about them on the hottest day of August will not be a helpful question. Keep your questions on target for the situation.

When Do I Ask?

You obviously need to ask questions before students and/or parents start asking you the very same questions! As you plan for the first week of school, think of questions that may be asked, and test yourself to see what you need to ask others. New teachers often say, "But no one ever told me." To avoid this trap, it's okay to ask your mentor or the teacher next door what issues or concerns they have experienced during the start of a new school year. Consider asking these questions, "What do you do to get the school year off to a smooth start? What challenges have you found during the first week of school that I should be aware of?"

As holidays or special events approach on the calendar (e.g., homecoming, parent–teacher conferences, delayed-start days), be sure to ask your colleagues about special schedules and issues for those days/weeks.

Where Do I Ask?

In a faculty meeting with other teachers, only ask the question if the other 89 people in the room would benefit from the answer. Do ask questions in your induction/professional development meetings that are on the minds of your peers. Always consider who is in the meeting, seminar, or classroom before asking questions. Mindfulness is an important attribute for professionals. When asking questions, be mindful of what is going on not only for you, but also for your colleagues.

How Do I Ask Diplomatic Questions?

Diplomatic questions often have a starting phrase or a pre-question statement. For example, "I've seen the fifth-grade curriculum guide. I know that everyone here spent a lot of time creating it. Is there a pacing guide for week-to-week topics?" That is much better than asking, "Why aren't there week-to-week topics in the guide?" The worst way to phrase that question would be, "Why didn't you write a week-to-week topic guide that is easy to find and follow?" Other diplomatic starters might be, "Could you share how you have …," "How have you …," "What have you found effective for …," or "What might work for …" To make a question even more diplomatic, consider asking it as a question to a group. "In the past, what steps did the group use to jumpstart success with the test reviews?" Being positive, rather than accusatory, is definitely a way to phrase questions.

Every communication that you have with your colleagues and administrators creates their image of you. Your well-developed questions, asked at appropriate times, are a part of your professionalism. See the download for Questions to Start Positive, Professional Conversations.

Chapter 5

Differentiation

Pretests: The Starting Blocks for Academic Differentiation

Vicki Phelps, EdD, NBCT
Lead Consulting Teacher for Gifted Education
Sumner County Schools, TN

Time. As a new teacher, you might feel as though there is never enough. You are given exhaustive lists of standards, students with diverse needs, benchmark testing, etc., and while you try to differentiate, it is possible to feel overwhelmed. The thought of sacrificing even more time for pretests and subjecting your students to additional testing may not be at the top of your priority list. As I work with new teachers, I regularly hear similar concerns, and quite honestly, I remember feeling the same way, until the day I was asked the following question: "*Without pretests, how are you able to accurately measure student progress or begin to differentiate for academic growth?*" Unable to answer, I knew that I needed to learn more about integrating pretests into my instructional practice.

Think of pretests as the starting blocks for student learning. By taking the "extra" time to pretest, you streamline differentiation to better meet individual needs and increase engagement. Consider the following students' performance during a unit of study:

Student A	Student B
• Inattention Issues • Behavior Problems • Summative Assessment: 100%	• Actively Engaged • Worked Collaboratively • Summative Assessment: 68%

After reading this, who would you say demonstrated the most academic growth and how might you explain the accompanying engagement levels? Now, consider if the students' pretest data were available:

Student A	Student B
• Pretest Score: 98%	• Pretest Score: 8%

With this information, it becomes clear that Student B demonstrated significant growth and Student A had little opportunity to progress at all, which also explains the behaviors. Not only would the data have helped in differentiation, but it would have also been extremely valuable in communicating student progress with parents and other school personnel.

I share this example to signify the power of pretests. Contrary to popular belief, pretesting *saves* time! Pretest data guide differentiation and allow you to work with smaller groups of students at their levels of readiness, increasing student engagement and vastly improving the classroom learning environment.

Here are some helpful hints to launch your students out of the pretest starting blocks toward differentiated student learning.

First Steps

Take advantage of pretests included with many curricular materials. If unavailable, consider using summative assessments as pretests or variations of the same questions through different text selections, data sets, etc. Concept maps are another way to assess for content knowledge. Ask students to construct concept maps including everything they know about a topic. It is amazing what you will learn!

Run the Race

If students demonstrate the need for differentiated content, integrate depth and complexity into the same content but at an advanced level. Depth is accomplished through the integration of advanced details, deeper vocabulary, data integration, and thinking as a disciplinarian. Complexity allows students to examine multiple components of learning at once, including differing perspectives, change over time, implications of assumptions, and multiple effects. Be an ACDC Rock Star: Advance Content with Depth and Complexity!

Keep the Focus

Whether you're adjusting text complexity or modifying math problems from pretest results, consider using Learning Folders. I found these to be extremely helpful with classroom management, as well as maintaining student focus. Each student's folder contains differentiated assignments to complete during independent work time, and students track their daily progress. At the conclusion of each work time, students set goals for next steps and remain focused on their own learning, not on that of their peers.

Having an agenda page in the front of each student's folder is key. Students retrieve their folders at the beginning of the week and reference the agenda (in the download) to see what tasks they need to complete. The agenda also includes a space for daily goal setting. Learning Folders help increase student engagement and accountability, provide uninterrupted small-group instruction, and organize student work. Your students will also have continued practice with goal setting and time management. Give it a try! Your students will thank you!

Differentiation: How to Meet a Moral Imperative

Dr. Will Dwyer
Principal
West Chicago High School, West Chicago, IL

American classrooms are more diverse now than they were 25 years ago. One quarter of children under the age of 18 in the United States come from immigrant families and nearly a third of all children live in poverty (Turner, 2015). These demographic changes have created a wider and more varied group of learners in classrooms across the country. While states, districts, and schools struggle for policies and programs to better serve so many diverse learners, classroom teachers and their ability to meet the different learning needs of children remain key to unlocking deep understanding for ALL students.

In many learning organizations, differentiating learning often means separating struggling learners from their more academically adept counterparts. Whether this takes the form of homogeneous grouping, tracked courses, or pulling students to work with specialists, the results are often damaging for struggling learners, who develop identities of inferiority and are deprived of academic exemplars to learn from. Differentiation that benefits all students can, and should, happen inclusively in classrooms in a way that brings all learners together.

There are three key strategies teachers can employ to create an environment conducive to differentiated learning. Use the download to reflect on your differentiation practices.

Create Worthy Problems

Rote learning, memorizing disjointed information, and repetitive basic facts are common aspects of education. However, these practices are not engaging to students when presented in isolation. When you create worthy problems full of challenge and interest with multiple pathways to solutions and ways to be correct, you help your students contribute to one another's learning without them competing to find the one right answer. Additionally, using complex and worthy problems allows you to create cooperative learning groups in which students of varying academic abilities and backgrounds can work interdependently on a shared task. This instructional strategy allows you to use various texts that students can access based on their reading levels and/or assigned roles.

Model Respect and Rapport

Offering differentiated learning opportunities without using grouping may present some challenges. Students may notice that they are engaged in different tasks than their peers. They may be more aware of the disparities of ability across students. However, by creating an environment of mutual respect where mistakes are celebrated as learning opportunities and not hidden, you can foster a classroom where students feel free to learn and take risks at their own pace and comfort level. You should be mindful to set an example of respect, decorum, and civility through classroom expectations you set along with your conduct with and around students. This requires the absence of sarcasm and the capacity to hear and value all voices in the room.

Leverage Feedback Effectively

Differentiation, at its core, is an acknowledgment that different students need different supports/materials to reach the nonnegotiable goals of learning. Therefore, your students will also require appropriate, personalized feedback and redirection to facilitate their learning. Helpful and timely feedback for all learners is essential for effective differentiated instruction. When crafting feedback for your students, be sure to address these three questions as identified by Nottingham and Nottingham (2017):

+ *What is the student trying to achieve?*
+ *How much progress has the student made so far?*
+ *What should the student do next?*

References

Nottingham, J., & Nottingham, J. (2017). *Challenging learning through feedback: How to get the type, tone, and quality of feedback right every time*. Thousand Oaks, CA: Corwin.

Turner, E. O. (2015). Districts' responses to demographic change: Making sense of race, class, and immigration in political and organizational context. *American Educational Research Journal, 52*(1), 4–39. doi:10.3102/0002831214561469.

Differentiating for Student Success

Sara Curran, EdD, NBCT
Fourth Grade Teacher
Community Unit School District 308, Oswego, IL

As a teacher, your primary role is to deliver instruction. Schools typically provide you with content standards, scope, sequence, and pacing guides to align your instruction with district expectations. However, students enter the classroom with various academic needs, social-emotional proficiencies, achievement levels, personal interests, and learning preferences. Since each student is unique, you must balance individual needs with the demands of the curricula. Differentiation is an impactful way to embrace the heterogeneity of a classroom while increasing success for all learners. Although differentiation can be daunting, you can achieve effective differentiation with thoughtful planning. The following tips will assist you in successfully differentiating your instruction.

Focus on Students' Needs

Students' needs should guide your decision making. You must know your students' interests, achievement levels, special education requirements, preferred learning styles, and social–emotional needs to effectively differentiate for them. Strive to maximize your interactions with students, gather information from exit slips, and use interest inventories to get to know your students well.

Use Data

Use data from classroom observations, formative/summative assessments, and standardized tests to plan your instruction. Adjust your lesson plans to include reteaching for students approaching proficiency, as well as enrichment opportunities for those who already exhibit mastery.

Reach Out

Seek guidance from other professionals at your school. Collaborate with teachers in your grade level/content area. Work with the reading specialist, gifted teacher, teacher of English Learners, social worker, or special education coordinator to discuss specific students' learning needs. Team teach or co-plan, when possible.

Scaffold or Tier Lessons

Tiering and scaffolding ensure all students are adequately challenged but not overwhelmed by learning experiences. Provide sentence stems, access to resources, picture cues, and/or enrichment opportunities to encourage a positive learning experience for all.

Differentiate Tasks

Tasks can be modified to differentiate for interest, achievement, or learning style. Offer choices whenever possible. Encourage students to self-select specific topics for research or written responses. Provide options for learning processes, such as partner work versus independent work, audiobooks versus independent reading, or hands-on learning versus textbook use. Permit students to self-select products to demonstrate their understanding. Allowing diagrams, paragraphs, slideshows, comic strips, or video clips will likely result in optimal outcomes.

Incorporate Flexible Grouping

You can group students based on student choice, readiness levels, or current achievement. Change groups often to ensure you are consistently meeting students' needs and promoting interactions with a variety of peers.

Promote Active Engagement

Engage all student groups in beneficial, motivating tasks. Aim for all groups to be involved in high-interest student-centered tasks that align with their current instructional needs. Set clear expectations for group work prior to beginning a task to promote on-task behaviors.

Pace Yourself

Differentiating curricula can be overwhelming and time consuming. Try one new differentiation strategy and get comfortable implementing it before attempting another idea.

Deliberately Reflect on Teaching

Use exit slips to monitor student understanding. Take notes on your lesson plans of changes you would like to make the following year (e.g., portions that went well, alterations to delivery, and areas of student difficulty). Ask students to reflect on their own learning and/or provide feedback on lessons.

By following these tips, you will be equipped to engage all learners in your classroom and achieve student success through differentiation. For additional support with differentiation, refer to the download accompanying this book. Student inventories, a reflection sheet, a lesson-planning template, open-ended questions, and lists of ways to differentiate instruction are available to assist you in meeting the unique needs of your students.

Providing Choice

Kylie Martin
English Teacher
Poland Regional High School, Poland, ME

Differentiation is one of my greatest challenges as a first-year teacher. Achieving successful differentiation is essential to having a productive and engaged classroom environment. Choice projects or assignments are the most significant component of my English classroom. For example, students build their knowledge of literary elements by analyzing novels they choose for themselves. This allows for learning through self-discovery and authentic engagement. Writing assignments ask students to express their individual voices by focusing on their own experiences, passions, or interests. Throughout the school year, my ninth graders have written memoirs; created websites, presentations, and posters on choice books and class-wide novels; analyzed self-chosen music videos; and written fictional short stories.

Providing choice of medium and content allows for genuine engagement and the opportunity to enter the class material at one's own intellectual level. Additionally, when creating projects, students often require different modes of entry and expression. Perhaps I offer the option of constructing an essay through templates that break down the introduction, body paragraphs, and conclusion. Or, I provide a visual map that helps them categorize their central claim and the two to three main ideas that support their central claim. It is important to offer a variety of ways for students to a) explore concepts relating to our learning targets, and b) demonstrate their understanding. Providing differentiated learning opportunities is often an exhausting challenge, but I am learning to adapt to my students' needs, strengths, and various interests as the year progresses.

Enhancing Learning for All Students: Using a UDL Framework to Create Expert Learners

Katrina A. Hovey, Assistant Professor
Western Oregon University, Monmouth, OR

Marla J. Lohmann, Assistant Professor
Colorado Christian University, Lakewood, CO
Twitter: @MarlaLohmann

Ariane N. Gauvreau, Field Director and Teaching Associate
University of Washington, Seattle, WA

Teachers are challenged with making content accessible for all, including exceptional and diverse students. Universal Design for Learning (UDL) is a research-based framework based on insights into how people learn. UDL emphasizes using three learning networks (e.g., multiple means of engagement, multiple means of representation, and multiple means of action and expression). Use of these three networks ensures that your students have access to the curriculum and can become expert learners (CAST, 2020).

Provide Multiple Means of Engagement

Dedicating time to increasing your students' motivation for learning and class participation is imperative. Research suggests that student motivation and engagement increase when teachers pique their students' curiosity (Stockall, Dennis, & Miller, 2012). Therefore, increasing student motivation and getting them excited about participating in your classroom community enhances learning. To increase student engagement, you can:

- Offer choices and options (e.g., seating preferences, forming student work groups, determining learning goals, demonstrating learning/mastery).
- Include problem-based learning (e.g., student work to solve authentic and culturally relevant problems, projects reflect student interests).
- Teach students to self-monitor and self-evaluate (e.g., use formative assessment strategies such as thumbs up/thumbs down, learning logs, and group rewards).
- Use classroom materials that reflect student culture and interest (e.g., diverse books, preferred activities, students teach classmates words from their home language, include decorations and curricular materials that reflect the community, share traditions, and acknowledge holidays celebrated by students).
- Build relationships with students (e.g., create a classroom handshake, make time for 1:1 conversation, celebrate student successes and birthdays, and take turns sharing about your weekend/family/pets/hobbies).

Provide Multiple Means of Representation

Multiple means of representation refer to the methods teachers use to present curriculum content (Glass, Meyer, & Rose, 2013). This practice benefits your students because they perceive and comprehend information in a variety of ways (CAST, 2018). For example, when presenting information, consider:

♦ Pairing verbal instructions with visual representations (i.e., show students photos, clip art, and step-by-step drawings to support verbal instructions).
♦ Including home language translation and representation in the classroom (e.g., use translation apps, label classroom materials in multiple languages, and encourage parents to read to students in English and in their home language).
♦ Incorporating hands-on learning activities (e.g., offer students manipulatives, include art and cooking projects, and set up a sensory table).
♦ Using think-alouds (i.e., you and your students think aloud while completing tasks).
♦ Modeling skills (e.g., role plays, technology integration, and audio and video recordings).

Provide Multiple Means of Action and Expression

Multiple means of action and expression is the "how" of learning and refers to the way students demonstrate understanding and curriculum mastery (National Center on Universal Design for Learning, 2018). Students have preferences related to participating and showing learning (CAST, 2018). You can incorporate the following strategies when checking for understanding and mastery:

♦ Incorporate dramatic play (e.g., role play, student skits, and puppet shows).
♦ Integrate technology (e.g., word process, presentation software, and create videos).
♦ Create visual representations (e.g., make posters, illustrate comic strips, create graphic novels, craft collages, and develop graphic organizers).
♦ Make audio recordings (e.g., use voice-over presentations, record responses, and/or readings).

When educators use the principles of UDL to optimize their teaching, they support all students through intentional, proactive, and reflective instruction (Lohmann, Hovey, & Gauvreau, 2018). Expert learners have an awareness of their learning needs and seek ways to meet those needs. Strategies for implementing UDL benefit students and are easily implemented by teachers at all grade levels and who work in all instructional setting (Gauvreau, Lohmann, & Hovey, 2019). For your convenience, a UDL strategy quick reference guide is available for download.

References

CAST. (2018). Universal Design for Learning Guidelines version 2.2. Retrieved from http://udlguidelines.cast.org

Gauvreau, A. N., Lohmann, M. J., & Hovey, K. A. (2019). Using a universal design for learning framework to provide multiple means of representation in the early childhood classroom. *The Journal of Special Education Apprenticeship, 8*(1), 1–13. Retrieved from http://www.josea.info/web/public/doc/archives/2019/Vol%208,%20No%201%20 (Jul,%202019)/vol8no1-2-FT.pdf

Glass, D., Meyer, A., & Rose, D. H. (2013). Universal design for learning and the arts. *Harvard Educational Review, 83*(1), 98–119. doi:10.17763/haer.83.1.33102p26478p54pw.

Lohmann, M. J., Hovey, K. A., & Gauvreau, A. N. (2018). Using a universal design for learning framework to enhance engagement in the early childhood classroom. *The Journal of Special Education Apprenticeship, 7*(2). Retrieved from http://www.josea.info/web/ public/doc/archives/2018/Vol%207,%20No%202%20(Jun,%202018)/vol7no2-5-FT.pdf

Stockall, N. S., Dennis, L., & Miller, M. (2012). Right from the start: Universal design for preschool. *Teaching Exceptional Children, 45*(1), 10–17.

Differentiation That Helps, Not Hurts

Hilary Dack, PhD, Assistant Professor
University of North Carolina at Charlotte, Charlotte, NC

How could differentiation hurt students? If you are giving students work at different levels to accommodate different entry points to learning, that's always a good thing, right? Not necessarily. As a former middle school teacher and researcher, I study new teachers' experiences using differentiation. I have spent hundreds of hours observing teachers as they "differentiate."

I have seen defensible differentiated lessons that are carefully structured to give all students in a general education classroom equitable access to rich, rigorous learning experiences. I have also seen teaching practices masquerading as differentiation that do the opposite. Two first-year teachers I know refer to these practices as "teaching that only sounds differentiated-y" or "fake differentiation." This article highlights the differences between these two forms of "differentiation," and poses three questions you can apply to any lesson to support using differentiation that helps, not hurts.

Defensible differentiation involves modifying instruction based on assessment-revealed differences in students' readiness, interest in different topics, or learning profile. You can do this by adjusting the content students explore, how students process content, or the products that display students' learning (Tomlinson, 2014). *Readiness* is a student's current level of mastery of a particular skill, while *learning profile* refers to students' preferences for how they approach learning. In a differentiated classroom, students frequently work on related but dissimilar tasks in the same space at the same time. This often means that students work in assigned groups that complete different tasks.

Is the Way I Group Students Fixed or Flexible (Tomlinson, 2014)?

In an effectively differentiated classroom, your student groupings should change often for two key reasons. First, just because your students share the same readiness level does not mean they share the same interests or learning profile. If some lessons are differentiated based on each of these three categories of student differences, groupings will necessarily change from lesson to lesson.

Second and more importantly, groupings can also shift across differentiated lessons based on student readiness. This is because readiness is a fluid concept. A student's proximity to a learning objective will change over time as the student gains more proficiency. Imagine that the targeted level of mastery is the learning destination or finish line that you want students to reach or move beyond. You can think of each student's readiness level as their location on the path toward that finish line at any given moment. One student may begin a unit close to that destination, but not actually advance much toward it from lesson to lesson. Another student may begin the unit far from the destination, but move quickly toward the finish line, and then beyond it, in several lessons.

Student readiness is different from student ability since teachers usually talk about ability as a fixed trait that does not change much over time. When your students are put into ability groups (e.g., "high-fliers," "middle-of-the-road," and "strugglers"), those groups often do not change throughout the year. Such fixed groupings do not support effective differentiation.

Is Assessment Data Guiding My Decision Making?

Flexible grouping must be informed by ongoing pre- and formative assessment data. Although you may be tempted to group students or assign differentiated-tasks based on hunches about student ability, defensible differentiation requires you to point to specific and current data about student readiness to justify your decisions. Telling yourself things like, "The student didn't show strong proficiency on this exit ticket, but I know he knows this," or "This answer makes it look like the student understands, but I don't think she really does," will not cut it. You must consider students to be innocent of learning until proven guilty by assessment data.

Are My Differentiated Tasks "Respectful" (Tomlinson, 2014)?

All differentiated tasks must be equally engaging and equally powerful. It is not respectful to have one group work on a task that most students their age would find engaging and another group work on a task that falls flat. Your students will notice if one group gets to work with technology or manipulatives while their group does not.

It is also not respectful if one group's task is more powerful in terms of offering a rigorous and rich opportunity to make sense of content while another group's does not. The task for students whose readiness with the lesson's objective is still developing must include scaffolding to help these students access the same rich opportunity. This is the opposite of having one group work with a hands-on/minds-on activity while the other group is drilled in rote facts and skills. Defensible differentiation requires "teaching up" for this latter group, not "watering down" (Tomlinson & Javius, 2012).

Conclusion

Ask yourself these three questions when you plan a differentiated lesson. Do you find your-self defending "teaching that only sounds differentiated-y," or can you answer each question with a strong "yes"?

To support the consistent use of differentiation that helps, download the document associated with this article, which includes a set of reflection prompts to spur your think-ing and space to jot down your ideas. If you repeatedly consider these questions as part of your regular teaching practice, they can offer a series of reflective "differentiation check-ins" when you begin to plan a unit, as you teach differentiated lessons within the unit, and when you consider the unit's efficacy after you have finished teaching it.

References

Tomlinson, C. A. (2014). *The differentiated classroom: Responding to the needs of all learners* (2nd ed.). Alexandria, VA: ASCD.

Tomlinson, C. A., & Javius, E. L. (2012). Teach up for excellence. *Educational Leadership, 69*(5), 28–33.

Find What Works for Them, and You'll Find It'll Work for You

Neil O'Reilly
Social Studies Teacher (9–12)

As a beginning teacher, one of the more stubborn misconceptions I have had to overcome is that differentiation involves too much effort when preparing a class of 30 or more students for success in a standardized test at the end of the course. Well, it didn't happen overnight, but I finally have it beat.

For me, starting small helped. I began by introducing choice boards for performance tasks designed to help students prepare for common assessment. This aligns work more closely with their individual interests. Additionally, I found learning stations a great way to begin to better understand my students' learning profiles. When delivering content to multiple student teams based on readiness, I might transition to jigsaw groups. This strategy allows me to pull together different learners with work that is appropriately challenging for each member while requiring all students to contribute equally to the group.

As I have grown as an educator and become more confident differentiating for my stu-dents, I always keep in mind that everyone is still making their way to the same learning goal. They are just getting there by different means. When differentiation is successful, stu-dents are far more likely to find the lesson engaging. Also, I spend less time managing the classroom and more time leading it. And on those occasions when my efforts fall flat, I still come away with valuable data on what works, and what doesn't, for my particular learners.

Differentiation Through Independent Study: The I-LEARN Process

Vicki Phelps, EdD, NBCT
Lead Consulting Teacher for Gifted Education
Sumner County Schools, TN

Whether you are looking to teach the research process through content differentiation, or you have one student out of 30 who has demonstrated content mastery on an entire unit, Independent Study is an excellent differentiation strategy. I have to admit, in my early years of teaching, I thought Independent Study consisted of allowing students to choose a topic to research and then present their findings to the class, without any true guidelines. This resulted in students having a great time finding obscure pictures of their topics, but most of the time, they did not learn anything new. I quickly realized that Independent Study did *not* mean students creating presentations on topics they had already mastered. Remember, the goal of differentiation is not only to engage students but also to provide them with opportunities for academic growth.

When you set it up correctly, Independent Study provides students with meaningful, rigorous units of study. That sounds great, but you might find yourself wondering where to begin! First and foremost, involve your students as much as possible in developing the unit as you follow the I-LEARN process:

Identify a Topic to Investigate

First, determine if the Independent Study should focus on a deeper, more complex examination of pre-assessment content (e.g., thinking as a content disciplinarian to solve a related world issue with applied skills) or on student interest. Once you and your student have settled on a topic, decide if the required research will be through a descriptive, cause/effect, comparison, or problem/solution approach, as well as what form the research will take: Case study, historical, correlation, experimental, action, and so on.

Lay Out a Learning Plan

During this phase, you will create the required learning components, along with applicable rubrics (e.g., Venn diagrams, journal entries, graphic organizers, PowerPoints, proposals, constructions, reflection sheets). Once you've identified those, create a list of needed materials and resources to successfully accomplish these tasks. Finally, construct a timeline of completion dates, along with preestablished check-in dates, as well as an Independent Learning Contract to be signed by the student, teacher, and parent.

Engage in Research

Next, focus on how your student will engage in research by establishing a guiding research question. This will be the essential question your student will answer as a result of the research. Next, identify how your student will organize and maintain the research, as well as how they will cite their sources.

Apply Learning

It is now time to create a culminating task for the synthesis of learned information, along with an accompanying rubric. This culminating task should include a real-world connection.

Reflect and Refine

Reflection is a key component in learning, so identify opportunities for your student to reflect throughout the Independent Study. In addition, specify how you, as the teacher, will provide additional feedback during the scheduled check-ins and throughout the research process.

Next Steps for Newfound Knowledge

Determine how your student will share the knowledge gained from the Independent Study with an identified audience and specify their potential next steps for future research.

In my experience, it has been very helpful to have an I-LEARN planning sheet (see download) as I conference with students during the development of their Independent Study. This interaction of ideas and insights is invaluable in engaging the students and getting them excited to move forward with this differentiation strategy. These planning sheets are also incredibly helpful in keeping track of each student's learning when you have multiple students working through Independent Study. As a bonus, you could even consider using the I-LEARN planning sheet as the learning contract!

Disaster Drills for Students with Exceptionalities

Deitra A. Kuester, PhD, Associate Professor
Bradley University, Peoria, IL

Lauralyn K. Randles, Doctoral Candidate
Illinois State University, Normal, IL

You will find that disaster drills are common in schools. These include two *types* designed to promote safety during disasters: "Get out," where you leave the building/structure and go outside, such as in a flood, a building fire, or wildfire, and "stay put," where you stay in the building or wherever you are, such as in an earthquake or tornado.

Title 20 of the Individuals with Disabilities Education Act (2004) addresses discrimination on the basis of disability, but some schools fail to include students with exceptionalities in evacuation procedures. For example, during fire drills, students unable to evacuate with peers are required to shelter in place on the landing of a stairwell and wait for EMS rescue (Scott, 2018). These students (e.g., those who use a wheelchair, special walker) are made to wait on a stairwell landing while others safely escape, because there is no emergency equipment available (e.g., evacuation chair, medical sled) to aid their transport.

In addition to fire, tornado, and other practice drills, as a result of the STOP School Violence Act of 2018, 90% of public schools also include active shooter drills (U.S. Department of Justice, 2018). These active shooter drills may include both "get out" and "stay put" procedures. School districts have their own procedures for practicing disaster drills, but there is no standard procedure across districts, and not all schools include active shooter drills (Hendry, 2015). Moreover, active shooter drills may be scaring students more than helping them, and schools are not preparing students with exceptionalities for active shooter scenarios (Chuck, 2019; Davidson, 2018). During disaster drills, in some cases, students with exceptionalities are being left out, told to stay home, and/or not accommodated (Smith, 2018). You must consider that students with exceptionalities need to be included in emergency procedures, too.

Preparing Students with Exceptionalities for Disaster Drills

Preplan! Practice! Include *all* students! Schools must plan for students who have a variety of needs (e.g., physical, sensory, intellectual, processing delays, visual, hearing, or a combination). It is your responsibility to ensure *all* of your students are accounted for and safe. Therefore, advocate for students with exceptionalities to ensure appropriate equipment is available. Desensitize your students by practicing as a class, prior to school-wide drills. Develop signs, signals, gestures, and so on as a way to get and sustain attention and relay directions. Speak with students and make appropriate accommodations for those with exceptionalities. Communicate and collaborate with parents about appropriate needs during Individual Education Program meetings. Table 5.1 provides an at-a-glance list of suggested strategies for use with students with various exceptionalities.

Additional checklists/resources are provided in the download to support your preplanning and advocating efforts for the safety of all students. You are encouraged to tweak these resources, make them appropriate and useful to best meet the needs of your students, and reproduce them for use in your classroom. Use these in conjunction with your school's procedures.

References

Chuck, E. (2019, April 14). Active shooter drills are scaring kids and may not protect them. Some schools are taking a new approach. *NBC News*. Retrieved from https://www.nbcnews.com/news/us-news/active-shooter-drills-are-scaring-kids-may-not-protect-them-n992941

Davidson, J. (2018, March 14). Schools aren't preparing students with disabilities for active shooter scenarios. *The Mighty*. Retrieved from https://themighty.com/2018/03/active-shooter-disability/

Table 5.1 Suggested Strategies for Inclusive Disaster Drills

Inclusive Disaster Drills
All Students
✓ Pretalk plans/expectations.   ✓ Create buddy systems.   ✓ Rename active shooter practices.   ✓ Make map. List procedures. Post by door.   ✓ Include "Checklist of Accommodations" in folders for substitute teacher and support staff. Post by door (Marin County Office of Education, 2010).   ✓ Use visual cue cards. Punch holes in them. Put on large notebook ring. Hang by door.
English Learners
✓ Make maps and list procedures in native language(s).   ✓ Use visual cues when giving directions.
Hearing
✓ If the student uses a Frequency Modulation (FM) system or other amplifiers, take microphone with you.   ✓ Practice silent drills. Allow questions/answers without auditory interruptions.   ✓ Americans with Disabilities Act (ADA) requires that fire alarms have flashing lights.   ✓ Consult the Teacher of Deaf/Hard of Hearing.
Mobility
✓ Ensure staff are aware of accessible exits/evacuation equipment and use.   ✓ Request training from administration for using evacuation equipment.   ✓ Let students explore equipment. Practice using it with staff.   ✓ Consult the Physical Therapist.
Multiple Needs
✓ When language, noise, lights (other stimuli) get in the way of a safe exit, teach students an emergency sign (draw "X" on their back with your finger, so they know to immediately stop, hold your hand/arm, walk with you without arguing or resisting).
Sensory
✓ Use *social stories* to help students learn what to do and why.   ✓ Create emergency box with the following items: Checklist of procedures, sunglasses for bright/flashing lights, noise canceling headphones, rewards, fidget toys, Kleenex, etc.   ✓ Gradually introduce sound and flashing lights.   ✓ If student cannot move due to sensory overload, use chair with wheels to transport.   ✓ Consult the Occupational and/or Behavioral Specialists.
Vision
✓ Post procedures/routes in Braille (or large print), whichever meets student needs.   ✓ If student is unable to follow visual cues (or visual exits), practice locating exit doors using clues (number of steps/cement blocks of hallway walls).   ✓ Practice having them ask for assistance from peers/staff around them.   ✓ Consult the Teacher of Visually Impaired, Orientation/Mobility.

Hendry, J. A. Jr. (2015). *The origin of lockdown: Enduring questions and one man's journey to discover where lockdown came from* [Brochure]. Medina, OH: ALICE Training Institute. Retrieved from http://www.alicetraining.com/wp-content/uploads/2015/11/Origin-of-Lockdown.1.pdf

Individuals with Disabilities Education Act. (2004). 20 U.S.C. § 1400.

Marin County Office of Education (2010). *Emergency plan for students with special needs for Marin County School District: Model annex to Marin schools emergency management plan.* San Rafael, CA: Author.

Scott, L. E. (2018, March 1). Emergency evacuation planning for students with disabilities. *Wrightslaw.* Retrieved from https://www.wrightslaw.com/info/emer.evac.plans.scott.htm

Smith, S. E. (2018, June 12). *In case of emergency, what happens to disabled students?* [Web log post]. Retrieved from https://rootedinrights.org/in-case-of-emergency-what-happens-to-disabled-students/

U.S. Department of Justice. (2018). *Student, teachers, and officers preventing (STOP) school violence program.* Retrieved from: https://bja.ojp.gov/program/stop-school-violence-program/overview

DIFFERENTiation

Christal Hoch
Fourth Grade Cambridge Teacher
Collier County Public School, Mike Davis Elementary School, Estero, FL

Real-world teaching is truly an art. There is no "one size fits all" approach to ensuring your students understand the critical content. When it comes to real-world teaching, it is so important to take the first couple of months and get to know your students. Each year brings a different group of students with different kinds of challenges. Before you can begin to teach, it is of the utmost importance to cultivate those relationships and gain trust of your students. Once you understand your students' home lives, motivations, and interests, that is when teaching really happens. I have to differentiate my instruction in order to meet all of my student's challenges and needs. One of the most helpful ways is utilizing technology. This generation was born with technology all-encompassing their lives. Websites like Flocabulary are very helpful. Kids love to sing and dance, whether they admit to it or not. Adding movement and song to a skill helps them memorize critical content. Another enjoyable way to differentiate is a partner scoot around the room where they help teach each other. I can teach a lesson 100 different ways, but sometimes it just takes a new person saying the same thing for them to grasp the concept. Your team, coaches, mentors, and sometimes even students can help you find new and innovative ways to teach a lesson. Always be willing to learn new ideas to reach every student, but ALWAYS trust your gut. You know your students best.

Using Choice Boards to Differentiate Instruction in the Classroom

Dr. Angela Danley, Associate Professor of Elementary Education
University of Central Missouri, Warrensburg, MO

Differentiating instruction is how you meet the needs of student learners by tailoring your lesson delivery. This includes your work with individual students or small groups. Your use of ongoing assessment and flexible grouping strategies makes differentiation a successful approach to instruction (Tomlinson, 2000). A differentiated classroom presents students with a variety of ways to learn and process the content in their most effective way (Tomlinson, 2017). You can differentiate instruction through a variety of ways based on student readiness, interest, or learning profile. When you differentiate instruction, your students take more responsibility for their learning.

Product Differentiation Using Choice Boards

One way you can differentiate instruction is through products. Product differentiation allows choice in learning to demonstrate acquired understanding of the content. One example of product differentiation is choice boards. Choice boards allow your students to choose how they will demonstrate learning of a key skill. Additionally, choice boards provide a variety of activities that focus on students' learning needs, interests, and abilities. Students are typically expected to complete at least three of the activities on the choice board. Creating this tool is a relatively simple process. Once you create one, you can edit and reuse it each year. The following steps are suggested when creating a choice board:

1. Identify the focus and learning outcomes in a unit of study.
2. Determine student readiness, interests, and learning styles.
3. Design approximately nine different activities centered on the unit of study based on student skills, interests, and learning preferences. Arrange each task in its own grid similar to a Tic-Tac-Toe board.
4. Provide directions on the number of tasks students are required to complete. Typically, three tasks are completed.

The use of choice boards in the classroom connects to the major principles of differentiated instruction shared by O'Brien and Guiney (2001):

1. Every child can learn.
2. Each child has the right to a high-quality education.
3. Progress for each child will be expected and recognized.
4. Each child in the classroom has distinct and individual needs.

Choice boards can be completed during station rotations, during classroom instruction time, or as a homework activity. This tool can be used with integrated cross-curricular content.

When differentiating instruction, it is important to remember that it is a pedagogy, not a structured program or worksheet driven (Robb, 2008). Furthermore, you can differentiate instruction to provide engaging and relevant learning experiences for your students. Since differentiated instruction is a student-centered approach, the use of choice boards gives students ownership of their learning. Every student is different, so you need to offer instruction in a variety of ways. Using the choice board in your classroom allows students to select activities that honor their learning preference and demonstrate that they understand the content.

See the download for examples of choice boards. The examples include fiction and non-fiction at the primary and intermediate grade levels. You can use the choice boards during centers or independent work time. You could also use this tool as a template for any content area.

References

O'Brien, T., & Guiney, D. (2001). *Differentiation in teaching and learning: Principles and practice.* London, England: Continuum.

Robb, L. (2008). *Differentiating reading instruction: How to teach reading to meet the needs of each student.* New York, NY: Scholastic.

Tomlinson, C. A. (2000). Differentiation of instruction in the elementary grades [ERIC Digest]. Retrieved from ERIC Clearinghouse on Elementary and Early Childhood Education website: https://files.eric.ed.gov/fulltext/ED443572.pdf

Tomlinson, C. A. (2017). *How to differentiate instruction in academically diverse classrooms* (3rd ed.). Alexandria, VA: ASCD.

Scaffolding Instruction to Support Student Learning

Anita S. Charles, PhD, Senior Lecturer & Director of Teacher Education
Bates College, Lewiston, ME
Facebook: Anita S. Charles, PhD
Twitter: anita_s_charles

Scaffolding is linked to Vygotsky's (1978) Zone of Proximal Development (ZPD), the conditions in which students can learn with support of a teacher, or the zone in which learning and teaching must happen. Anything "below" the zone is what the learner can already do. Anything "above" the zone is not (yet) accessible, even with supports. Teachers must adapt and adjust learning within the ZPD for every learner, using scaffolded instruction that is responsive to individual students. These scaffolds are stepping stones to support progress toward goals for your students. The download includes web links and sample templates.

Break Longer Assignments into Smaller Parts

For a project, you might first have students complete a worksheet with their ideas and a title. The next assignment might be to locate three sources, then to build an opening paragraph. You don't need to grade each step along the way, just check them off as they complete each one. Students who fall behind on a given step must be given every opportunity to complete it with support. The intent is to help build student success toward the final project/paper, not to create a cascading backlog of smaller assignments. If a student gets stuck, you might need to break that bit into even smaller tasks. Use an assignment planner to help students stay on track.

Use the Think–Pair–Share Strategy

This strategy ensures that all students are engaged and empowered to have a voice, and you can adapt it for any age, grade, or content area. First, students are given a quick moment to think—I sometimes ask them to jot down a quick response on scrap paper. Then they quickly pair with a neighbor to share ideas or responses. Finally, they report to the group with one or two ideas. I use this to review key information, to go over main points of a reading, to answer a challenging question, or to boost lagging energy. You can shorten, lengthen, or eliminate one of the steps depending on your purpose and time constraints. This strategy can go quite quickly as a check-in. You do not need to call on every pair to share. Simply engaging in the process allows students to feel connected.

Use Templates or Graphic Organizers for Readings, Media, or Lectures

You can use this strategy to support scaffolded learning. A template is a structure to help your students anchor key points, review material, and organize their thoughts to support them during class discussions. For example, they can use them for lecture support, note taking, pre-reading, prewriting, and assessment. Also, you can use graphic organizers throughout your curriculum. They can assist your students in making connections across content areas and between concepts. The visuals you can create are endless. You can provide your students with a completed visual or have them complete parts as you are teaching using media sources in your classroom.

Help Students with Writer's Block

When students feel unable to get started on an assignment, have them share an idea out loud that you write down for them. I've used this with students who say, "I just can't think of anything," or "I don't know how to start." Here is what it might look like:

TEACHER: Tell me one thing you remember. (OR: "One question you have is…"; "What was the main point of…"; "What word pops into your mind…"; "What was the character doing when…") Use question probes to jar an idea.
STUDENT GIVES ONE SHORT THOUGHT.
TEACHER WRITES DOWN WHAT STUDENT SAYS.
TEACHER OFFERS ANOTHER PROBE.

Continue this process. The point is to write down what the student says, more or less verbatim, and then, after five or six lines say, "You've got a great start, keep going."

Provide Tiered Reading Assignments

Websites exist that allow you to locate or build multileveled reading assignments. Ways to adapt a reading passage include providing summaries, making the text less dense, increasing print size, using simpler vocabulary, and having vocabulary or comprehension guides/tools available. One biology teacher I know sets out three different levels of readings and activities, all of which aim for the same goals and standards. You might offer students a choice or give them the one best suited to their current level. Teacher-friendly websites for tiered readings include Newsela, TextProject, and ReadWorks.

Use Tiered Questions

Have a set of questions at the ready, running from simple to complex, that enable all of your students to participate during whole-class discussions. Carefully consider who gets what question during classroom discussion. Your struggling students can answer fact-recall or subjective questions around their opinions, beliefs, or feelings. You can encourage more advanced students to dig more deeply into themes, depth, or breadth of material.

Use Flexible Grouping

Use varied methods of grouping students depending on purpose and context. Try to allow for heterogeneous groups whenever possible, and limit to no more than four students per group. It can be helpful to assign roles to students, and to ask groups to submit a summary of who did what during the group work.

Reference

Vygotsky, L. S. (1978). *Mind in society: The development of higher psychological processes* (M. Cole, V. John-Steiner, S. Scribner, E. Souberman, Eds.). Cambridge, MA: Harvard University Press.

Finding a Different Way: Differentiation

Calla Stroh
Middle School Teacher
Steward School District #220, Steward, IL

In your classroom, do you have a wide variety of student learning levels? Is just breezing through lessons not your style? Are there some students behind grade-level expectations, while others already know the information and are ready to move on? If you answered yes to one or more of these questions, then it is time to learn more about differentiation. Being able to modify lesson plans to best educate your students puts you on the pathway to becoming an accomplished teacher.

Differentiation can be as simple or as complicated as you need it to be. There are multiple ways that you can differentiate in your classroom. You can differentiate the content of lessons to achieve student growth. You can also vary the process by choosing different strategies to deliver lessons. Or, you can give your students some choice, and differentiate the products they complete.

Guided reading programs are one example of how you can involve differentiation in the classroom and are representative of ways to differentiate your content. Find and administer a pretest to group your students according to need, reading levels, or any variety of measurable skills. From there, create your groups. Target their needs based on skill level. My small, rural school district uses a kindergarten through eighth grade guided reading format. All classrooms teach reading at the exact same time every day. Students are assessed at the beginning of the year and placed into groups that may cut across age levels. Then, we rotate students through different sets of standards-based skills. No matter what grade level the students are currently in, students are reading at an appropriate instructional level. They are assessed twice per quarter on reading levels, and once a month on skills. Based on these data, we regroup students, and if needed, use Response to Intervention when students are not making sufficient gains.

Another way to differentiate is to consider how students learn. We all know that students have different learning preferences, and by changing the process for them, you can reach more of your students. For example, if you are trying to teach students about nouns, you can have one group watch and listen to videos about persons, places, and things. Another group can work on a school-wide scavenger hunt centered around nouns. A third group can write mad libs using nouns to complete sentences. By changing the way content is delivered, you'll have your students working in ways that complement their learning preferences.

You can differentiate and increase motivation in your classroom by capitalizing on your students' interests. As you build effective teacher–student relationships, your awareness grows about who they are and where their interests lie. This awareness supports differentiation of products students complete. You are giving your students more ownership of their learning based on your understanding of their interests.

How do you start differentiating? Assessing your students and having data is key. Constantly having up-to-date data about your students will aid in the process of grouping and knowing their exact needs. Additionally, the more you utilize differentiation, the more parents will express interest in your classroom. Therefore, you need ample data and clear expectations when communicating with parents.

The graphic organizer download addresses three categories in which you can differentiate. You can change the content of the lesson, modify the process, and offer choice about the product. Each category contains a list of things you can try to differentiate. The list is by no means exhaustive, but it gets you started on your journey.

Chapter 6

English Learners

Family Engagement: For English Learners

Jennifer Jaros, NBCT
EL Teacher at Holmes and Hatch Schools
District 97, Oak Park, IL
Twitter: @JarosEsl

Engaging with Families of English Learners for the Classroom Teacher

These tips are specifically written for schools and districts where many languages are spoken and there is no one predominant language of English Learner (EL) students. Communication in bilingual programs may differ.

1. Speak with the EL teacher about his/her knowledge of the student's family and background. Then determine what useful information the EL teacher has. By doing so, you can help the family feel more connected. This contact will support initial needs as the family joins the school community.

2. Use TalkingPoints, as both an app and on your computer at talkingpts.org, to communicate with all families. This family communication system is similar to Bloomz or Class Dojo, but with an added multilingual feature. When setting up parent information for your class, click on the home language for each student. When messages are sent to parents, each message is translated into the chosen home language. Yes, there may be grammatical errors, but being able to convey important information to all families with the click of one button is useful. For multilingual families, ask in which language they prefer to receive the messages. Parents of EL students may be fluent in English and prefer to use English as their primary contact language.

3. Add all religious holidays to your calendar/Google calendar. Be sure to not schedule important tests, culminating activities/trips, PBIS celebrations, or parent volunteer opportunities on any religious holiday. Google calendar has a simple feature under *Other Calendars* that adds religious holidays from many faiths, allowing you to have

the information you need in one place when scheduling events. Never assume a family from a certain country practices a specific religion. Respect all religious holidays.

4. Ask parents for their participation, especially when translating information about school events. Parents want to be involved, and multilingual families have a unique skill set they can share. If there is a school or classroom event that needs to be publicized to the larger school community, ask a parent to translate the written communication. Note: For privacy reasons, do not ask parents to translate about specific students, families, IEP information, behavior issues, etc.

5. Individually invite parents to school events, emphasizing that emerging English skills do not exclude them. For example, in many schools, parents come in to read to the class. Encourage parents to read in whatever language they are most comfortable. Everyone benefits from hearing a read-aloud, regardless of the language. Listening to a read-aloud in any language strengthens reading skills in all languages.

6. Make sure all your students have a local library card. In most communities, the local library is not only a place to get books and information in various languages, it is a community center. In some countries, the public library system as we know it does not exist. There might be fees, so parents may be unsure how to access free library services. Make a connection with the local librarian to assist families with getting a library card. The librarian can also answer other questions parents may have.

To gather pertinent information about families, use and personalize the download document.

Know Your English Learner Students as Individuals

Rebekah Young
ESOL Liaison
Woodland Middle School, Sarasota County, FL

As a new teacher supporting English Learners (ELs), where do you start? Should you consider focusing on language acquisition, family and community building, social–emotional support, scaffolding instruction, differentiation, or something else entirely? In trying to weigh the value of each, all are impactful. Keep in mind, knowing your students as individuals gives an entry point into each of the strategies so you can acclimate students into the learning environment.

Getting to know your EL students is the most important tip I can offer. Each EL student comes with their own unique background and experiences. Some students were born in the United States but have a language other than English spoken at home. These students will generally have a strong concept of conversational English, having been surrounded by music and television, but lack the academic language necessary to be successful in school. Other students come from a culture where education is the primary focus and have already been learning English in their home countries. Given their strong educational backgrounds, these students just need exposure to language rather than support with academic concept attainment. They may simply require a language frame or word bank when assessed to show their understanding. Then there are students who have interrupted or limited schooling before entering the United States. These students need the most support as they balance learning a language, academic concepts, and the culture of school. To foster their transition, those students need support that is strategic, collaborative, academic, and social–emotional.

When learning about your students, become familiar with their educational histories. For instance, if a student is a fluent reader and writer in their first language, the literacy transition to English is usually much smoother. Additionally, knowing the alphabetic principles involved in the student's first language is a good indicator of how specific the initial phonics instruction will need to be to begin acquiring English.

For example, I'm currently working with a Ukrainian student who has been in the United States for less than a month. Although he was successful academically before moving here, the Ukrainian alphabet is written in a variation of Cyrillic script, not the variation of Latin that is used in English. Therefore, a Ukrainian speaker's needs are different than those of a Spanish-speaking student who has the same academic history. The student from Ukraine needs to learn basic alphabetic principles before he can engage in reading and writing. A Spanish-speaking student can quickly learn letter pronunciation and go on to learning grammatical structure and English vocabulary. If you have students with mixed backgrounds and languages, which you will, the best thing to do is ensure that you are building a literacy-rich environment. Modeling the habits of successful reading, writing, listening, and speaking daily will create an easier and more organic transition into learning English.

Ultimately, EL students have such varied experiences that you must get to know their personal backgrounds and educational histories to support their acquisition of the English language and our culture. You must tailor each student's language-acquisition plan to their specific needs. This will be the most expedient scenario for helping your students transition into school. Use the download to assist you in collecting information about each student. Then, utilize this information as you plan to support students' individual needs.

High-Impact Strategies for Teaching English Learners: Scaffolding for Success

Carla Huck, MA/MEd
ELL Instructional Leader
The School District of Lee County, Fort Myers, FL

Scaffolding is key to effective classroom instruction for English Learners (ELs), as it enables students to access grade-level texts and concepts while they are still in the process of acquiring language skills. You can support learning and student performance of specific tasks through modeling, questioning, feedback, visuals, graphic organizers, and more. Gradually withdraw supports so your students become more independent as they gain proficiency in English and demonstrate strategic behaviors during learning activities.

The following guidelines are critical to successfully scaffolding content and academic language learning for your ELs.

Step 1: Identify the Language Proficiency Levels of Your Students

Thoughtful planning with consideration of your students' individual needs leads to effective teaching. You need to present content that it is comprehensible to the student, given their level of language proficiency.

- ♦ Use your state's annual proficiency assessment scores to create a map of your class with performance descriptors for listening, speaking, reading, and writing. Know what to expect linguistically from students at each level of proficiency. Remember that students in the first two phases of language acquisition—entering and emerging—will require supports for each learning task.
- ♦ For students new to the country, use your language screener assessment data. Review each student's educational background through an oral interview with the parent. This information can help you learn about cultural, experiential, and socio–emotional dimensions as well as pinpoint academic strengths or gaps in formal education. You may have students with limited and/or interrupted formal education (SLIFE) who require interventions to build foundational literacy skills.
- ♦ If available, consult native language proficiency assessments. These data will indicate the student's level of literacy in his or her own language. Proficiency in the first language has significant influence on second-language acquisition.
- ♦ If data are available that span a number of academic years, review student growth annually in each domain of language.

Step 2: Build and Activate Background Knowledge

All learners have background knowledge they have acquired through school and life experiences. Connecting current learning to previous learning is activating prior knowledge. With ELs, it is critical that you use techniques to also build students' knowledge of a topic and fill in any gaps they may have.

- ♦ Connect new concepts to prior knowledge, learning, and experiences by asking students what they already know about the topic.
- ♦ Use visuals, realia, and brief video clips to activate prior knowledge or build background on a topic that may be completely new. Consider topics specific to American culture that your students from other countries may not know: Historical figures, cities and states, traditions, holidays, etc.
- ♦ Create anticipation guides for texts, videos, and mini-lessons. This assists students in thinking about and discussing main ideas or concepts prior to presentation of content.
- ♦ Introduce a conceptual framework, such as a graphic organizer, to help students understand text structure along with main ideas. Make charts of key information and post for reference. Have your students use learning logs to record key ideas. Regularly ask them to locate information from previous lessons.

Step 3: Explicitly Teach Vocabulary

Vocabulary is critical for understanding a text or concept. Present key words using both linguistic and nonlinguistic representations. Students should have multiple meaningful interactions with these words. The essence of effective vocabulary instruction is creating contexts in which students constantly use relevant vocabulary across the four language domains (listening, speaking, reading, and writing).

♦ Select the most essential words for the student(s) to understand the text and the task. Determine words from the three tiers of vocabulary. Then, add words needed for process/function, word parts (prefix, roots, suffix), and multiple meaning words. You can copy and paste text into websites such as https://vocabularytool.airprojects.org or https://wordsift.org to have the words categorized.

♦ Develop word knowledge with reference to cognates. Post and teach logical transition words. Incorporate word-generation activities.

♦ Help your students create and update personal dictionaries. Depending on their grade level, they can write words and/or draw pictures, add a definition you have provided, and record the word in their native language.

♦ Build deeper word knowledge and make semantic connections through Frayer models, concept maps, word sorts, or list-group-label activities.

Step 4: Support Oral Language Development and Productive Language Skills

If you provide regular, structured opportunities for students to interact with the content and one another, they will gain academic and social language proficiency along with content and skills mastery.

♦ Use sentence starters and language frames specific to your learning task to foster writing and constructive conversation skills.

♦ Combine note-taking strategies with listening (e.g., video viewing guides, graphic organizers, and Cornell notes). These can all be differentiated, with partially teacher-completed sections and/or word banks.

♦ Plan a variety of peer–peer interactions for students to practice and discuss content through think–pair–share, information gap, mix and match, or inside–outside circle. You can also consider using a variety of cooperative learning activities.

♦ Provide access to meaningful and diverse texts. Adapt the Lexile level. Add an illustrated glossary. Highlight key words. Find native language text. Utilize technology resources to translate and read aloud.

Utilize the download as a reminder of the three types of scaffolds, with examples. The second part of the download includes critical questions to ask yourself when planning for ELs.

Teaching English Language Learners

Beatriz Dillman
Sheltered English Instruction
Old Post Elementary, Oswego, IL

I teach a fifth grade Sheltered English Instruction class. I have students from eight different countries in my classroom. The primary goal for my students is to grow in the four domains of language acquisition: Listening, reading, writing, and speaking. Differentiation is very important since students are at various levels of learning English. I have newcomers who are refugees. I also have students with an Individualized Education Plan.

Differentiation is important to meet students at their level. Grouping students by reading ability to work on different skills is vital. My class has students ranging in reading levels from first grade to fifth grade. Having teacher assistants in the classroom is extremely helpful during small group time so all students can have support. Collaboration with special education teachers, reading teachers, resource teachers, and teaching assistants is essential. They will help support your students' various needs. The English Learner (EL) resource teacher helps newcomers learn foundational skills.

As an EL teacher you may bring a student to a Multi-Tiered System of Support (MTSS) meeting. Be prepared to advocate for your student if you see learning difficulties that go beyond language. In my experience, many times the MTSS team believes learning difficulties come from a language barrier. A motivated student without learning difficulties will learn the language.

People define success in different ways. I feel successful seeing students make progress. My students feel successful when they pass the Assessing Comprehension and Communication in English State-to-State for English Language Learners (ACCESS) test and exit the program.

Vocabulary Instruction for English Learners: Providing Opportunities to Practice

Rhonda D. Miller, PhD, Assistant Professor
Coastal Carolina University, Conway, SC

Vocabulary is an essential part of learning to read, but it is also an essential aspect of communication. Without an understanding of essential vocabulary, students cannot begin to understand concepts. For English Learners (ELs) and for ELs with disabilities, you must provide multiple opportunities to practice carefully selected vocabulary words through listening, speaking, reading, and writing activities (Gersten et al., 2007; Jitendra, Edwards, Sacks, &

Jacobson, 2004). Pre-teaching that vocabulary before teaching the content can help create background knowledge that is essential to comprehension (Francis, Rivera, Lesaux, Kieffer, & Rivera, 2006).

Vocabulary Selection

It is important to choose words from your text or from your content area lesson that are essential to understanding the text or lesson (Echevarria, Vogt, & Short, 2008). Think about the reading passage or lesson you are teaching. What vocabulary words keep occurring in discussion or in test questions about the topic? Which words are hard to pronounce or decode? For example, if the topic is the life cycle of a butterfly, the word *chrysalis* would be essential to understanding that topic, and it may be hard to pronounce. Are there words that have multiple meanings? For ELs, the word *fly* may be confusing since a butterfly can fly, and a fly is also another kind of insect. What about words found in other content areas? A life cycle is explained in stages. The word *stage* is an important concept that appears in other contexts. Understanding these types of words will help students develop background knowledge across content areas. The vocabulary planning sheet (in the download) helps you select words to teach in a lesson or unit.

Speaking and Listening Practice

Explicit instruction. When students are familiar with vocabulary, they are more likely to participate in discussions/activities and are better able to make connections. You can use explicit instruction to teach both the pronunciation and the meaning of new words quickly while providing multiple opportunities for students to interact with the vocabulary. Table 6.1 contains an example script for teaching a new vocabulary word. During explicit instruction, students can see the word, hear the word, and speak the word multiple times while making connections to its meaning. Think about a lesson of your own where you could use this technique.

Table 6.1 Sample Script for Explicit Instruction

Target word: *factor*	
Teacher	(Points to word *factor* on the board) This word is *factor*. What word?
Students	Factor.
Teacher	Yes, factor. Factors are numbers that multiply together to make another number (Points to the four and the seven in the math problem $4 \times 7 = 28$ written on the board). Four and seven are factors of 28 because they multiply together to make 28. When numbers multiply together to make another number, what do we call them?
Students	Factors.
Teacher	Yes, factors. Two and three are factors of six because $2 \times 3 = 6$. Two and three are also factors of 12 because $2 \times 3 \times 2 = 12$. Numbers that multiply together to make another number are called factors. What are factors?
Students	Numbers that multiply together to make another number.
Teacher	Correct.

Table 6.2 Word Cards for Word Sorting Game

habitat	organism	worm	ecosystem
produce	nutrients	predator	survive
beetle	creature	decompose	prey
consume	shelter	soil	forest

Word games. Working with partners is engaging and motivating. Using class-wide interactive activities allows all students to have multiple opportunities to connect with vocabulary. The following list of suggested game formats can be tailored to the specific content area or text passage that your students are reading. Many of these games are patterned after TV game shows or board games. In the download, see Directions for Word Games and more information on how to play three of the games.

- ♦ Twenty Questions
- ♦ Outburst
- ♦ I Have, Who Has
- ♦ $25,000 Pyramid
- ♦ Family Feud

Reading and Writing Practice

You can tailor the following list of suggested activity formats to the specific content area or text passage that your EL students are reading. The activities in this list have a reading and/ or writing focus.

- ♦ Word sorts (categories such as people, places, things, and actions). See Table 6.2 for an example of a group of word cards developed from a reading passage about food chains.
- ♦ Memory game (match picture to word or match word to definition).
- ♦ Quizlet.com (teachers can create and save word lists).
- ♦ Graphic organizers (Venn diagram, word splash, word map).

Vocabulary instruction is critical for ELs as it is the key to making content comprehensible. The activities described above incorporate speaking, listening, reading, and writing in ways that support language development and engage students, providing multiple opportunities for practice in an engaging way.

References

Echevarria, J., Vogt, M., & Short, D. J. (2008). *Making content comprehensible for English learners: The SIOP model* (3rd ed.). Boston, MA: Pearson.

Francis, D. J., Rivera, M., Lesaux, N., Kieffer, M., & Rivera, H. (2006). *Practical guidelines for the education of English language learners: Research-based recommendations for instruction and academic interventions.* Portsmouth, NH: RMC Research Corporation, Center on Instruction. Retrieved from http://www.centeroninstruction.org/files/ELL1-Interventions.pdf

Gersten, R., Baker, S. K., Shanahan, T., Linan-Thompson, S., Collins, P., & Scarcella, R. (2007). *Effective literacy and English language instruction for English learners in the elementary grades* (NCEE 2007-4011). Washington, DC: National Center for Education Evaluation and

Regional Assistance, Institute of Education Sciences, U.S. Department of Education. Retrieved from http://files.eric.ed.gov/fulltext/ED497258.pdf

Jitendra, A. K., Edwards, L. L., Sacks, G., & Jacobson, L. A. (2004). What research says about vocabulary instruction for students with learning disabilities. *Exceptional Children*, 70(3), 299–322. doi:10.1177/001440290407000303.

Assessment of English Learners: How to Make Tests Less Stressful

Carla Huck, MA/MEd
ELL Instructional Leader
The School District of Lee County, Fort Myers, FL

As you plan formal and informal assessments, keep in mind that language and content are intertwined for English Learners (ELs). Therefore, separating one from the other in the assessment process can be challenging. The following are possible assessment adaptations for ELs to reduce the language demands and potential student frustration, while at the same time increasing the validity of your tests.

♦ **Range:** Adapt the number of items the student is expected to complete, such as even or odd numbers only. Reduce the number of options in multiple choice response items.

♦ **Time:** Allow additional time for completing assessment tasks. Consider breaking longer tasks into manageable chunks. Longer assessments can be given over two days rather than during one sitting.

♦ **Home language support:** Provide scaffolding during assessments by asking an aide, peer assistant, or colleague to read aloud and explain the test. Provide a bilingual dictionary or content area glossary. Translate the test, in full or just the directions, depending on the proficiency level of your student. Remember: There is a difference between assessing an EL's ability to read and follow written directions versus his or her ability to complete a task or answer questions on a content topic.

♦ **Linguistic complexity:** Reduce the level of the assessment's complexity to make it easier for the student to demonstrate understanding without reducing the rigor of the content. Keep sentence structures as simple as possible. Avoid colloquial and idiomatic expressions. Provide sample problems for each task type, along with images, diagrams, word banks, sentence starters, or writing frames.

♦ **Format:** Use clear and consistent formatting for tests. Students should be familiar with the directions and types of questions used. Be clear with your expectations for completing the test. If the assessment is administered on a computer, make sure students have practiced with the platform and have been taught keyboarding skills. If a technology-based test has accommodations, such as translation or text-to-speech, practice with students so they are comfortable applying them independently.

♦ **Cultural lens:** Preview your assessment for any items with potential cultural bias. For example, regard names, places, sports, holidays, or historic events that are specific to a particular group, region, or culture with which ELs may not have background knowledge. Make changes when possible. When creating fictional scenarios, such as those used in mathematics word problems, use a school context with familiar names and vocabulary to make the items more comprehensible.

- ◆ **Product:** Whereas native speakers may be required to write a paragraph summary or essay, it may be more reasonable for an EL to show mastery in different ways. Your students could produce an illustration, a completed graphic organizer, a model, or verbal response that does not rely on sophisticated English usage.

- ◆ **Participation:** Actively involve your students in monitoring and assessing their own performance. They can co-construct rubrics or complete test corrections. Plan how you will share assessment results with students in a meaningful way.

- ◆ **Scoring:** Differentiate your scoring by grading content knowledge and language skills separately. Have high expectations, but set realistic goals for growth based on student language proficiency levels. It is important to look at a student's overall learning progression with a focus on growth rather than test scores.

Download the infographic as a reminder of ways to make testing less stressful for your ELs.

The Importance of Activating Background Knowledge

Katie Tice
Kindergarten Teacher
School District of Lee County, Fort Myers, FL

As a kindergarten teacher, it can be challenging working with an EL who has had little to no formal schooling. However, every student brings life experiences regardless of educational exposure. The trick for the teacher is to find ways to extract that information and connect it to the lesson concepts.

Once you know your student's language proficiency level, you can then begin to build on his background knowledge using linguistic scaffolds. I recently received a new student from Haiti, and he is in the beginning stages of proficiency. He is able to understand familiar words and sentences and can express himself using simple phrases, but his vocabulary is below grade level.

We recently read a story about a duck. I first showed the class a picture of a duck. We discussed where we have seen ducks before. My EL student was excited to see the duck and expressed that he knew what one was. When we transitioned into centers, my small group used picture–word cards from the story to help retell the events and identify characters and setting using the correct vocabulary. When it was time for the assessment of sequencing events, I made sure to provide my EL with those picture cards as well. By the end of the lesson, he was able to retell the story with and without the picture cards. These small wins for a student help build confidence, motivate them to participate in class discussions, and accelerate their acquisition of language and content.

Developing Vocabulary Skills with Your English Learners

Jeanne Okrasinski, EdD, Professor
Eastern Illinois University, Charleston, IL

English Learners (ELs) are just like the other students in your classroom. They want to make friends and share funny stories at lunchtime. They want to be accepted by their peers, and they want to learn. What is most daunting for new teachers is helping with the last piece: How do we help ELs learn in the traditional classroom alongside their native language peers?

There is a vast difference in students being able to speak with their peers in casual situations (e.g., lunchroom, hallways, and playground) than speaking and interacting in a classroom academic setting. In official terms, we call this Basic Interpersonal Communication Skills (BICS) versus Cognitive Academic Language Proficiency (CALP). When students talk with each other, they don't need to use big, heavy, clunky academic words and really don't care if their grammar is correct (BICS). In the classroom, however, students often feel as if they will be reprimanded for using improper grammar or cannot quite remember the actual word that should be used (CALP). BICS can be developed by students in a relatively short amount of time. CALP usually takes at least a few years (sometimes as much as 5–7 years!) for students to develop a sufficient background in the English language to be comfortable enough to participate as fully as most native speakers. Be patient.

The most important tip I can offer is to make friends with the English as a Second Language (ESL) coordinator for your building or district. If you have a bilingual specialist in the building for the language(s) in your classroom, this is also an important person with whom to build a relationship. When you have staff in the building who have expertise in a topic, use them. ESL-trained specialists have a bag of tricks they can share with you. If you can explain to them what you are trying to do in the classroom, they can help you adapt those strategies for your ELs. In addition, the ESL coordinator may be able to show you how to transform quizzes, tests, and other assignments so that they are more "friendly" to students whose language skills are not at grade level.

Vocabulary is one of the greatest gifts you can give to your ELs. Here are three strategies to help you develop your students' vocabulary skills.

Strategy 1

Picture dictionaries for students with limited English skills are some of the most helpful resources for the classroom. Rather than pull out dictionaries all the time, create a simple one-page document with pictures of the most common items or people/resources accessed daily. Take the pictures yourself of the items/people that are meaningful to your EL students! Be sure to include a picture of a toilet. The words *bathroom* and *restroom* may mean very different things and not translate well, but the word and picture of a toilet is fairly universal. Figure out what is most critical for your students—notebook, textbook, pencil, lunch, recess, nurse, sick (that's a fun picture), telephone, and other necessities or emergency types of words are crucial for a student to be able to point to if they do not yet have the word in their vocabulary for the item. A sample is provided in the download. However, the pictures are most effective when taken from your own classroom/school building.

Strategy 2

Word wall or personal dictionary for older students or those that switch classrooms: Don't settle for the boring, average, run-of-the-mill word wall. Make your word wall pop! Use synonyms and antonyms to expand the vocabulary of your EL students. A very easy and effective way to learn words is to group them by similar meaning. For instance, if students need to learn the word ARGUE, put with it the idea of DISCUSS, DEBATE, and REASON and then add some fun words like SQUABBLE, BICKER, or HASH OUT. Squabble is a seriously fun word for students to say out loud. Once they've practiced the meaning of the actual word a bit, throw in an antonym, or two, like AGREE or MAKE PEACE. You can find a sample page of the personal dictionary in the download.

Strategy 3

Deciding whether to teach vocabulary words prior to reading a passage of text is not a debate for your ELs. They need to get comfortable with the academic words they will be reading, so use pre-reading strategies to prepare them to learn the new information. A good first step is to have your student(s) write the word in a manner that helps them to pronounce it correctly. Asking your ELs to spell words phonetically is great, but it does not necessarily need to be in standard phonetic form. It's alright if they write it phonetically in their home language. Drawing a picture to show the meaning or use of the word, writing the definition in their own words (in whichever language they prefer), and possibly including synonyms/antonyms are all helpful tools in personal dictionaries or word journals.

You can use these three strategies with different levels of ELs. Word walls and personal dictionaries help support no matter how proficient they become in English and are easy options for students to develop on their own. Developing confidence and skill in academic English takes time and can be frustrating during the early stages of language development. Stay positive and supportive.

Culturally Relevant Children's Books as a Path Toward Critical Consciousness

Marisol Diaz, PhD, Visiting Assistant Professor
Skidmore College, Saratoga Springs, NY

Every person who reads this article has an accent. Your accent carries the story of who you are—who first held you and talked to you when you were a child, where you have lived, your age, the schools you attended, the languages you know, your ethnicity, whom you admire, your loyalties, your profession, your class position: traces of your life and identity are woven into your pronunciation, your phrasing, your choice of words. Your self is inseparable from your accent. Someone who tells you they don't like the way you speak is quite likely telling you that they don't like you.

(Matsuda, 1991, p. 1)

I begin with this quote by Maria Matsuda, to remind *all readers* that we *all* carry an accent. As Matsuda reminds us, an accent extends beyond a sensory dimension and into an essential part of our identity. This is why it is a teacher's responsibility to honor a student's language(s), because in doing so, they communicate validation.

Books are powerful tools. They carry stories that can be used to empower or suppress. The books a teacher chooses to read to their students say a lot about the teacher's beliefs. I use books as a way to develop students' critical consciousness about the world and their sociopolitical contexts. Before I share my lesson idea, I want to state that there are many great books out there, some of which I have read and some of which I have yet to read. Compiling a list would be inexhaustible. There are also many ways a story can be read and presented, with millions of questions to ask the students and cover an academic standard. Creating a "formula" for how to teach a lesson is not part of my goal. Rather, my goal in sharing this lesson idea is to encourage you to systematically think about ways you can take any book and engage your students to think more critically about the world. The most important thing before planning any lesson is to know your students, their families, their communities, and their sociopolitical histories within a larger context.

One day I read the book *What Can You Do with A Paleta? Que Puedes hacer con una paleta* (Tafolla, 2009). The characters and themes in the book authentically reflected the neighborhood and people familiar to my students. The book, written in Spanish and English, is about the shared experiences of enjoying a *paleta*/popsicle. Before reading this story to the class, we discussed our favorite paleta flavors and where the best locations were to get one. Then I read the story to the class, stopping at each page, to soak up the illustrations. Once we finished reading, we continued discussions. I asked the students, "If your life was a paleta, what flavor would it be?" Many students paused and started sharing. I told students that everything they have experienced made them each a unique *sabor*/flavor. Using this metaphor, students made the connection that their way of "being" allowed them to be unique. Once our conversations slowed down, students wrote a journal reflection about what we discussed. Then I handed out a cardboard cut-out of a blank paleta pattern. (See download.) On one side students drew about their life, important people, and experiences they had. On the other side they wrote a "flavor of life" poem. I hole-punched the top of the paleta and used yarn and paper clips to make them easy to hang from the ceiling to see both sides.

There are many English Language Arts components in this lesson that benefit all students, not just language learners. However, when we connect culturally relevant materials, learning increases for all. Extending the book theme into science and math is simple. Students learn about the different states of matter, liquids and solids, in science. Students can also make their own paletas, learning about measurements and fractions in math. Depending on the grade, there are endless possibilities of what you can do with a paleta.

Language is directly connected to how we think. Stopping language or suppressing it, in essence, stops learning. Using a book that demonstrates culturally relevant themes is a great way to validate student identity. In doing so, you take a stand to resist oppressive messages that state there is only one correct way to exist in the world.

References

Matsuda, M. J. (1991). Voices of America: Accent, antidiscrimination law, and a jurisprudence for the last reconstruction. *The Yale Law Journal, 100*(5), 1329–1407.

Tafolla, C. (2009). *What can you do with a paleta? Que puedes hacer con una paleta?* Decorah, IA: Dragonfly Books.

Escaping English Only

Megan Freeman
First Grade Teacher
Oliver Wendell Holmes School, District 97, Oak Park, IL

Throughout the year, all parents are invited to come into the classroom as a guest reader. Parents are welcome to read a book in any language, if they wish. Students light up when hearing their first language being used in the classroom, and it gives the student and their family an opportunity to teach the rest of the class. In writing, I've seen students become frustrated when they can't express their ideas in English. If they've learned how to write in their first language, I encourage students to try this as an initial step. They sometimes seem surprised at this suggestion. I don't want students to develop an idea that school is only for English. My hope is that students and families feel our classroom is a community where all languages can flourish.

Celebrating Classroom Diversity

Judy Matuszewski, EdD, Retired Professional Educator
Madisonville, TN
Twitter: @JudyMatuszewsk1

There is such excitement to receive your class list. The list you have waited for, worked for. Wait, some of these names are unfamiliar. How do you pronounce this one? Why is there a άή accent over some of the letters?

Seeing this diversity, how confident are you in working with students whose primary language is not English? Begin with a deep breath. Grab this opportunity. Start by engaging families. Ask for their native language greeting. You may not be familiar with or speak the language. Asking for this greeting opens a line of communication between you and the family. Talk with the student and family about the correct pronunciation and meaning of the child's name. True, there may be some laughter and giggles (at least there was when I tried to pronounce a Korean student's name), but you are learning, yourself, as well as modeling that you expect your students to call peers by their given names.

To bridge the language gap, encourage parents to label items with both native and English versions of their child's name. By pairing the names, the native version is recognized along with the English equivalent. As a kindergarten teacher I also labeled anchor charts with numerous native languages. How supportive it was to see Arabic, Korean, and Chinese characters alongside red and *rojo* on the color words anchor chart. I asked parents to help me with this task as another small attempt to welcome them into our classroom community.

You need to make an effort to communicate, even when there are language challenges on all sides (teacher–student, student–student, and teacher–family). Everyone can learn from one another. However, there will be challenges and mistakes made. It is okay and how everyone learns. This effort shows your students and their families how much you care about them, their culture, and their native language. This may encourage your students who struggle with English to feel just a bit more comfortable making mistakes: *If my teacher can, so can I.*

Finally, I found that for some of my quietest students, giving them a camera (I used an old cell phone) and asking them to "photograph things that help you learn" offered some insights. For some, I was able to spark short conversations about the resources they used on a frequent basis. This did not work for all, and some could not articulate clearly what the photograph represented, but I was still able to glean an idea of what the student meant. For the student who took photos of anchor charts with pictures, I created additional picture representations of topics (e.g., lunch choices). You could use this same idea in the upper grades by developing anchor charts with photographs for technology tools, math symbols, periodic table, and more (see download). For the child who simply photographed friends, I looked for peers who spoke a similar language, which sometimes meant finding an older student to join us for a project. I also sought out a good English-speaking role model (great speaker who is patient) to join us. Even with these supportive peers, I would check in with my student to see how confident they were with the lesson or project. Photographs are a window into a student's thinking, especially when they cannot articulate those thoughts in English.

When one of these ideas doesn't work with a family or student, continue to try others. Few of these strategies will put *all* students and their families at ease. However, by finding ways to support most of your students, you can focus your slightly less divided attention on those having the most difficulty. Families will appreciate your heartfelt interest in helping their child. If you want your EL students to ask questions, try, and fail at times, you must be willing to do so yourself.

Welcome, Share, Celebrate: Creating a Safe and Inclusive Classroom for English Learners

Erin Laverick, PhD, Professor
English Concordia University, Ann Arbor, MI

For a student who speaks a language other than English at home, the first few days, months, and even years at school can be overwhelming. When entering a classroom for the first time, an English Learner (EL) is exposed to a new culture, language, and routine. In addition, it is common for ELs to go through what Krashen (1982) has defined as the "silent period." Most go through this stage when they first acquire the new language, because they are listening to and absorbing it. Specifically, they are processing what they hear and may not have the vocabulary to express themselves yet. When an EL demonstrates signs of the silent period, allow the student to soak in as much of the language and culture as possible. If you practice patience, eventually the student will begin to use the language, participate in class, engage with his/her peers, and have a comprehensive learning experience. As they acclimate, continue to help the student feel welcome.

Welcome

If the student begins in the middle of the school year, consider having classmates make a welcome sign. It is also supportive to assign the new student a peer who can assist in helping him/her navigate the school beyond the classroom: Finding the restroom, returning library books, going to the principal's office, buying lunch, finding the school bus, and so on. A responsible peer will lessen the EL's anxiety and model proper use of spoken English. In addition, the native speaker can experience a new culture and language, which has the potential to begin to break down stereotypes, fears, and assumptions in the classroom (Zuñiga Dunlap, 2015). Therefore, there are benefits for both the EL and his/her peer.

During this time, you want to determine whether the student is feeling academically and emotionally "okay." You could create a check-in (see below and download) to assess the student's feelings, fears, questions, and more. If they don't yet have the language skills to communicate thoughts and feelings, you should encourage them to sketch and/or write in their native language. You might use a translator or Google Translate. Ask the EL to complete the check-ins on a regular basis. Doing so will help you assess their needs. In addition, as their English improves, completing the chart gives them the opportunity to improve their metacognition about what they've learned.

Today, I felt...	I liked it when we...
I did not like it when we...	I need help with...

Share

As ELs develop their language skills and begin to become accustomed to the classroom, encourage them to share their culture with peers. For example, if teaching a unit on how to write an informative paragraph, you could ask students to write about a family tradition. As a pre-writing activity, students could discuss their traditions and brainstorm in small groups. The focus of the assignment and pre-writing will make learning more meaningful because you are connecting content to the students' home lives, cultures, and languages. In addition, you are offering them a platform to share their culture(s) with their peers.

Celebrate!

When students are comfortable in the classroom and using the target language with confidence, find ways to celebrate their culture(s) and home language(s) in ways that deepen students' understanding of one another. Depending on the students' language proficiencies, celebrations can take place in many forms. Look for ways that members of the school population can come together for the good of the wider community (Aronson & Laughter, 2016). For example, students may:

- Create a video or photo collage to share images from their home countries
- Give a short presentation about a tradition
- Attend family events
- Present in student-work showcases
- Participate in game nights
- Hold cultural events
- Take part in community service projects

These activities and others will offer students a way to share and celebrate their cultures. Through celebrations, sharing, and welcoming students, you can continue to create a safe and inclusive learning environment for all your students and their families.

References

Aronson, B., & Laughter, J. (2016). The theory and practice of culturally relevant education: A synthesis of research across content areas. *Review of Educational Research, 86*(1), 163–206.

Krashen, S. D. (1982). *Principles and practice in second language acquisition.* Oxford, England: Pergamon Press.

Zuñiga Dunlap, C. (2015). *Helping English language learners succeed* (2nd ed.). Huntington Beach, CA: Shell Education.

The Noisy Classroom

Socorro Garcia-Alvarado, PhD, Adjunct Professor
University of Texas at San Antonio, San Antonio, TX

In a school setting, most students enter an environment that is unfamiliar. This new environment now requires them to focus on specific areas of academics such as reading. Included in the new requirements students face are rules of when to talk or be silent. Nevertheless, classrooms today should not be soundless, rather noisy with student chatter.

Contrary to former beliefs, you must have an overview of language as a whole and understand that oral language precedes written language. It is with this foundation that literacy skills develop. For English Learners (ELs) in particular, acquiring a new language comes with receptive and expressive skills that must be enhanced in your classroom.

Oral language is defined as the listening and speaking modes of communication, which will provide the basis for acquiring written language such as reading and writing (Otto, 2014). As you foster students' oral language, there are many benefits for them. Language development is critical to literacy skills (García & García, 2012). Oral language is the foundation to reading; thus, oral language development within the first five years of a child's life determines their success in reading comprehension in elementary school (Neuman, Roskos, Wright, & Lenhart, 2007).

Oral language can be cultivated when we purposefully promote student talk (García & García, 2012). Specifically, for ELs, opportunities to converse must be included in the classroom. As a new teacher, it takes deliberate lesson planning to integrate stopping points for your students to talk and process information.

In previous years, a quiet classroom was considered an ideal environment for learning. However, research has shown that a learning community must allow responses in the learning process (Christie, Enz, Vukelich, & Roskos, 2014; Kostelnik, Soderman, Whiren, & Rupiper, 2015; Otto, 2014). This requires a mind shift to get rid of the idea that a learning environment equals silence.

Encourage your students to talk so they can engage in conversation, process, and express their thinking. Conversations can take place before, during, and after instruction. Furthermore, they can also occur during social interactions such as morning meeting, circle time, or bellringer (warm up activity at the beginning of class). Sometimes students may just want to engage in conversation with a friend. Providing time for that engagement is also beneficial. However, be mindful that ELs also go through a silent period of expression but are still acquiring receptive language.

Talking plays a big role in learning, as it is a medium of thinking (Vygotsky, 1978). The more occasions students can engage in conversations, the greater their thinking and learning develops. Students' talk organizes their thinking. Furthermore, it provides a context for learning. Conversations allow them to learn how language works by communicating in an authentic setting with peers.

With the idea of integrating talk in the classroom, a crucial part of developing language is active listening on your part. It is through this time that you develop an awareness of the understanding and the comprehension levels of each student as well as their strengths and needs. During this time, you can also serve as an active language partner.

Linguistic scaffolding refers to a supportive manner in which the partner engages with and assists the student in their language to achieve a higher level than they would independently (Otto, 2014). For example, as a language partner, you will scaffold the student's language. Students naturally want to express their ideas either in their first language or the second language they are learning. As they do so, you can scaffold their language through questioning in order to maintain the verbal interaction and make discourse flourish.

The following interaction provides an example of a teacher as an active language partner using questions to extend the dialogue.

STUDENT: Ms. Rosas, I went to the panadería (bakery).
TEACHER: Really, what did you do there?
STUDENT: We bought bread and tacos.
TEACHER: I love tacos! What kind of tacos did you get?
STUDENT: The kind with meat inside. You know the asada (grilled) ones.
TEACHER: Oh, the grilled tacos.
STUDENT: Yes, grilled.
TEACHER: Do they sell other kind of tacos?

This simple interaction between teacher and student was not focused on academic content, yet through the teacher's questioning the student offered further explanation about his experience at the bakery. Additionally, the student heard the word "grilled" in a relevant context that will allow him to connect to the term. As the student repeats the new terminology, he is now aware how to use the word in his language repertoire.

As you enter your classroom, many demands are placed upon you that interfere with the important task of planning. Use the download to reflect on how you are planning to include opportunities for oral language. Implementation of oral language that includes time for conversations, active listening, and engagement in discourse through questioning is an essential element in the lesson planning process. Ultimately, keep in mind that students are also coming to a new classroom experiencing the same apprehensions about the unfamiliar setting. Genuine conversations break the ice.

References

Christie, J., Enz, B. J., Vukelich, C., & Roskos, K. (2014). *Teaching language and literacy: Preschool through the elementary grades* (5th ed.). Boston: Pearson.

García, E. E., & García, E. H. (2012). *Understanding the language development and early education of Hispanic children*. New York, NY: Teacher's College Press.

Kostelnik, M. J., Soderman, A. K., Whiren, A. P., & Rupiper, M. Q. (2015). *Developmentally appropriate curriculum: Best practices in early childhood education* (6th ed.). Boston: Pearson Merrill/Prentice Hall.

Neuman, S. B., Roskos, K., Wright, T., & Lenhart, L. (2007). *Nurturing knowledge: Building a foundation for school success by linking early literacy to math, science, art, and social studies*. New York: Scholastic.

Otto, B. (2014). *Language development in early childhood education* (4th ed.). Boston: Pearson.

Vygotsky, L. (1978). *Mind in society: The development of higher psychological processes*. Cambridge, MA: Harvard University Press.

Chapter 7

Professionalism/ School Culture

Teacher Leadership and the New Teacher

Nathan Bond, PhD, Professor
Texas State University, San Marcos, TX

As a new teacher, you bring enthusiasm and fresh ideas to the classroom when you start your professional career. You are excited and ready to work with students, to get involved in school activities, and to make a positive impact in your new environment. In other words, you want to serve as a teacher leader. By definition, a teacher leader "maintains K–12 classroom-based teaching responsibilities, while also taking on leadership responsibilities outside of the classroom" (Wenner & Campbell, 2017, p. 140).

Like teaching, leadership is a developmental process that requires time, preparation, and support. Although new teachers generally do not serve in traditional leadership roles during their first few years, they can begin serving as leaders and laying the groundwork for more sophisticated leadership opportunities in the future. Below are some small but important ways to begin your teacher leadership journey.

Teach Well

During the first year, everything is a new experience. You are learning about your students, the curriculum, and the school for the first time. Rather than overcommitting yourself, spend time perfecting your pedagogical skills and getting off to a positive start with your teaching. You are the leader of the students in the classroom, and you will have more credibility as a leader in your colleagues' eyes if you deliver effective instruction (Ado, 2016).

Work Closely with a Mentor

Most schools assign an experienced teacher to work with a new teacher during the first few years. A mentor will help you to implement the curriculum, deliver effective instruction, teach students with diverse needs, and carry out the school's policies (Stanulis & Bell, 2017). When you work well with a mentor, you demonstrate the leadership skills of listening and accepting feedback.

Build Positive Professional Relationships with People in the School

Smile, greet, and speak to teachers, administrators, staff members, and students when you encounter them. In addition to developing a positive learning community with students in your classroom, aim to establish a similar atmosphere throughout the school. A leader's effectiveness hinges on rapport and the quality of their relationships with others (Bond, 2011; Crippen, 2010).

Be a Good Follower

New teachers have many opportunities to participate in school activities such as team/departmental meetings and professional learning communities. When you are a member of these groups, demonstrate good followership by participating actively, listening to others, working collaboratively to solve problems and reach consensus, and completing assignments. Learning to follow well is a way to discover how to lead well (Pucella, 2014).

Learn About Leadership

Leaders are not born. Instead, they become leaders by acquiring "an observable set of skills and abilities" (Posner, 2009, pp. 1–2). As a way to learn the fundamentals of leadership, read credible online materials or popular print books about leadership. Find a person in a formal leadership position who will be an additional mentor and guide you in the area of leadership. Teacher leaders are well versed in both pedagogy and leadership.

Keep Learning

Teaching is a dynamic profession with new ideas to discover and innovative teaching strategies to master. Attend professional development workshops offered inside and outside your school district. Maintain memberships in professional organizations to stay abreast of the latest information about your field. Be curious about your own teaching, reflect on your effectiveness, and explore areas for growth (Snyder, 2015). Teacher leaders challenge themselves continuously to improve.

People mistakenly think that only experienced teachers can be teacher leaders. This is simply not true. All teachers, even new teachers, can serve as teacher leaders (Barth, 2013). If you take the steps mentioned above, you can begin the journey to become a teacher leader and make a positive difference in your school. See the download for a teacher leader self-assessment tool.

References

Ado, K. (2016). From pre-service to teacher leader: The early development of teacher leaders. *Issues in Teacher Education*, 25(1), 3–21.

Barth, R. S. (2013). The time is ripe (again). *Educational Leadership*, 71(2), 10–16.

Bond, N. (2011). Preparing preservice teachers to become teacher leaders. *The Educational Forum*, 75(4), 280–297. doi:10.1080/00131725.2011.602578.

Crippen, C. (2010). Serve, teach, and lead: It's all about relationships. *Insight: A Journal of Scholarly Teaching*, 5, 27–36.

Posner, B. Z. (2009). From inside out: Beyond teaching about leadership. *Journal of Leadership Education*, 8(1), 1–10. doi:10.12806/V8/I1/TF1.

Pucella, T. J. (2014). Not too young to lead. *The Clearing House*, 87(1), 15–20. doi:10.1080/00098655.2013.818524.

Snyder, J. (2015). Teacher leadership and teacher preparation: A personal narrative. *The Educational Forum*, 79(1), 5–11. doi:10.1080/00131725.2015.972801.

Stanulis, R. N., & Bell, J. (2017). Beginning teachers improve with attentive and targeted mentoring. *Kappa Delta Pi Record*, 53(2), 59–65. doi:10.1080/00228958.2017.1299543.

Wenner, J. A., & Campbell, T. (2017). The theoretical and empirical basis of teacher leadership: A review of the literature. *Review of Educational Research*, 87(1), 134–171. doi:10.3102/0034654316653478.

Becoming a Teacher Leader: Four Steps and a Simple Framework

Jana Hunzicker, Associate Professor
Bradley University, Peoria, IL

I get it. Right now, the last thing you are thinking about is becoming a teacher leader. Yet most teachers develop into leaders without even realizing it, so why not at least entertain the idea?

York-Barr and Duke (2004) define teacher leadership as "the process by which teachers, individually or collectively, influence their colleagues, principals, and other members of school communities" (pp. 287–288). Danielson (2006) refers to it as a "set of skills demonstrated by teachers" who influence student learning beyond their own classrooms (p. 12). Katzenmeyer and Moller (2009) describe teacher leadership as identifying with, contributing to, influencing, and accepting responsibility for effective teaching practices and student learning outcomes. So, teacher leadership is a process, a skill set, and a commitment to making contributions and accepting responsibility. You can do that!

I know what you are thinking. As a new teacher, you have a lot going on. Between learning the curriculum, preparing engaging lessons and activities, testing, and dealing with a myriad of classroom management issues, your days are full – and that doesn't even include obligations outside the classroom. So how can you at least begin thinking about the possibility of becoming a teacher leader? Four steps and a simple framework are all you need!

Step 1: Begin with yourself.

Leadership begins with a mindset. You are no longer a college student. As a teacher, what moral and professional standards will you set for yourself? What personal rules will you establish for things like communicating with others, dressing for work, and meeting deadlines? How will you address challenges and deal with conflict? To intentionally develop your professional identity, it may be helpful to make an always/never list. For example, I will always tell the truth; I will never use profanity. Creating and committing to such a list will help you develop a level of professionalism that others will respect and admire.

Step 2: Get good at teaching.

Teacher leaders are teachers first. Before you can positively influence other teachers, you have to be a good teacher! This is going to take a while because teaching is so complex. The key is continuous learning. Apply and adapt what you learned in college. Go to workshops. Read blogs. Observe experienced teachers. Try new ideas, and when something doesn't work, reflect and try something else. Persevering in spite of setbacks is how novice teachers develop into experts. But please be patient with yourself. Getting good at teaching is a career-long endeavor.

Step 3: Actively participate.

Teacher leaders gain experience through job-embedded collaboration, so while you're getting good at teaching, be sure to actively participate in initiatives beyond your own classroom. Is your grade level analyzing data? Use this opportunity to learn from others. Have you been asked to serve on a committee? Don't just show up to meetings; offer your ideas and volunteer for committee-related tasks. Does the principal need assistance with professional development? Offer to help. In addition to being a team player, actively participating beyond your classroom will allow you to build relationships and develop your leadership skills.

Step 4: Take initiative.

Demonstrating professionalism, being a good teacher, and staying involved all support the ultimate act of teacher leadership: Taking initiative. Do you notice a problem? Meet with fellow teachers to discuss possible solutions. Do you have an idea for a school-wide project? Run it past your principal and offer to take the lead. Sometimes, taking initiative involves even smaller acts. No one is speaking up at the faculty meeting? Be the first person to say something constructive. Regardless of scale, teachers who regularly take initiative are likely to become teacher leaders (Hunzicker, 2019).

A Simple Framework

Useful as these four steps may be, becoming a teacher leader is not quite that simple. You see, not every teacher-led initiative can be considered teacher leadership. This is where the five features of teacher leadership come in handy (Hunzicker, 2018). Such a simple framework makes it easy for new teachers to recognize acts of teacher leadership when they occur (see Figure 7.1).

From speaking up at a faculty meeting to leading professional development, acts of teacher leadership large and small have five features in common: Teacher leadership is student centered, action oriented, beyond one classroom, a positive influence, and collaborative.

1. Teacher leadership is *student centered* because its ultimate objective is student learning and well-being.

Figure 7.1 Five features of teacher leadership.

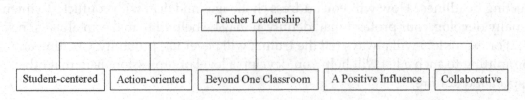

2. Teacher leadership is *action oriented* because it involves hands-on effort and engagement toward a specific purpose.
3. Teacher leadership extends *beyond one classroom* because it involves, affects, and/or benefits students across classrooms, grade levels, teams, schools, and/or districts.
4. Teacher leadership is *a positive influence* because it benefits students, builds relationships with colleagues, and encourages participation (as opposed to requiring it).
5. Teacher leadership is *collaborative* because teacher leaders work together with others to accomplish tasks, address challenges, and resolve problems.

With these five features in mind, teacher leadership can be defined as an action-oriented, collaborative process through which effective teachers positively influence student learning and well-being beyond one classroom.

So, new teachers, as you begin thinking about the possibility of becoming a teacher leader, follow the four steps and keep the five features of teacher leadership in mind. Someday soon, when you take initiative and discover that all five features are present, you will know you are on your way to becoming a teacher leader! Use the download to track your progress in becoming a teacher leader.

References

Danielson, C. (2006). *Teacher leadership that strengthens professional practice*. Alexandria, VA: ASCD.

Hunzicker, J. L. (2018). Five features of teacher leadership. *Illinois ASCD Journal, 64*(1), 53–57. Retrieved from http://publications.catstonepress.com/i/950370-spring-2018

Hunzicker, J. L. (2019). What makes a teacher a leader? *Kappa Delta Pi Record, 55*(3), 130–136. doi:10.1080/00228958.2019.1622384.

Katzenmeyer, M. H., & Moller, G. V. (2009). *Awakening the sleeping giant: Helping teachers develop as leaders* (3rd ed.). Thousand Oaks, CA: Corwin Press.

York-Barr, J., & Duke, K. (2004). What do we know about teacher leadership? Findings from two decades of scholarship. *Review of Educational Research, 74*(3), 255–316. doi:10.3102/00346543074003255.

Building Your Brand in the Classroom and Establishing a Professional Identity

Vincent T. Laverick, EdD, Assistant Professor and Chair of Education Division
Lourdes University, Sylvania, OH

Like any business or organization, you are a brand. Remember when you sat in the student's desk and would Google or ask older friends and siblings about a specific teacher? Were there teachers you were excited to work with? How did their actions match their brand? What will be YOUR brand?

Here Are Ten Standards to Live by to Build Your Brand in the School Community

1. **Treat people well.**
   - Treating students well does not mean providing what they want but rather what they need. Treat your students well by nurturing them and meeting their educational needs in order to find success. Sometimes saying no and holding firm on a decision is treating students well.
   - Treat support staff at your school well. They hold vital responsibilities in the building as well as in the lives of students. Often, without their effort, you would find it hard to achieve success.
   - Brand yourself as someone who treats people well.

2. **Listen.**
   - We have two ears and one mouth for a reason. Use them in correct proportion. Listen to others and learn from their positive and negative outcomes.
   - Listen to the comments and insights of parents/caregivers about students. They often know what is best for the long-term development of their child. As a teacher, your role in the growth of the child is often limited to one year. Keep this in perspective.
   - Brand yourself as a listener.

3. **Avoid negative talk.**
   - If your thoughts are negative and related to your school, classroom, colleague, student, or parent/caregiver, it is best to keep them to yourself. Negative comments do not improve your brand.
   - If you are on the receiving end of negative comments, find ways to separate them from the challenge you are facing. Then, focus on addressing the challenge rather than the negativity.
   - Brand yourself as someone who is positive.

4. **Invite others into your classroom.**
   - Invite administrators and parents/caregivers into your classroom, especially when students are presenting projects.
   - Use technology to digitally invite others into classroom experiences by sharing student successes through personal communication and social media.
   - Brand yourself as welcoming.

5. **Celebrate successes.**
   - Take time to celebrate student success at school. Recognizing when individuals achieve success helps show you care about them.
   - Share success in your classroom with local news outlets.
   - Brand yourself as someone who celebrates others.

6. **Attend extracurricular events.**
   - Attending a choir concert, art fair, soccer match, or debate team event allows you to see the student in a different light. Often, students are excited to see you.
   - This visibility provides an opportunity for parents/caregivers to see you supporting their child outside the classroom.
   - Brand yourself as someone who supports students outside the classroom.

7. **Connect the community to the classroom.**
   - Think of ways you can use acquaintances to connect the real world to the classroom. For example, invite the local banker to your class to talk about budgeting money.

- Consider how your class can support community initiatives; for example, recycling or service projects.
- Brand yourself as community conscious.

8. **Find a mentor.**
   - If a mentor is not provided, find a colleague with more experience than you whom you can trust to maintain confidentiality and talk to when there are times of challenge or uncertainty. A mentor can provide the confidence you need to move forward successfully.
   - A mentor can provide valuable insight into your teaching pedagogy. Ask your mentor to observe classes and provide feedback to encourage your continued growth as an educator.
   - Brand yourself as open to professional growth.

9. **Laugh.**
   - Laughter is typically the best medicine. Laugh at yourself when you make mistakes.
   - People are drawn to individuals who exhibit happiness and positive emotions.
   - Brand yourself as someone who has a sense of humor.

10. **Take care of yourself.**
    - Get enough sleep. Eat well. Exercise. Pay attention to your grooming. Dress professionally.
    - Make time to decompress. Consider taking a walk, a quick yoga session, or 15 minutes of quiet time sitting outside. Sometimes taking a few minutes for yourself can help maintain a healthy balance in life.
    - If you do not take care of yourself, you will not have the energy to build your brand.
    - Brand yourself as healthy.

You can build a brand for yourself by working to address each of these ten items. Use the download to document what you are already doing to reach these standards. Then, every few weeks, spend some time planning how you will implement ideas from these standards into your daily practice.

Mr. Mansfield, There Is a Male Member on the Board

Jace Mansfield
English Teacher
Pekin Community High School, Pekin, IL

A student comes in and obnoxiously draws a rainbow on the board as I am greeting other students entering my class. As I see her (not-so) spectacular art written over my daily agenda, I make an off-the-cuff remark about how rainbows aren't so special to me. See, I am color blind, and blues and purples, greens and yellows, simply don't stand out as different for me. So, as I mention this to my student, she launches into 5,000 questions about color-blindness, all while other students enter the room and become enamored with the questions as well. So, amidst the "Can you see this color?" storm that was quickly brewing, I decide the best course of action is to take the first two minutes of class to dispel this tempest of questions so that the rest of the period might be saved.

I quickly type "color blind test" in the Google machine and click images, not thinking for a moment something might go wrong before throwing it onto the smartboard for the class to see. With a page full of various dot tests on the screen, I launch into a brief explanation about my colorblindness as students start to smile and snicker. The more I explain and point out various images, the more the laughter becomes unabashed. Something is wrong. "What's so funny?" I insist. A brave soul comes up, points at a green-dotted blob and asks, "Do you see *anything* in this image at all?" Of course I don't, I am color blind! "Why, what's there?" I ask with a sinking feeling. "Mr. Mansfield, there is a male member on the board."

Laughter erupts in full force. I scramble to remove the tab from the board, red as I can be and fearing my job security. After several minutes of laughter, we eventually are able to get class started with only minor chuckles for the rest of the hour.

Three things worth pulling from this anecdote:

1. **Know your shortcomings.** I am color blind, and I literally put things on the board I KNEW I couldn't see. Rarely will things be so cut and dry. Recognize your strengths and capitalize on them.
2. **Build rapport, and own it.** This ended up being a total nonissue. I immediately told my department chair, and she laughed, saying that was one of the greatest blunders she had heard. In some schools, an issue like this may have been catastrophic, but because the students and I had built trust, along with my superior, it ends up just being a funny story.
3. **Learn from your own blunders.** I made this mistake because I am young, and the line between being the professional in the room and the buddy is sometimes blurred as a younger teacher. Take examples like this, and make conscious choices to avoid similar issues in the future. Just remember, if it detracts from student learning, it's not worth doing.

Beyond Survival: Three Tips for Thriving in Your First Year of Teaching

Megan Porter, Fourth Grade Teacher
Hillsborough County School District, Tampa, FL
Instagram: tampateacher
Twitter: @dayteach12

Rebecca West Burns, PhD, Associate Professor
University of South Florida, Tampa, FL

Students are in need of passionate, dedicated teachers like you. Being a new teacher will bring its share of challenges, but your students may be facing ones that are much greater.

Beginning teachers in low-performing, high-needs schools are warriors. Many teachers fear such schools because they come with a long list of challenges. We, on the other hand, feel like we are meant to confront them. Together, we have over two decades of combined experience working in schools and supporting new teacher learning, particularly in urban schools that support families and students living in poverty. What we have learned, over time, is that these students are not "bad," and these schools are not "failing." Instead, the system is failing them, and they need teachers who are committed to addressing inequities in order to close the opportunity gap.

Although working in low-performing schools may be challenging, they can be some of the most rewarding places of employment. If you are fortunate enough to work in such a school, thriving in this environment takes a special level of patience, love, understanding, and compassion. To help you be successful, we'd like to offer three survival tips based on our experiences. You can use these tips no matter what school you are teaching in – urban or rural, high- or low-performing, elementary or secondary, it does not matter. These tips can help you not only survive but thrive in your first year and beyond.

Survival Tip 1: Remember Your Priorities and Be Kind to Yourself

If you feel like your to-do list is constantly growing while the hours in a day are shrinking, don't worry–those feelings are normal. However, it is easy to become overwhelmed, which can lead to increased stress and burnout. To avoid these outcomes, it is best to remember your priorities. Reflect on why you came to teaching in the first place: The students. One strategy to manage the stress from an ever-growing to-do list is to prioritize. Students always come first. That paperwork can wait until tomorrow. There will be times where you forget to call a parent back, turn in paperwork, or sign up for training. It happens. Be kind to yourself and realize that you are human. Admit your flaws and come out with a smile. Your students will even see how you handle challenges, and they will learn from you.

Survival Tip 2: Go with Your Gut

As a new teacher, it is crucial to build relationships with your colleagues and ask for support when you need it. However, being a new teacher could also mean you receive unsolicited advice. It is easy to second-guess yourself and drown in the suggestions and advice from others. Remember, these are your students. Do not listen to what they did last year, for that substitute, or whatever other horror stories may come your way. When inundated with tons of advice, trust your gut. No one knows your students better than you do.

Survival Tip 3: Embrace All Students as Your Students

There is no "my kids" or "your kids." They are all "our kids." The most successful schools are those that come together as a close faculty. This means opening your doors, building relationships with colleagues, and making your school feel like a home. How do you do this? Start small. Say hello to students, other teachers, AND staff. Every. Single. Day. Invite other teachers to co-teach or co-plan with you. Model for students how to collaborate and how to build a strong team. You will be surprised by how much students watch and learn from you. Extend the open-door policy to all students and their families, even if they are not in your class this year. You never know if that student or their sibling may be in your class in the future. Embracing all students as *your* students demonstrates kindness and compassion. It illustrates for students, families, and other teachers that school can become more than just school. It can become a true community.

Thriving Not Surviving

Teachers are the most important part of a student's academic success, but such success comes only when students' (and teachers') social–emotional needs are met. When times get stressful, remember to prioritize your to-do list, trust your gut, and embrace all students as your own. No matter what, love your students. Have their backs and show them that you care. Even if you slip up on the content, they will remember you as someone who deeply cared for them and made them a home for at least a school year. You've got this!

   Use the download to collect pertinent information about "your kids."

It Is Okay to Not Know Everything

Julie Padilla
Social Studies Teacher and Literacy Specialist
John V. Lindsay Wildcat Academy Charter School, Bronx, NY
LinkedIn: www.linkedin.com/in/padilla-j-julie

Being a new teacher is stressful. You want to hold your own. You want to impress others. You want to make a difference with your students. Success, though, involves taking a step back at times and admitting you may not have the answer. Creating professional relationships with your colleagues, whether in your department, your grade level, or even your classroom neighbor is necessary. Collaboration, honesty, and communication are integral to your success as a teacher. It is human nature to need to consult someone and bounce ideas off them! The mentors and colleagues who you seek out for advice will become your trusted advisors and allies in the long run.

   Professionalism does not mean you are perfect; it means you are willing to make mistakes. It means you are eager to listen to others when they have ideas for how you can move forward. Once you accept the fact that it is okay to not know everything, then you can ask for assistance and be receptive to guidance. Within your building are plenty of knowledgeable individuals who can help you, and it may be difficult to determine who exactly to consult. Your colleagues and administrators often want to assist you. They want to lend a hand, but you have to be willing to hear what they have to say, and you may even have to seek them out yourself! Beginning a conversation may make you feel uncomfortable, but just be yourself. Be genuine. The heartfelt manner in which you are asking for guidance will come naturally.

When thinking about professionalism and establishing your identity as an educator, don't limit yourself to asking for help from colleagues and administrators. Some of the most informative and helpful people in the building are the support staff. These individuals often interact with students and families in different capacities than your fellow educators do. The school secretary, the custodian, and the lunch supervisor can provide unexpected insight.

Consult students and their families when you have questions, concerns, or issues. Develop rapport with them. For example, think about a student concern or issue. Consulting the parent or guardian may seem like the last resort, but the reality is, that individual knows the child in a different capacity. Seeking that perspective can assist you in resolving the concern or issue.

Refer to the download for suggestion on who to consult for particular reasons. The download also contains easy conversation starters. As a new teacher, it is okay to admit you may not know what to do. It is okay for you to ask for help. It is okay for you to ask questions of others.

Success Really Has Three Cs

Stephanie Morrison
Kindergarten Teacher
USD 383, Manhattan, KS

A first-year teacher is flooded with advice from administrators, veteran teachers, parents, and others. Being able to implement the wisdom can be a stressful process. My advice is to be a) a strong **communicator**, b) **coachable**, and c) a **champion** for students.

Having an open line of **communication** with my school team and family stakeholders is essential to having a dynamic classroom environment. It avoids creating misunderstandings and establishes a strong team. For instance, when I dealt with a student with strong behavior needs, I expressed my concern for alarming choices, but more importantly, I enlightened the parents with the positive behaviors. By reporting the superb behavior, my student felt a sense of success, which created a more positive and safer environment.

Additionally, being **coachable** is a wonderful way to improve your first year. By being coachable, you are providing yourself with the opportunity to improve and excel as an educator. I listened to advice my team teacher and administrator provided me. Take advantage of professional learning and collaboration opportunities by truly investing in learning and implementing new ideas. My teacher toolbox is now more precise, and I've created a more successful environment.

Lastly, and most importantly, I teach like a **champion** for my students. The majority of teachers begin their career full of joy, love, and passion because little eyes watch you every day. They know when you are committed. Your personality and attitude create the classroom environment, so make it a beautiful one.

Look for Your Growth Moments

Rashad J. Talley
Assistant Principal
Washington Irving School, Chicago, IL
Facebook: https://www.facebook.com/shad.t
Instagram: https://www.instagram.com/klass_akt_1911/

As a novice in the profession, it is imperative to first understand that you are who you are. You should not feel like you have to change for anyone, but you must adapt, and those are two separate actions. At your core, you come with your own set of skills, talents, notions, as well as quirks and idiosyncratic behaviors. I encourage you to take a professional work personality quiz, such as https://www.proprofs.com/quiz-school/story.php?title=ode5otk4vxz5, or a free version of the Color Code personality test (https://www.colorcode.com/choose_personality_test/). These tools will help you navigate in spaces with other colleagues and help you understand what your needs are and how you fit into to the fabric of your professional community.

Even as you will constantly evolve in this space, you must be hyperconscious of your thoughts, words, and actions. No, I don't want you to be fearful, but there is a very intentional lens that you must have when coming into a new space as a professional and a part of a school community. Know that you belong, but just as a baby enters the world, you must find your space and place and get adjusted. It takes time, so allow yourself those moments. Rome wasn't built in a day, and neither was the best teacher ever, whoever he or she is! It takes a reflective nature to make the adjustment, knowing that you are made for this, and are cut out for the job.

Most of what takes place in a school building is all about perception. When reflecting, you should always think, "What could this look, feel, or sound like to others?" before taking any action. At first this may be daunting, but it's a social competency to be self-aware, to be introspective in this work and in life. Many people miss growth moments because they are not aware of their blind spots. Once you recognize that they exist, you should routinely check for them, and be honest about what is revealed and uncovered.

You should not be afraid to ask questions. This is key to your self-development. Be observant and cross-check with a trusted colleague when you are unsure. New teachers often don't know what they don't know. The opportunity to be vulnerable in that space allows for growth to happen. Also, build an open line of communication with your administrators and building leaders. You should also see them as coaches. These are the people in the building who look out for your best interests. Trust that. Build professional relationships with colleagues, but do not compromise your reputation or be known as the one with loose lips because you share too much. There is also value in having someone outside of the building to speak with. It is good to have someone you trust who is unbiased and neutral.

Build a relationship with some of the unsung heroes in the building: The school secretary, custodian, teacher assistant, security guard, and lunchroom manager. Those are relationships that some educators take for granted. These connections will help you understand the larger picture, and help develop your lens for systems thinking, and how all stakeholders play a part in the work of schools. See the download for a calendar of events that can spark possible growth moments throughout the school year.

Overall, your position as the new kid on the block can be intimidating, but there are some sure ways to combat those anxieties. Take that personality test. Learn your building inside and out. Build relationships with key players. Ask questions. Reflect. Finally, don't be afraid. You are there for the purpose of shaping the minds of young people who are watching your every move. Remember that, and you will always be mindful of your actions and words as a model for all.

Professionalism and School Culture: An Act of Predeciding

Rose Johnson, MEd, Instructional Specialist
Midway Middle School, Hewitt, TX

Beth Brabham, EdD, *Curriculum Coordinator*
Midway Independent School District, Waco, TX

Predeciding your actions determines your professionalism and your interactions with those around you. In turn, predecisions ultimately impact the school culture. As a new teacher, you face constant situations that require you to act and respond quickly. When you observe veteran teachers who adopt a continuous professional attitude, they have likely predecided their reaction to most situations. In beginning your professional career, this is the time to consider what kind of predecisions you are going to make.

Future Challenging Situations

Predeciding your attitude and behavior prepares you for future challenging situations. You will likely endure stress, difficult situations, difficult decisions, and difficult people every school year. Changing your circumstances or other people's behavior may not be possible, but determining how you respond or behave is something you can control. Making the decision about your own behavior or response to others has to occur before you know what lies ahead. Predeciding your attitude comes from the following:

- ◆ Reflecting on how you handled yourself when faced with adversity;
- ◆ Deciding ahead of time how to change in future situations, if necessary;
- ◆ Ensuring your motive is not about selfish gain, but rather born out of an attitude that drives you to desire a culture of humility, kindness, and compassion; and
- ◆ Possessing your willingness to listen, desire to compromise, and hunger to make the world of education a place where all students and adults thrive.

When you follow these recommendations, you honor professionalism and promote positivity as well as pride in your school.

Building Relationships

Predeciding your attitude and behavior also builds relationships. In the world of education, trusting one another is of utmost importance. Most would likely not argue that point, but building trust and genuine comradery takes time and action. As a new teacher, strive to learn how to work through adverse situations, how to humbly give and take, and how to celebrate others. Difficult situations occur with more than just students and parents. Difficult situations can occur within your grade-level team or department. Consider your behavior with colleagues ahead of time to prevent pride and negativity from seeping into relationships. In joining an existing team, predecide your own contribution. As a team member, contribute to the culture by earning trust and comradery through your individual actions.

Contribution to Education

Another act of predeciding is determining what overall contribution you want to make to the field of education. Every school has unhappy educators, so be careful not to be caught up in that negativity. When you decide ahead of time that you want to continue learning, growing, and improving your craft as an educator, you will succeed. To contribute to the field of education in a positive manner, educators can do the following:

- Practice the act of constant reflection.
- Learn from experienced, more accomplished teachers.
- Collaborate with and learn from new teacher peers.
- Realize your attitude influences others.

A predetermined willingness to be open to all knowledge and experience of others further enhances the contribution you will make to the field of education.

Predecide. This seems simple, yet it is quite difficult. By posting the downloadable document in your workspace you can view it as a daily reminder. The act of predeciding cannot happen occasionally. Establish your routine for predeciding so you are consistent in your actions and choices. Others will notice your consistency and see you as a professional. Adopting the practice of predeciding allows you to reflect and better handle situations, build relationships, and enhance your contribution to this incredible profession. The commitment to decide ahead of time makes all the difference.

Teach Like Yourself

Brittany John
Biology Teacher
Cumberland County Technical Education Center, Vineland, NJ

One of the most challenging aspects of being a new teacher has been staying true to who I am as an educator. During my first year, I often felt like there were things I was "supposed" to be, instead of embracing my own uniqueness as a teacher. Though I envisioned myself teaching from a place of joy and strength, I sometimes found myself teaching from a place of fear and insecurity. Instead of reflecting on my practice, I started listening to messages like "You're too nice." and "Do they respect you?" leading me to believe that I can't be who I am and still have the respect of my students. Though maintaining authority was something I needed to improve, the insecurity I felt from these voices led me to make decisions that were out of character and regressive, none of which made me a better teacher.

What I have learned is that the more in tune I am with myself, the stronger I am as an educator. Going into my next year, I am committed to taking my reflective practice seriously—listening to my own voice—no longer treating it as optional. Reflecting daily on my decisions, though uncomfortable, will help me to cultivate a strong sense of self. Although I am still working on embracing my own identity as a teacher, I now understand that my presence in the classroom will look different from another's, and that is okay.

Establishing Your Professional Identity: Transitioning from Student to Working Professional

Mary Frances Thomas
Assistant Principal
Chicago Public Schools, Chicago, IL

The transition from being a student to being a teacher can be overwhelming. All those years, YOU were the student, learning and taking directives from your teachers. Now the roles are reversed. It's all on you now. So, how do you make that transition as smooth as possible? These are the keys to making that transition.

Project Confidence

Many college students struggle with finding an appropriate voice in their undergraduate classroom interactions. Some are naturally shy and shrink from public speaking. Others have a comment to offer on every topic. Whatever their natural impulse, many choose to play a passive role. The transition to teacher requires a dramatic change to an active and confident voice.

You have probably heard the expression "first impressions are everything." If you think about how quickly you have sized up a professor, you may see the truth in the saying. And, as others will quickly form impressions of you, work to project confidence. Timid teachers tend to inspire thoughts like "Can they make it through the first year?" Confident teachers make students and parents think, "This is going to be a great year."

Consider how your confidence has grown over time. Remind yourself of what it took to land this teaching job. Throughout your teacher preparation program, you have gained experience and confidence in your ability to work with students, colleagues, and families. Over the course of your first years in teaching, your confidence will continue to grow and become more natural as you learn things about yourself as a teacher.

Be a Team Player

Being a team player is essential to successful teaching. You will need to join more than one team when you assume your first position. You have to team with students you teach and their families, as well as with your co-teachers, administrators, and staff. Membership on each of these teams requires you to find a role.

The most important team you need to build is with your students and their families. You have chosen a profession where much of your students' success will depend on the connections you make with them, both inside and outside your classroom. Thus, another critical transition for you will be to learn effective ways to build trusting relationships with your students and their families. Take time to get to know who your students are as people. Incorporate their interests and learning styles into your classroom. Go to students' athletic events or recitals. Communicate with students' families about positive things as well as concerns. In most cases, your reward will be increased cooperation and open home-to-school communication because you are working together as a team for the benefit of each of your students.

There are benefits to working as a team with other teachers. Seminal research suggests that collegiality not only makes your job easier but also is linked to continuous improvement in successful schools (Warren Little, 1982). One of the quickest ways to earn respect from colleagues and administrators is by showing that you work well with others. All teachers are provided with time to plan. Using some of this planning time to work with colleagues will prove to be time well spent. Whether you are analyzing student work or data, searching for the best resources for your next unit, or trying to figure out a better strategy for a behavioral issue, some of your best resources are right down the hall. Teachers with varying levels of experience all bring valuable input to the table. Veteran teachers have knowledge about what works and what doesn't work, while teachers with just a few years under their belts aren't so far removed from the newness of teaching and can relate to early career teachers. Your role is to bring knowledge of innovative resources and strategies.

Do Your Job Well, Yet Maintain a Balance

The first couple years of teaching are often characterized by too little sleep, frequent illnesses, and a sense of emotional isolation. If you want to stay in the profession for the long haul, you need to find balance. You need to remember that teaching is your profession, but it is not your life.

There will be times when students, parents, colleagues and administrators will want to meet with you before or after school (and evening!) even though you might want to use that time for lesson planning. There will be times when you have to consider saying no to requests or scheduling a time that works better for you. Make sure the time you spend planning/prepping does not overtake the time you need with family and friends. It is crucial that you learn to balance your workload with your home life.

Reference

Warren Little, J. (1982). Norms of collegiality and experimentation: Workplace conditions of school success. *American Educational Research Journal, 19*(3), 325–340.

Get Empowered: How to Use Your Professional Learning Community

Marygrace Farina, EdD, Reading Specialist
Archdiocese of Chicago, IL

Arleen P. Mariotti, PhD, Adjunct Instructor
Hillsborough Community College, Tampa, FL

Kimberly A. Schwartz, PhD, Reading Coach
Hillsborough County Public Schools, Tampa, FL

Lori Sue Grieb-Severino, PhD, Literacy Coach
Hillsborough County Public Schools, Tampa, FL

What Is a Professional Learning Community (PLC)?

A PLC is a group of educators who meet regularly and work collaboratively to improve their teaching skills and positively impact student learning (Johnson, 2017). PLCs are a form of embedded professional development. Many school districts offer PLCs as a way for teachers to increase their pedagogical content knowledge and skills. Effective PLCs foster teachers' deep conversation, reflection, and collaborative problem solving to strengthen their teaching skills and increase student learning.

PLCs come in different forms based on their purposes and goals, which are guided by the professional needs of the team members. PLC teams often focus on the shared mission of curriculum, lesson planning, and classroom procedures. Some PLCs develop support strategies for students who are struggling or create assessments as part of data gathering. For example, your PLC might choose to learn more about a topic of professional interest based on student data through a study of the professional literature. When PLCs function well, they have shown a strong link to student achievement and professional growth (Botha, 2012; Carpenter, 2015; Wang, 2016).

In a PLC, you can expect

♦ student-focused meetings where goals are set to improve instructional practices;
♦ increased student learning (Botha, 2012; Carpenter, 2015; Wang, 2016);
♦ a community of new and experienced professional educators to engage with you in camaraderie, affirmation, empathy, and mutual respect (Farina, 2019);
♦ open discussions surrounding the challenges that exist in your classroom or school;
♦ more engagement with other teachers;
♦ support by administrators;
♦ emergence of teacher leaders through distributive leadership;
♦ growth as an educator in a safe environment; and
♦ opportunities to put theory into practice, and then share your experience and challenges with peers (Botha, 2012; Carpenter, 2015; Farina, 2019; Wang, 2016).

As a member of a PLC, you should

- become knowledgeable about PLC procedures and organization;
- acknowledge and welcome contributions from each member;
- read blogs and research articles connected to the goals of the PLC and share with your team;
- utilize your PLC as a professional resource;
- exhibit a growth mindset by asking questions to stretch your own theories and practices;
- work toward observable and achievable learning goals for students, yourself, and the other PLC members;
- show a willingness to share leadership roles with team members (Farina, 2019; Fullan, 2005; McAlister, 2016).

What if Your School/District Does Not Have PLCs?

As a new teacher, look for like-minded individuals. Initiate a conversation in real time or online regarding the possibility of starting a PLC focused on shared needs or interests. Informal PLCs can be comprised of two or three educators, so you do not need many colleagues to begin one. If you would like to start one in your school/district, approach your administration with information about PLCs and the area(s) the team might want to set as their purpose(s)/goal(s).

Through your membership in a PLC, whether you join an established one or initiate your own, your focus should be on optimizing each member's capacity. In the most effective PLCs, members establish relationships so that the collective strengths of the team support each member's individual growth. Utilize the two-part download to evaluate your current PLC or for resources to start your own.

References

Botha, E. M. (2012). Turning the tide: Creating professional learning communities (PLC) to improve teaching practice and learning in South African public schools. *Africa Education Review, 9*(2), 395–411. doi:10.1080/18146627.2012.722405.

Carpenter, D. (2015). School culture and leadership of professional learning communities. *International Journal of Educational Management, 29*(5), 682–694. doi:10.1108/IJEM-04-2014-0046.

Farina, M. (2019). *The study of evaluating teacher perspectives of collective efficacy in the high school professional learning community* (Doctoral dissertation). Retrieved from ProQuest Dissertations and Theses Global database (No. 22617469).

Fullan, M. (2005). *Leadership & sustainability: System thinkers in action.* Thousand Oaks, CA: Corwin Press.

Johnson, N. N. (2017). Effectively managing bias in teacher preparation. In U. Thomas (Ed.), *Advocacy in academia and the role of teacher preparation programs* (pp. 146–160). Hershey, PA: IGI Global.

McAlister, M. (2016). The creative nature of communities of practice. *Transformative Dialogues: Teaching & Learning Journal, 9*(2), 1–7. Retrieved from https://www.kpu.ca/td

Wang, T. (2016). School leadership and professional learning community: Case study of two senior high schools in Northeast China. *Asia Pacific Journal of Education*, *36*(2), 202–216. doi:10.1080/02188791.2016.1148849.

You Are a Role Model: Considerations for Teachers in the Area of Professionalism

Dr. Mary Rebecca Wells, Assistant Professor
Georgia Southern University, Armstrong Campus, Savannah, GA

Dr. Jana Underwood, Lecturer
Georgia Southern University, Armstrong Campus, Savannah, GA
junderwood@georgiasouthern.edu

As a new teacher, focus on these seven attributes critical to developing your professionalism. They are: 1) content competence, 2) teaching performance, 3) personal conduct, 4) disposition, 5) professional standards and ethics, 6) self-reflection leading to professional development, and 7) contribution to education. You are a role model for your students, so showing professionalism in these areas sets the best example for them. In addition, time and again teacher evaluators and administrators have deemed these attributes as crucial components contributing to teacher effectiveness.

Familiarize yourself with each area of professionalism. Take time to ask yourself critical questions and reflect on your work as a professional educator:

Content competence: How well teachers know their content area for their grade level or subject matter. This should be easily observable in your lesson plan and during lesson facilitation.

Ask yourself:

- Do I really know this content?
- How well do I know how this content develops beyond the grade level (above and below) and beyond the subject level?
- Can I demonstrate how this content fits with other courses in the content area?

Teaching performance: How well teachers know appropriate teaching strategies that match their content as well as their students. This should be observed in the pedagogical choices you make and the data you collect and use.

Ask yourself:

- Am I able to ensure that students can learn this content?
- Am I up to date on the research-based best practices for teaching my content?
- Are lessons I develop age and developmentally appropriate for my students?

♦ Do I differentiate for all my students, not just those with IEPs or 504s?
♦ Do I use data to plan instruction and interventions?

Personal conduct: How teachers act in school and personal settings. This includes how you dress, meet deadlines, show respect for others, and conduct yourself on social media, as well as outside school.
Ask yourself:

♦ Do I dress for success?
♦ Do I meet deadlines?
♦ Am I on time to school, classes, meetings?
♦ Am I mindful of what I post on social media?

Disposition: The attitude that teachers present toward content, students, school, community, and so on. These are a reflection of your personal qualities as a teacher and can lend insight as to whether or not you respect diversity, demonstrate fairness, believe you can make a difference in students' lives, show enthusiasm for the content, and set high personal goals.
Ask yourself:

♦ What do I value regarding my students, community, and school?
♦ What do I believe about my students' potential and ability to learn, grow, and develop?
♦ How do I motivate my students?
♦ How do I shape student learning experiences to ensure that learning takes place?
♦ What are my personal and professional goals and do the two areas overlap?

Professional standards and ethics refers to teachers maintaining student confidentiality, adhering to all legal guidelines, keeping commitments, keeping students safe, respecting diversity, and so on. This is observed when you interact with others in formal and less formal settings (e.g., fellow teachers, parents, and students).
Ask yourself:

♦ Do I maintain student confidentiality?
♦ How do I show respect for diversity?
♦ How do I address student safety (physical and emotional)?
♦ Am I familiar with the local, state, and federal laws that impact my students' rights?

Self-reflection leading to professional growth: When teachers model self-reflection that leads to improved performance. This is observed when you self-reflect on your own strengths and weaknesses then take professional learning actions based on analyzing those reflections.
Ask yourself:

♦ Do I regularly (at least weekly) reflect on how I can improve my content knowledge, pedagogy, communication skills, and overall craft?

♦ When I identify areas of weakness, do I seek professional learning opportunities to help strengthen my skill set?
♦ If I am really strong in an area, do I offer to mentor another teacher who may be struggling in that area?

Contribution to education: What a teacher does to "give back" to the profession. This is observed when your contributions take the form of service and membership.
     Ask yourself:

♦ Do I have the opportunity to serve on committees or school councils?
♦ How can I get more involved?
♦ What professional organizations do I need to join that will help me connect with other educators and community stakeholders?
♦ Am I a member of the PTA? If not, how do I sign up?

You can use the downloadable document to self-reflect in order to determine your level of professionalism and steps for growth.

Chapter 8

Navigating Teacher Evaluation

Teacher Evaluation: An Ongoing Conversation

Amy Howerton, EdD, NBCT
English Division Chair and Secondary English Teacher
Oswego School District #308, Oswego, IL
Twitter: @amy_marie1201
LinkedIn: www.linkedin.com/in/amy-howerton-edd-8b497810

As a teacher evaluator for more than 15 years, I have experienced several changes in teacher evaluation. Currently, my district's process includes student learning data as an element of teacher performance (Assembly, 2010). What has *not* changed in evaluation is that it remains a conversation occurring between two or more professionals. As a new teacher, use the following tips to make the most of those ongoing conversations: Ask for help. Prepare. Listen. Continue the conversation. These tips are supported by guided questions in the download to assist you in preparing for teacher evaluations.

Ask for Help

Teacher evaluation is often daunting. Forms, procedures, data, timelines, and criteria can be overwhelming to tackle independently. One of the best supports as a new teacher is a mentor or trusted professional you can ask for help. Well before your first evaluation, ask a trusted professional in your own school—or even your evaluator!—to help you understand the evaluation process. Although schools are often required to share detailed information on teacher evaluations with educators, having a personal conversation with a colleague can tell you much about the process. Ask about evaluator preferences or school norms for evaluation *not* documented in the official evaluation tool. For example, some evaluators or schools prefer printed copies of files *and* electronic submission. It can be helpful knowing these details from someone who has gone through the process.

Prepare

When completing evaluation forms, continue the conversation with your mentor or trusted professional. A second pair of eyes is helpful, especially when you are completing documents for the first time. In addition to serving as a peer observer, your mentor also may have ideas about how to best showcase your teaching strengths. Finally, consider the criteria against which your performance will be assessed. An oft-used model in teacher evaluation is the Charlotte Danielson Framework for Teaching (The Danielson Group, 2017). Knowing the criterion language used by your evaluator(s) can help calm nerves about formal evaluation. Feedback from your evaluator(s) will likely include language and descriptions about areas of teaching (Danielson calls them "domains"). You will be more confident if you understand the language used in the criteria. Knowing this language also allows you to "talk the talk" in evaluative conversations.

Listen

Although you will need to speak with your evaluator during evaluation meetings, be prepared to *listen*. I strongly recommend bringing something to the meeting(s) with which you may take notes. This small yet meaningful act prepares you to listen to your evaluator's feedback and demonstrates your commitment to professional growth. Often, evaluators will provide ideas for you to try in continually improving your teaching practice. Take note of these ideas! As you listen and take notes, consider what questions you have for the evaluator, or prepare some in advance. Rather than making you appear unknowledgeable, questions demonstrate your desire to grow and learn from and with your evaluator. Especially if your school is implementing a new initiative or program, asking questions about these elements shows your evaluator that you are interested in the goals of the school and want to be a part of its success.

Continue the Conversation

You will likely have more than one formal observation early in your career, in addition to informal observations. All of these are opportunities for you to engage with your evaluators as you continue the conversation about student learning and your own performance as an educator. Although I have known teachers who wait to be informed of when evaluations will happen *to* them, I encourage you to invite your evaluator(s) into your classroom when you want to demonstrate an interesting lesson, a new activity, or show off one of the ideas recommended by your evaluator. By taking an active role in the ongoing evaluation conversation, you are empowered to realize the evaluation results and professional growth you want!

References

Assembly, I. G. (2010). *Performance Evaluation Reform Act: Laws of Illinois, 2010*. (Illinois Public Act 096-0861). Springfield, IL: Author.

The Danielson Group. (2017). *The framework for teaching*. Retrieved from https://www. danielsongroup.org/framework/.

The Real Value of Teacher Evaluation

Lori Abbott, NBCT
Professional Learning Specialist
High School District 214, Arlington Heights, IL

Performance evaluation is one of the most stressful components of a teacher's job, especially if the teacher is not yet tenured. It can feel like a task done "to" the teacher rather than a learning opportunity "for" the teacher. If you are willing to own your evaluation (rather than receive it from your supervisor), it can be a rewarding experience that promotes your continued professional growth.

How Do I Own My Evaluation?

Goal Setting

The first step toward owning your evaluation is to write a goal that is not only challenging and important to you but also aligned to building and/or district goals. You must articulate how your work with students contributes to the overall achievement of the school or district. Whatever protocol you use for developing your goal, consider the following guidelines:

♦ Use specific language—it is difficult to achieve a goal that is vague or unclear.
♦ Create a timeline for success—break the larger goal down into discrete steps or lessons.
♦ Determine how to measure progress—this will help you decide the type of feedback you need from your supervisor.
♦ Focus on student learning—emphasize effectiveness over implementation.

Once you have submitted your goal and had it approved by your supervisor (if necessary), you can plan your lessons accordingly. Not every lesson must be directly aligned to your goal. You may have other initiatives you need to address, as well as a specific curriculum that is required. You should intentionally plan goal-aligned lessons on a regular basis. However, you can work toward achieving your goal and allow for opportunities for your supervisor to collect evidence of your progress during one or more formal observations. The Formal Observation Cycle usually consists of a Pre-Observation Conference, Lesson Observation, and Post-Observation Conference.

Pre-Observation Conference

During the Pre-Observation Conference, you will share your rationale for planning as well as the connection between the lesson being observed and your goal. Do not assume that your supervisor will make that connection. Be prepared to justify your decision making (i.e., lesson objectives, instructional activities, and informal assessment strategies) based on what you know about your students (readiness levels, motivation, and learning preferences) as well as instructional best practices. There should be clear alignment among the learning objectives, instructional activities, and the assessment strategies you have planned to implement. Use the download to prepare for your Pre-Observation Conference and bring it with you for talking points.

You should also communicate the type of feedback that would be helpful to you. This is the second step in owning your evaluation. Some examples of useful feedback are levels of questions, patterns of discourse, student engagement, time on task, and bias (i.e., gender, racial, and socioeconomic). Your supervisor will most likely be documenting evidence of specific teacher or student behaviors (based on the instrument used for evaluation). By giving them a focus for the observation, you ensure that you receive feedback that is meaningful to you and will help you to improve your professional practice.

Lesson Observation

You may be tempted to try and plan the "perfect lesson" for your observation. There are two reasons you should avoid this temptation. First, there is no such thing as a perfect lesson. Second, in order for the feedback from the observation to be useful to you, the lesson must represent your authentic practice. Otherwise, the feedback will not transfer to future lessons. Owning your evaluation includes owning the successes as well as any challenges that arise during the observed lesson. Deviating from your lesson plan is not necessarily a bad thing. It can demonstrate flexibility and responsiveness to your students. During the Post-Observation Conference, you can clearly explain these choices to your supervisor.

Post-Observation Conference

The Post-Observation Conference may occur immediately following the observation or at a later time (possibly even the next day). If you are not going to meet right after the lesson, you should use the download to jot down your immediate impressions (positive and negative) and reflect on the overall effectiveness of the lesson: Did the students achieve the learning objectives? How do you know? You should also consider other ways to teach the lesson (even if it was successful), as well as things you would do differently moving forward. This is a chance to demonstrate to your supervisor that you are a reflective practitioner who is consistently trying to improve.

The final step in owning your evaluation is to receive the requested feedback from your supervisor and carefully analyze it to construct new learning. The conclusions you draw from this analysis will prompt you to commit to one or more applications that will influence your future planning and instruction. Not only will this impress your supervisor but it will also cause you to grow professionally through the process, which is the real value of teacher evaluation.

Six Steps to a Smooth Evaluation

Amie Livengood, MSEd, NBCT
Instructional Coach
District 428, DeKalb, IL

As you begin your professional teaching career, you will experience multiple evaluative observations. The process can be stressful and tricky to navigate. By breaking down the process into these six steps, you will feel more prepared and confident.

Step 1: Review your evaluation rubric and process. The rubric should give you a strong indication of what is expected of you. Make a copy of the evaluation tool/rubric your school has adopted and use it to assess yourself. Be honest and humble as you think about how you can both celebrate strengths and reflect upon weaknesses. As you work through the rubric, consider how you can highlight areas in which you are confident. Similarly, consider how you can begin goal setting for areas in which you need to improve.

Step 2: You'll notice that some of the areas your evaluator will be looking at will not be so obvious in your observation. For example, your rubric may include a descriptor for parent communication. If so, your evaluator will not observe this during your lesson, and you may want to provide evidence of your communication. Start collecting early. Gather parent contact logs, a list of your professional development activities, unit plans, assessments, and so on. This evidence shows your evaluator ways in which you are meeting the standards on the rubric that are not observable. You may even want to show your evaluator the rubric on which you self-assessed to think systematically about your practice.

Step 3: Brainstorm observation ideas and plan your lesson. Think of the areas you already identified as your strengths and play to them. A few tips:

a. Now is not the time to roll out a brand-new classroom management technique or a new structure in your class. Although your content may be new to you, the procedures and techniques within the lesson should be tried and tested.

b. Be able to identify where the observation fits into the overall lesson/unit sequence. Show your evaluator what you taught before the observation date and what comes next, including where the lesson fits into a summative assessment. This provides context for the evaluator before your observation and may help clarify some of your instructional decisions.

c. Be able to showcase what is important to your evaluator and/or school. Was the last institute day devoted to building student relationships? Show it! Is a building goal to improve reading scores? Show how you incorporate literacy skills! Is your principal a huge techie? Showcase an effective use of technology in your lesson.

Step 4: Have a plan for the "what ifs." Here's the thing: A student will probably blurt out, or someone might say something completely inappropriate. A good evaluator knows about students in your school and is going to look at HOW YOU respond, not simply that a student acts out. To ease some pre-evaluation stress, visualize certain scenarios happening in your classroom and have a plan for how to respond to each. For example, consider these common interruptions:

a. A student refuses to do the work.
b. Students will not participate/answer.
c. A student says an inappropriate answer.
d. A student comes into class crying.
e. Your smartboard/projector/computer stops working.

Step 5: Take a deep breath. It's not helpful to tell you to just relax – of course you'll be nervous! As a new teacher, having someone extra in the room who is judging your teaching is nerve-wracking. However, assume the best of your evaluator and think of them as someone who can give you feedback on how to grow as an educator. You have spent a lot of time preparing for this moment. You are ready and any feedback that you get will help you on your next observation.

Step 6: Your observation is done! During your first few years, you will probably have multiple formal observations each year. Think of the first observation as your pretest, or formative assessment of your teaching. Use that feedback to adjust your teaching before your next observation. Evaluators want to know that you are a reflective practitioner, not someone who is on the defensive. Similarly, administrators do not expect teachers new to the profession to be perfect on all aspects of teaching.

Although evaluation can be a stressful part of the job, it is also important feedback that can help guide you into becoming a successful and effective teacher. Good luck!

Take a Deep Breath

Rebecca Lehman
Kindergarten Teacher
Madison School, Skokie, IL
Instagram: @mslehmankinder
Twitter: @msrebeccalehman

Veteran teachers have always told me, teaching gets easier each year. They are comfortable in the classroom and their classroom management techniques have improved over time. So, thinking about your first evaluation might be a little scary. Take a deep breath. Your principal hired you because they believe you can do the job. They know it is your first year teaching, and it's okay to make mistakes. You are nervous and trying your best. So, when it's your time to be evaluated, do what you were meant to do: teach.

I felt prepared and confident for my first post-informal observation meeting. I shared what went well and areas that needed improvement. I absorbed advice like a sponge and returned to my classroom with new ideas. The most beneficial feedback I received was focusing on student problem solving rather than interrupting during guided reading groups. The first time my principal watched guided reading, I was working with a small group who required my undivided attention. Unfortunately, other students in the class were interrupting me with questions, causing a distraction. During my post-observation meeting, my principal discussed strategies to minimize this issue. She said other teachers wear a hat to indicate they should not be interrupted. I chose to wear a safari hat during guided reading. During my next observation, she noticed I was wearing a hat, and no interruptions occurred! When you are being observed, remember, your principal not only hired you but also hired who you will become.

Formal Evaluation: Process, Not Product

David Perrin, EdD
Assistant Principal and Instructional Coach
Rochelle Township High School, Rochelle, IL
Twitter: @DavePerrin4

Every teacher wants a "good evaluation," but new teachers must understand that their evaluation is a formative assessment, a roadmap for improving instruction as well as student experiences and outcomes. Teacher evaluation is about the process of getting better, not the product of a performance rating. These five tips will help you focus on your own process of self-improvement and hopefully make your first evaluations less daunting and more impactful.

Embrace the Role of Lifelong Learner

The administrators who hired you believe in your ability but understand that you are still learning. All teachers are. Your first formal evaluation is a "big test," but there will be others. And learning from your successes and failures on those tests is part of your own educational process, just as it was in your preparation program, and just as it is for your own students. Remember that administrators are teachers, themselves, and are invested in finding ways to help you improve, just as you are doing with your own students.

Develop an Eye for Effective Teaching

Observation of other professionals is a vital part of any preservice teaching program. After all, improving at anything is difficult without first observing a model of someone at more advanced stages of the process. So why should modeling stop during such a crucial stage of the process as the first years of teaching? Many districts are beginning to recognize the importance of creating opportunities for teachers to observe one another (please see the download as one example). Teacher and presenter Robert Kaplinsky issued a call to action in 2016 that began the #ObserveMe movement (https://robertkaplinsky.com/observeme), eliciting a groundswell of institutional support for teachers to observe one another. Chances are that your school has a similar program to encourage you to watch other professionals at work, and for them to watch you. If your district does not offer these formal opportunities, seek them out on your own by asking your mentor, instructional coach, or another veteran teacher if you can observe them during your planning period.

Practice to Build Confidence

Informal evaluations or "walk-throughs" are part of the overall evaluation process, yet surprise visits can feel awkward or stressful even for experienced teachers. Just as you should observe other teachers, ask your mentor or another colleague, even another new teacher, to pop in to watch you for a few minutes early and often during the first month or so of school. Soon you will begin to feel more at ease with the idea of being observed. Practice also applies to the lesson you choose for the formal evaluation. Choose a lesson for the formal evaluation with which you are at least somewhat familiar, not something you're trying out for the first time. If you teach the same prep several times a day, request your evaluation for later in the day so that you have time to deliver the lesson earlier in the day and make adjustments as you go.

Realize You're the Director, Not the Lead

An evaluation is about what the *students* do, not what the *teacher* does. This is one of the most prevalent misconceptions of the evaluation process. New teachers often assume that an evaluator wants to see them perform and that their students need to be quiet and attentive to demonstrate good classroom management. What evaluators actually want to see is active student engagement, not passive compliance. It may initially seem uncomfortable or even counterintuitive, but you need to give up some control of your classroom by limiting lecture and other teacher-centered activity in favor of cooperative learning, class discussion, project-based learning, and so on.

Engage in Meaningful Reflection

At its best, an evaluation provides qualitative data for the purpose of improving instruction. You should use feedback from an evaluation to set explicit goals. Review your evaluation with your mentor or another veteran teacher whom you trust and ask for their guidance to help you interpret the document. Engage in "how to" discussions with your evaluator and ask for concrete, actionable steps for improvement. Request follow-up visits to keep the feedback loop open after you have had a chance to address areas for improvement. After you have observed others and practiced some new techniques, ask your evaluator to come back and give you feedback on how they are working.

Realize that the evaluation process begins well before the day of the evaluation. Observe others and ask them to observe you, practice to gain comfort with the methods you choose for the formal evaluation, begin to relinquish control of the classroom to make it more student-centered, and solicit feedback at every step to set goals. Do the work up front and the evaluation will take care of itself.

Preparing for Observations with a Growth Mindset

Melissa Dudic, NBCT
Assistant Principal for Teaching and Learning
Maine South High School, Park Ridge, IL
Twitter: @mdudic1

For all teachers, novice and veteran, feedback is a critical component for continuous improvement of your practice. Although the observation process can be stressful, when viewed as an opportunity for feedback and growth, the experience can be both positive and motivating.

When you're preparing to be observed by a supervisor, intentional planning is key. You should design with intention every component of the lesson plan, from objectives to engagement activities to assessment, using your knowledge of the unique strengths and challenges of the individual students in your class. Each decision you make about one will affect the other. The planning process is not always linear, and you must consider both individual components of the lesson as well as the lesson as a whole.

A well-planned lesson begins with clearly defined objectives for what students will know and be able to do at the conclusion of the lesson. With these objectives in mind, consider the learning activities that will support your students in achieving those objectives. Also consider formative assessment techniques you will integrate throughout the lesson to provide both students and you with information about progress and next steps in learning. Formative assessment might be informal, including one-on-one conversations with students or listening in on small group discussion, or it may be more formal assessments, such as using a technology tool that organizes instant student responses.

The sequence of learning activities should invite your students into the lesson with a launch that allows for all to participate regardless of their skill level. Plan for a variety of activities throughout the lesson that provide opportunities for your students to explore, discover, collaborate, and take ownership in making meaning of their learning. Be sure to also include an opportunity for your students to summarize and consolidate learning at the end of the lesson.

A formal observation usually includes both a preconference and post-conference meeting. Take advantage of the preconference conversation to explain to your evaluator the rationale behind each part of the lesson. Explain why you have chosen particular methods or strategies and what you hope your students will learn as well as what you hope to learn as their teacher. Showcase your pedagogical and content-area expertise by sharing the context about individual students in your classroom. For example, rather than simply telling the supervisor that there are 15 girls and 5 boys in the class, explain how this demographic affects the dynamics of the group and influences your design of the lesson.

As soon as your observed lesson is over, jot down some informal notes of what went well and what you wish had gone differently using specific evidence from the lesson. Do this while the lesson is still fresh in your mind. Be as specific as possible, zooming in on small details as well as zooming out and viewing the lesson as a whole, always keeping student learning at the forefront. And remember, no lesson is perfect. Typically, your evaluator will share evidence or notes from the lesson prior to the post-conference meeting. Review these notes with an open mind and compare them to your own reflections. Did anything surprise you? Do the notes align with your own perceptions of how the lesson went?

During the post-conference conversation with your evaluator, do not be afraid to critique the lesson or facilitation decisions that you made during the lesson. This is what reflective practitioners do. Be sure to also include strengths of the lesson and how they positively impacted student learning. Familiarize yourself with the evaluation framework used by your school, which typically includes a descriptive rubric for important elements of planning, instruction, classroom environment, and professional practice. By being familiar with the rubric, you will be able to use a common language with your evaluator and understand what the next level of improved practice looks like.

The observation process should not be viewed as something that is done to you, but rather, a process in which you actively take part and learn alongside your evaluator. Take a moment at the end of the post-conference to summarize two to three key takeaways and action steps from the conversation and how you might apply them to future lessons. It can be easy to get bogged down by the feedback about a particular lesson, but the ultimate goal is to view the areas of growth and strength as learning opportunities to improve future lessons.

The associated lesson planning tool can be used to organize the major components of your lesson and provides questions for consideration at each stage of the process. On the last page, you can record your thoughts after the lesson, as well as your reflections from the post-conference. With thoughtful planning and a growth mindset, you can look forward to a positive evaluation experience that moves your practice forward and supports student learning.

A Bad Observation: A Learning Opportunity

Shaunna Alcorn
First Grade Teacher
Clark County School District, Las Vegas, NV

Choosing the right lesson for an observation can be tricky. There have been several occasions when I chose a lesson that was not the best choice. During my first year, I was told I needed to present a math lesson for my upcoming observation. My administrator told me she only had a specific day available to observe me. We met for my preconference the day before my scheduled observation. We discussed differentiation, what meaning-making strategies I would use, how I would ensure all my students were learning, and how I would know that my students learned the intended standard. Unfortunately, there was one thing we never discussed: Managing materials.

I had planned a calculator lesson for math that day. This was a new concept for me to teach, so I felt very uneasy about how this lesson would unfold. That uncertainty was my first mistake. The lesson was already in my plans, and all the other first grade teachers were teaching the same lesson that day. I felt obligated to use this lesson. This was my second mistake. I went in feeling unsure. My observation went downhill from there. It was more than bad; it was horrible! In a very amateur move, I passed out my materials before I set expectations. This was my third mistake. Turns out, none of my students had ever seen a calculator. They were mashing buttons. They were pretending they had cell phones. They were texting their BFF's across the room. I was completely unprepared for the level of excitement that a simple calculator would bring my students. Once those calculators touched their little fingers, it was over. The lesson was a loss.

I learned two valuable lessons from this observation. First and foremost, never pass out materials before establishing expectations. Expectations need to be clear, simple, and enforced. More importantly though, I learned that I need to say something if I have any uncertainty. I should have talked to my administrator and told her about my hesitation. We could have come up with a plan together for using a different lesson, a lesson that I felt more confident in tackling for my observation. I worried that if I admitted I was unsure about how my lesson would go, I would be viewed as incapable and unprepared. Instead of asking for help, I went ahead with the lesson. My lack of confidence was evident.

Once I got over my fear of appearing unprepared, I finally started asking for help. I created a preconference planning sheet (see download) with questions regarding the following:

- ◆ Resources
- ◆ Common student misconceptions
- ◆ Differentiation
- ◆ Supporting my EL students
- ◆ Classroom management

My administrators have never made me feel like my questions were unimportant. They are always willing to answer any question I have. Now, when I walk into a preconference, I come prepared. I have a mental list of questions at the ready. I used to worry about annoying my administrators with too many questions. Instead, I have come to realize that part of their job is to help me become a better educator. Administrators evaluate your performance as an educator, but they are also there to mentor and advise. Do not wait for the post-conference to ask questions!

Navigating Teacher Observation: Strive for Five

Marsha Black-Chen, EdD, Senior Lecturer
The Mico University College, Kingston, Jamaica

Are you nervous about being observed by your administrator? Do you wonder how your students will respond? How will you handle those planned and unplanned visits to your classroom? In preparing for your teacher observations, consider these five suggestions.

1. **Enter the classroom by being prepared**
   Entering a classroom comes with the duty of impacting student learning, so you should always be prepared. Being prepared allows you to:
   - Sustain a positive classroom culture.
   - Create every lesson as if it were fit for an observation.
   - Be consistently present, confident, and engaging.
   - Know that your students depend on you for accurate information.
   - Organize the learning environment to enhance student–teacher interaction.
   Being prepared allows you to execute your lesson plans while formatively assessing your students' learning. Teaching and learning are complicated, but, by being prepared, you have an opportunity to emphasize incremental learning, which in turn generates long-term understanding.
2. **Choose the right lesson for observation**
   As you prepare the right lesson for observation, consider your past professional learning. Utilizing what you have learned helps you improve your practice as you prepare for your observation.
   - Analyze the curriculum and consider your instructional methodologies.
   - Set high goals at this time for your students and for your classroom setting.

- Value your students' points of view.
- Encourage your students to be autonomous and innovative.

It is possible for each lesson to be the right lesson for observation, if you are activating what you know about how to teach.

3. **Prepare students for classroom visitors**

Consider preparing your students for classroom visitors. This can be culturally relevant because in some cultures students stand when a visitor enters the classroom, while in other cultures students remain seated. With your students, determine how you will greet visitors. Also consider how you will:

- Explain the purpose of classroom visitors.
- Communicate clear expectations about behavior and participation when visitors come to your classroom.
- Ensure that students have been previously exposed to the lesson structure and topic.
- Maximize opportunities for your students to express their points of view.
- Equip your students with the necessary resources.

Prepare your students for classroom visitors ahead of time. This will affect the willingness of your students to reveal their thinking when visitors enter the classroom. Strive to make this a positive experience for you and your students.

4. **Be prepared for unplanned observations**

Unplanned observations should not be a challenge. Create an educational environment where your students assume responsibility for their behavior and participation even when unplanned visitors arrive. You should:

- Commit to your instructional approach.
- Encourage student learning and self-regulation.
- Nurture your students' natural curiosity.
- Respond to students' understanding and misconceptions during the lesson.

Even with unplanned observations, being prepared and executing the planned lesson should reduce your anxiety, thereby creating a fluid, consistent, and purposeful learning environment.

5. **Advocate for your teaching**

One very powerful way you advocate for your teaching is by owning your professionalism. Do this daily through intellectual discourse with your students, colleagues, and observers about your practice. Here's how to do this:

- Share your own ideas about teaching, including your philosophy.
- Align your teaching practices to your philosophy.
- Reflect and analyze your personal perspectives on learning to improve your practice.
- Encourage your students to be metacognitive.
- Hear and reflect on the ideas of others.

As an advocate, focus attention on your students and yourself. Through this, you can communicate your professionalism through intellectual discourse, even with observers.

As a new teacher, navigating teacher observation is easier if you enter the classroom as ready as you can be, choose the right lesson for an observation, prepare students for classroom visitors, handle unplanned observations, and always advocate for your teaching. See the download to help you prepare to Strive for Five.

Day One Sets the Tone

Alisa M. Ross, EdD, Assistant Professor
Southern University and A & M College, Baton Rouge, LA

I truly believe the first day of school sets the tone for the entire year. Besides greeting my students at the door and checking their schedules to make sure they were in the correct class, I posted and followed an agenda as well as assigned homework on the first day!

As a new teacher, I knew I would be evaluated at least two times throughout the school year. This was yet another stressor to add to my list. How did I prepare? To begin, I met with my mentoring teacher on a weekly basis. I asked her to explain the evaluation process to me and what our administrators would look for. Next, I printed a copy of the teacher evaluation form to become familiar with the rubric. Third, I changed my mindset. In other words, instead of waiting to prepare for and teach for my observation, I started to think of each day as my observation day. This helped me because once I became comfortable with my teaching and the evaluation rubric, I was able to "teach like a rock star every day!"

I included my students by getting them involved on Day One. From passing out instructional resources to collecting papers, my students played an active role in the classroom. I also stressed to them to continue working, even though a visitor may enter the room. After an observation, I praised my students and thanked them for being on their best behavior!

Teacher Evaluations: What Does "Good" Look Like?

Meghan A. Kessler, PhD, Assistant Professor
University of Illinois Springfield, Springfield, IL

> I have concluded that classroom teaching ... is perhaps the most complex, challenging, demanding, subtle, nuanced, and frightening activity that our species has ever invented.
> —Lee Shulman, *The Wisdom of Practice*

It is no mystery that teaching is one of the most complicated tasks we humans do. Researchers have been fascinated with this complexity for decades, even comparing it to the skillful improvisation of jazz musicians or the rapid-fire collaboration of basketball players when rebounding the ball (Cuban, 2011). In fact, studies have found that teachers make about one decision per minute during a typical lesson (Clark & Peterson, 1986), and engage in hundreds of unplanned interactions with students all day long (Jackson, 1990)! Therefore, it is understandable that figuring out the "best" way to evaluate teachers is difficult. However, we have come a long way. We know now that teacher evaluation should be an educative, *not punitive*, part of teachers' jobs, and that teacher voice should be central to the process (Danielson, 2013). Therefore, this article provides a few quick tips to help you evaluate your evaluations.

What Do Good Teacher Evaluation Practices Look Like?

If you are on the job market, consider using the following list as a way to vet the school you are applying to or interviewing at. Teacher evaluation practices can tell you a lot about school culture, administrative values, and the implementation of district or state policies. You also may use this list to prepare for that inevitable, final interview question: "So, what questions do *you* have for *us*?" Or you could use the following list to guide conversations with administrators, mentors, or colleagues. If you have already accepted a job (or have been teaching for a few years), this list can also be a way to examine whether evaluation practices are helping you and your colleagues reflect and improve.

They Put Teachers in the Driver's Seat

Teacher evaluation should *never* result in a "gotcha" moment. The process should be transparent and empowering. Therefore, ask your administrators about the tools or rubrics they use, resources available to you, what they typically look for during walk-throughs or observations, and what practices are followed before/during/after observations. Consider evaluations as a time for you to do a deep dive on your professional goals. Be inquisitive about where you are, where you want to go, and how your administrator or evaluator (and the evaluation process) can support you.

They Are Collaborative

If you teach in a school, district, or county that has a teachers' union, it is likely that your evaluation methods were collaboratively designed by union and district leadership. If this is the case, you may ask your building union representative about what interests were central to the development of the evaluation tool. If you do not teach in a unionized setting, ask building leaders how teachers were involved in the construction of the evaluation methods. In either case, do not hesitate to rely on support from your colleagues. For example, ask colleagues about how they are organizing their materials, what formatting is typical for lesson plans, what platforms or tools are used to provide evidence to evaluators, and what they wish they had known the first few times they were evaluated.

They Are Growth Oriented

Just as you want your students to develop a growth mindset, consider framing problems of practice as a new opportunity to improve and leverage your evaluation process towards this end. Some evaluation methods even follow a kind of instructional coaching model, which has been shown to be one of the most powerful forms of professional development (Kraft, Blazar, & Hogan, 2018). Put simply, evaluations should be the launchpad for guided professional learning. Therefore, think of your evaluator as a "critical friend" who is interested in what is best for you and your students.

Inquiring about teacher evaluation will show that you care about your professional growth and are curious about school policies. Taking an active stance will not only help you prepare but also help reduce some of the anxiety that evaluation can bring. See the download, "A Worksheet for Evaluating Evaluations," as a helpful structure.

References

Clark, C. M., & Peterson, P. L. (1986). Teachers' thought processes. In M. C. Wittrock (Ed.), *Handbook of research on teaching* (3rd ed., pp. 255–296). Washington, DC: American Educational Research Association.

Cuban, L. (2011, June 16). *Jazz, basketball, and teacher decision-making.* Retrieved from https://larrycuban.wordpress.com/2011/06/16/jazz-basketball-and-teacher-decision-making/.

Danielson, C. (2013). *The framework for teaching evaluation instrument.* Princeton, NJ: Danielson Group.

Jackson, P. W. (1990). *Life in classrooms.* New York, NY: Teachers College Press.

Kraft, M. A., Blazar, D., & Hogan, D. (2018). The effect of teacher coaching on instruction and achievement: A meta-analysis of the causal evidence. *Review of Educational Research, 88*(4), 547–588.

The Five Ws of Teacher Observations

Maryellyn Friel, NBCT
Special Education Teacher
U-46, Elgin, IL

I find the most critical aspect of teacher observation, often undervalued in terms of time, is the preparation. A successful lesson starts with a plan. A successful observation starts with a plan, too. Let's plan!

Start *With* the *When*

When will I be observed? This is how most observations start. You will be asked if a certain time or class period works. Time is often the first conversation in the observation process. You might have limited choices in the when of an observation. Administrators will have time constraints and might only be available during specific parts of the day. They might also have an interest in observing a specific subject area due to school initiatives such as adoption of a new curriculum. So, if you are asked when you would like to be observed, think about the subjects, class periods, or group of students you are teaching. With which subject/class period/group do you feel most confident? Which subject/class period do you feel most proud of? If you are restricted in when you will be observed, use this same approach. What do I feel most confident about for this class/group of students? What do I feel most proud of? Use this as your guide as you tell the story of your practice.

Followed by *Where*

Where will I be observed? This is probably an easy response since teachers tend to work in the same space daily. However, think about the place and space. Is the space arranged the way you like it? What would you change and why? What do you like about the way the space is organized when you teach? Do you change the space during lessons such as moving desks? Would an alternate space be better, such as the library? Keep space in mind as you prepare. You may want to revisit space as you finalize your lesson plans.

Next Is the *Who*

Who are your students in this subject? Now that you know when you will be observed, begin by describing your students' strengths in this subject. What needs do they have? Who works together well? Who needs "extras"? You may want to consult with colleagues who also work with your students who need extras, such as the special education teacher or school social worker. They may have insights to consider or information to be aware of, such as emotional or learning strategies to keep in mind. Consider how this information about your students impacts your instruction and the decisions you make. You may want to create a chart as an artifact to represent your knowledge for your preconference (see download). Keep your description focused on the subject area. For example, if you are teaching a writing lesson, ask yourself what you know about your students' abilities and needs in writing. Then, think about how you support this analysis.

Now Comes the *What*

What am I teaching right now with this group of students? Now that you know when your observation will take place and which students will be part of the observation, think about the lesson goal(s) you taught today and what you will be teaching when observed. Ask yourself:

♦ Why did you choose today's goal?
♦ How successful was today's goal?
♦ What learning goal do you intend to work on when observed?
♦ What do you want your students to understand next or more deeply?
♦ What state or district standards do your goals support?
♦ Are your goals clear?

It is often easier to think about what students will *do* during the lesson instead of what they will *learn*.

Finally, the *How*

How will you know your lesson was successful? Be sure your assessment connects back to the goal. Also think about how today's assessment contributes to the formal assessment at the end of the lesson series or unit. Will you use an exit slip or perhaps a checklist? Will you use student work produced during the lesson to provide insights?

Be Kind to Yourself: Be Your Own Critical Friend

Lynn Williams Leppich, MA (Cantab) MA
High School Teacher, Liestal, Switzerland
Affiliate Lecturer PH FHNW Northwestern Switzerland

Newly qualified teachers and interns involved in initial teacher education programs are kept constantly on their toes—by students, materials, curricula, deadlines, and so on. Observations by teacher educators, mentors, and management representatives are frequent and regular. In fact, as an aspiring or new teacher, you might well end up feeling that you are constantly being observed—and perhaps experience some degree of nerves, pressure, and even stress because of these visits.

And yet, each of these visits—whether scheduled or unannounced—by a teacher colleague, department chair, or administrator will provide you with invaluable feedback on your teaching. Once the observations slowly dwindle in number as you progress through your teacher education program and licensure and gradually settle into life at your school, you may find that you will miss them—though not the nerves, pressure, and stress! Teaching can be very lonely, even when you're surrounded by the students in your classroom. Isolation comes from the busyness of the day, leaving little time to gain insight from peers. New teachers will be left to look to the expressions on students' faces, engagement in certain tasks, and the quality of work as lesson feedback. You are likely to find this is simply not enough. Students' expressions can be hard to interpret, and the quality of work often reflects the lesson's effectiveness.

This is why it is important to fill that feedback void. To a degree, you can simulate the feedback process by becoming your own critical friend. By stepping aside and reflecting on both your planning and the subsequent execution of your lesson, you can create the necessary distance to make a relatively objective assessment.

As a *critical* friend, you study your lesson documentation carefully ahead of teaching the material. Keep an open mind and force yourself to look for inconsistencies, anomalies, and omissions. At the same time, you are a critical *friend*. So, without making excuses for any inconsistencies, anomalies, and omissions, or becoming inwardly defensive or defeatist, show yourself the respect you would show a real-life friend. Acknowledge your effort. Give credit where credit is due. Offer a realistic perspective on the time and energy a lesson or unit might ask of you. Encourage yourself in your endeavors. Reassure yourself and regroup when you fail.

What will be missing, of course, if you become (at least on occasion) your own *critical* friend, is genuine interaction. For this reason, it will be invaluable to have a resource to jumpstart your thinking and direct your thoughts in the direction a critical *friend* might when reviewing your lesson planning or observing you as you teach. Use the accompanying checklist (download), "Five Prompts to Help You Become Your Own Critical Friend," to review your lesson planning and teaching with the necessary distance and direction.

Lastly, remember to really be that friend. Be kind to yourself. Remember that you are just starting out, and that teaching is also a learning business.

Chapter 9

Relationship Building/ Communication

Know Your Network: Advice to Beginning Teachers on Relationships and Support

Lynn Sikma, PhD, Assistant Professor
University of North Carolina at Wilmington, Wilmington, NC

Teaching is difficult. Your teacher preparation program often cannot prepare you for every situation. You graduate with the tools and knowledge to plan engaging lessons and manage your time and your classroom. However, you do not learn how to deal with the day-to-day demands and challenges of the job, like how to deal with a difficult parent, what to do when one of your second graders throws up in the middle of a lesson, or what kind of offenses warrant an office referral. As a result, it is easy to get burned out or feel inadequate. During these times, it's important to tap into your resilience.

Resilience can be described as your ability to bounce forward after facing adversity (Walsh, 2002). Some people have high levels of resilience because, over time, they have successfully overcome numerous hurdles. Others have low levels, perhaps because they have gone through life relatively smoothly and have not had many setbacks from which to bounce back. Regardless, it is possible (and important) to improve your personal resilience by building up your protective factors. These protective factors help you get through difficult times. As a new teacher, you might want to check out the BRiTE program (www.brite.edu.au), a series of online modules used in teacher preparation programs in Australia to build resilience in preservice teachers (Mansfield, Beltman, Broadley, & Weatherby-Fell, 2016). These modules have been used successfully with beginning teachers in the United States.

One protective factor is your social network. This network is not an online platform like Instagram or Facebook, but rather a compilation of all the people you interact with on a regular basis. Who are the family, friends, and colleagues who support you on a daily basis? As a new teacher, you need to have an active support network, both in and out of school. Equally important is knowing the role each person plays in your network, with whom you interact and for what purpose. Being aware of who fulfills each role is helpful; it allows you to see where your support network might be lacking.

Try setting aside 20 minutes every few months (suggested: September, November, February, April) to do the following activity: Start by brainstorming a list of everyone who comes to mind when you think of the word *support*. This means different things to different people, so define support as you see fit. This list can include anyone (Mom, principal, neighbor, etc.) who you feel supported by. Once your list is complete, indicate what kind of support you receive from each person on your list. Some people may provide more than one type of support, while others may serve a very specific purpose. Use the downloadable document to get you started.

Most beginning teachers list supports that fall into one of five categories:

- **Emotional:** This is often identified as the most needed support by new teachers. Who are the people, both in and out of school, you can go to when you are having a rough day? Who can you vent to about a frustrating exchange with a parent? These should be safe people who are in a nonsupervisory position (i.e., not your administrator).
- **Relational:** This refers to support from another new teacher in the same career phase as you. This type of support is paramount because it helps you maintain your confidence during moments when you feel like you don't know what you're doing. Optimally, this would be someone else in your school or district since they can relate to your particular context, but it does not have to be.
- **Contextual:** This relates to support you need to navigate your specific school context. These people help with questions like, "How is open house handled? How do you fill out a referral? Who do you go to if the copy machine is jammed?"
- **Instructional:** This kind of support focuses on your instructional practice. "Who are you collaborating/sharing lesson plans with? Where are you getting ideas for classroom management? How are you locating and utilizing non-text resources for your teaching?"
- **Social:** This helps ensure you are maintaining some work–life balance. "Who are you hanging out with after work? What activities are you finding time for on weekends?"

Once you are aware of who you seek out for support and what your needs are, you can grow your network. Is there a particular type of support you are lacking or would like more of? Who can you connect with to fulfill that need?

One way to connect with others is to be a strategic extrovert. Become aware of colleagues' strengths (and what they think they are), and ask them for help in those areas. People inherently love when others recognize their talents, so approaching them for help in one of those areas will create a more personal connection.

New teachers like yourself tend to underestimate the value they bring to a school and to their veteran colleagues. Remember that you have talents that you can also offer to others. This is an effective catalyst to know and grow your network.

References

Mansfield, C., Beltman, S., Broadley, T., & Weatherby-Fell, N. L. (2016). Building resilience in teacher education: An evidenced informed framework. *Teaching and Teacher Education, 54,* 77–87. doi:10.1016/j.tate.2015.11.016

Walsh, F. (2002). Bouncing forward: Resilience in the aftermath of September 11. *Family Process, 41*(1), 34–36. doi:10.1111/j.1545-5300.2002.40102000034.x.

The Power of Humor in the Classroom

John Lando Carter, EdD, Assistant Professor
Middle Tennessee State University, Murfreesboro, TN
Twitter: @cartersensei

> In every classroom there should be some form of laughter. If the students are sitting through an entire lesson and no one laughs or smiles, then that classroom is missing something.
>
> —Ron Clark, *The Excellent 11*

Ron Clark, famed principal of the Ron Clark Academy, makes humor, among other wonderful, must-have teacher qualities, a top piece of advice in his 2004 book *The Excellent 11*. He's right! How often students laugh and smile is a signal of your classroom culture. Daniel Coyle (2018), author of *The Culture Code*, reveals that "laughter is not just laughter; it's the most fundamental sign of safety and connection" (p. 88). Leveraging the power of humor, as Professor Daniel C. Allen (2019) notes, can indeed create a positive learning environment. Allen says it can also enhance learning itself and reduce test anxiety. In fact, one of my own education professors would play "Every Breath You Take" by the Police before we took a test. We laughed every time and immediately felt at ease just before the test.

So, how do we do it? Let's begin with some important ground rules. We want to utilize humor as a mechanism to deepen relationships instead of diminishing them. Clark (2004) provides a careful warning: "It is important to be able to joke with students and have fun, but at the same time teachers need to make sure that the type of humor they are using isn't hurting or embarrassing any of the students" (p. 175). Avoid even seemingly innocent approaches, such as nicknames (which may not be humorous to the student) and sarcasm (which can easily be misinterpreted). Teachers should always aim to stay positive and productive with humor at all times. You should never engage in humor that degrades or downgrades students or their sense of belonging.

Here are some ways to employ humor in your classroom. From this list, find the strategies that fit your personality and style. Brainstorm ways to use them in your classroom:

- Goofiness or silliness
- Singing and dancing
- Costumes
- Storytelling
- Impressions
- Memes

♦ Self-directed jokes
♦ Pop-culture connections

It's all about finding your own style when weaving humor into daily lessons and interactions with students. For example, I employ a general sense of goofiness paired with content-related *memes*. Students speak in the language of *memes*, so designing custom *memes* to help ease students' anxiety over tough texts such as *Macbeth* can be powerful. Kevin Kruse, one of Twitter's star *twitterstorians*, uses his signature dry sense of humor to help students stay engaged during history lectures at Princeton. My children's principal at their elementary school dances in the drop-off line and dresses up in hilarious costumes, such as Piggy from the wonderful Mo Willems book series. These little efforts to make students laugh pay huge dividends in student engagement and minimizing classroom management issues. The ultimate goal is to have students beat you to the door because they cannot wait to laugh and learn in your classroom.

We are not just goofing around by making humor a regular staple in our classrooms. We are setting the cognitive conditions for optimal learning and developing authentic relationships with students. According to Kounios and Beeman (2009), neuroscience research "demonstrates that individuals are more likely to solve complex problems when they are in a positive mood, as measured by signature activity in the brain's cingulate cortex" (Seelig, 2012, p. 146). Not only do we help students enter a more conducive mood to learn through humor, but we also forge relationships by laughing together (often at your expense), which can help all teachers move into the deeper role of mentoring, a role defined by reciprocal learning, sharing, and interacting in a genuine way.

Finally, Conan O'Brien recently gave some great advice new teachers can use in a 2019 *Rolling Stone* interview: "To really have a sense of humor, you have to be able to laugh at yourself" (Doyle, 2019). As a new teacher, laughing at yourself will be crucial to your survival because you will not get everything right the first year, or even the first few years. So, laugh at yourself and gain credibility through vulnerability in your classroom. Students will see you not only as human but also as a human who is learning along the way, just like them.

Post the download infographic to remind yourself of the ways humor supports student learning.

References

Allen, D. C. (2019, July 22). Bringing authentic humor into the classroom. *The Teaching Professor*. Retrieved from https://www.teachingprofessor.com/topics/teaching-strategies/bringing-humor-into-the-college-classroom/

Clark, R. (2004). *The excellent 11: Qualities teachers and parents use to motivate, inspire, and educate children.* New York, NY: Hyperion Books.

Coyle, D. (2018). *The culture code: The secrets of highly successful groups.* New York, NY: Bantam Books.

Doyle, P. (2019, January 22). Conan O'Brien remembers when Trump stormed off his show. *Rolling Stone.* Retrieved from https://www.rollingstone.com/

Kounios, J., & Beeman, M. (2009). The aha! Moment: The cognitive neuroscience of insight. *Current Directions in Psychological Science, 18*(4), 210–216.

Seelig, T. (2012). *inGenius: A crash course on creativity.* New York, NY: HarperOne.

Promoting Parental/Family Involvement

Jameelah R. Wright, MA
Early Childhood Family Literacy Specialist & Parent Educator
East Orange School District, East Orange, NJ

In the field of education, there is a common adage, "Parents are their children's first and most important teachers." The facts are clear: Parental involvement in student's education is pivotal, paramount, and key to their success in school and in life. Research has consistently shown that "one of the most effective ways to increase student achievement is for parents to be actively involved in the education of their children" (Martinez, 2004, p. 1). Also, family involvement positively impacts students' cognitive and social development through active participation in classroom and school activities.

With all we know about the importance of parental and family involvement in education, many schools, especially those serving urban areas and students of color, report that parental and family involvement is dismally low or basically nonexistent. If parents know they are an important part of students' success in school, why aren't families flocking to schools in droves to ensure this? According to Martinez (2004), there may be barriers or perceived barriers that prevent parents from becoming fully involved in schools, such as attitudes, logistics, lack of skills, and system barriers.

The first perceived barrier, attitude, can be defined as a lack of trust between schools and families. Families may feel that the school does not really want them to be involved. Consider these examples. Attitudes develop when little effort has been made to build a partnership with families. When parents enter the building or classroom, they are not greeted warmly. For families whose first language is not English, attitudes may develop if every document sent home is in a language they do not understand.

Logistical barriers, the second perceived roadblock, are those such as schools hosting meetings and school events at inconvenient times for parents. Additionally, not providing childcare services or transportation for meetings and events can be problematic for families who would like to participate. Often, parents are unable to attend meetings if they cannot take time off from work. Other parents who do take time off from their jobs are seldom acknowledged for doing so.

The third potential barrier that families face is their own perceived deficit of skills. They may be reluctant to volunteer for, or participate in, school meetings or committees because they feel uncomfortable doing so. Perhaps there is an absence of information about the roles families play in the school, or maybe they are unaware of school procedures and policies. The paucity of information coming from the school to inform and educate parents about their rights, privileges, and expectations leaves them feeling too inadequate to participate in meaningful ways.

The fourth perceived roadblock is system barriers, which can be a lack of resources to support parent and family involvement. Perhaps there is no funding for activities and programs targeted to parents and families. School staff are not paid for the time they put in after regular working hours. Parent leaders are not compensated for their time, contributions, or expertise. Another example of a system barrier is a school with express drop-off and/or pick-up for students. Parents simply drive up and drop-off or pick-up students, and never have the opportunity to enter the school building or classroom. Although this system was probably created to alleviate parking issues, it may unintentionally send families the message that they are not welcome inside the building.

Parents will not want to become involved if the culture and climate of the school or classroom is not welcoming, or if teachers or administrators have shown themselves unworthy of trust. This, in turn, negatively affects student learning. If schools do not go out of their way to involve families, then families will not go out of their way to fit into an environment where they feel uncomfortable or unwanted.

Sometimes you, as the teacher, are so busy lamenting parents who are not involved that you overlook the parents who are, or who want to be. Some ways that parents/families show interest in building a sustained relationship with you and the school include, but are not limited to, attending parent–teacher conferences, participating in extended class visits, and helping with class activities (Weiss, Caspe, & Lopez, 2006). There might be just one or a few families who are deeply committed and involved in the students' education. They attend every event, donate supplies, time, and money to the classroom, and are generally there when needed. Why not embrace these parents, fully engage them, and ask them how you can get more parents on board?

Parental involvement can exist in many forms. It does not have to be limited to attending assemblies or parent–teacher conferences. You can help promote parent engagement through workshops and trainings that you design and host. Through regular and ongoing workshops and trainings, parents can be informed about how pertinent their participation is in many ways, such as homework, discipline, health, nutrition, and so on. Teachers who provide more opportunities for family involvement and occasions for nontraditional contact (such as parent discussion groups, parent resource rooms, and home lending libraries) enjoy increased levels of family participation (Weiss et al., 2006).

With all we know about the importance of parent participation, there is reason to believe that more families can be involved in their child's learning, classroom, and school through your effort as a teacher. If families do not know the importance of their involvement, then as the teacher it is your responsibility to tell them. Clearly, if we do not want to leave any students behind, then we surely cannot leave their families out.

For ideas on how to develop parental/family interest and involvement, and to set meaningful goals for family involvement in your classroom, see the "Parental/Family Interest and Involvement Reflection and Checklist Form" (download).

References

Martinez, J. (2004). Parental involvement: Key to student achievement. *National Center for School Engagement.* Retrieved from http://schoolengagement.org/wp-content/uploads/2014/03/ParentalInvolvementKeyToStudentAchievement.pdf

Weiss, H. B., Caspe, M., & Lopez, M. E. (2006). *Family involvement in early childhood education* (Research Brief No. 1). Retrieved from Global Family Research Project, Harvard Family Research Project website: https://archive.globalfrp.org/publications-resources/browse-our-publications/family-involvement-in-early-childhood-education

Parent Tips from the Teacher for Having a Successful School Year

Jennifer Wellberg, Researcher
Duke University, Raleigh, NC

The beginning of the year can be filled with both excitement and anxiety for many families. Communicating the expectations to parents ahead of time will help to build a successful relationship with them and ensure an enjoyable school year experience for all involved. Here are a few tips that I would strongly recommend passing along to parents:

- **Attendance matters!** Children need to attend every day unless they are sick. When your child is sick, inform the school that morning and send a note to excuse the absence when your child returns to school. Learn the school's attendance policy and make regular attendance a priority.
- **Be on time when dropping off and picking up your child.** Know the arrival and dismissal times at your child's school and make it a habit to arrive on time or even early!
- **Take note of deadlines.** Failing to return items such as permission slips or library books will negatively impact your child and you. Keep a calendar of important dates and deadlines.
- **Familiarize yourself with school and classroom policies.** Understanding the rules and expectations for behavior, volunteering, birthday parties, attendance, homework, severe weather, and arrival and dismissal will allow you to remain compliant and be involved in your child's school.
- **Maintain open communication with school professionals.** Know how to contact the teacher and other school professionals. Find out their planning time and learn when they are available to meet with you or have a conversation.

Creating a Caring Culture in the Classroom

Deepti Kharod, PhD, Assistant Professor
Dreeben School of Education, University of the Incarnate Word, San Antonio, TX

Caring is often presented in schools as part of a values-based character program. Some believe that caring is an intrinsic quality, whereas others look at caring as something we do, not something we are. In the latter, caring is viewed as learnable and teachable, including the relationship with the teacher and the culture in the classroom. So, how can a new teacher like yourself create a culture of caring in the classroom, and what is the best age to start?

Who Are the Participants in a Caring Relationship?

There is a carer (someone who gives care) and a cared-for (someone who receives care). Both are active agents in a two-way relationship because the cared-for gives feedback, which in turn encourages the carer. However, each relationship determines how individuals learn to express caring.

What Actually Happens, and How Does the Process Unfold in Your Classroom?

- ◆ **Receive care:** Your students need to have the experience of receiving care to help them learn how to give care. This could include your relationship in caring for them. Your students could also act as the carer in relationships with classmates that support your classroom culture.
- ◆ **Focus on others:** It is important for the carer to know about the cared-for, including their needs and preferences. As a new teacher, encourage your students to value others by recognizing each person's individuality, cultural and family background, and developmental and emotional needs. In your classroom, emphasize helping students develop dispositions that support caring relationships. Then, the focus is on others, not on themselves.
- ◆ **Learn skills:** Your students need to learn skills to put caring thoughts into action. The action can be tangible, for example like helping a classmate with a problem, or intangible like welcoming a new student by sitting with them at lunch. Carers use these types of skills. You need to help recipients of care learn skills to give feedback, such as ways of expressing appreciation and gratitude with smiles, words, or other reciprocations.
- ◆ **Practice receiving and giving care:** Similar to learning other skills, the capacity and ability to care grows when students observe and experience modeling. Adults are important but not the only models. Many students engage in caring behaviors, which can be explicitly identified to build awareness and give feedback. (*Thank you, Esteban, for moving over to make room for Ally. That was a caring thing to do!*) Your students need time and opportunities to practice receiving and giving care.
- ◆ **Reflection:** Raising awareness about caring behaviors builds dispositions, which undergird communities of care in classrooms. This starts with you, the teacher, who sets the tone through personal reflection which you can share through methods such as thinking aloud or role play. Similarly, students can learn to pause and think about how an interaction feels. Documenting those feelings through a journal prompt or making them public by expressing appreciation to another strengthens awareness, habits, and dispositions.

How Can This Approach Support Caring Behaviors in Other Contexts?

Experts say relationships of care can involve a person and other living and nonliving things, such as animals, objects, and even ideas!

Building Rapport Drives Successful Teaching

Chantelle Grace, PhD Student, Graduate Teaching Assistant
University of Georgia, Athens, GA

Building rapport with your students is an imperative step toward creating a classroom culture conducive to learning. As American author and speaker John C. Maxwell said, "Students don't care how much you know until they know how much you care." Reflecting on my own teaching experiences, I can attest to the value of Maxwell's words, as I found relationship building to be the main factor that brought my teaching efforts to fruition. When my students knew I cared about them as individuals, they were more willing to engage in my meticulously planned lessons, because they trusted me as their teacher and did not want to let me down. How will you show that you care about your students as individuals?

As a new teacher, you may not initially prioritize relationship building since other demands are often fighting for your attention (e.g., lesson planning, required meetings, and supervision duties). Don't get me wrong, all of these demands need responsiveness, too, especially when you are the "newbie" in a school. However, none of them will make as big a difference as taking the time to communicate with your students and becoming familiar with their lives and community. Relationship building is the driving force behind all successful teaching. Once you establish a positive rapport with your students, what you can accomplish in the classroom is unlimited.

There are several ways to approach relationship building with your students. One way you can develop positive connections is through weekly "speed dates." Don't announce these "dates" out loud, but instead accomplish them in subtle ways that are genuine to your students. Each week set a goal for how many students with whom you want to meet throughout a class period, as well as the amount of time you can dedicate to each one (usually around 2–3 minutes). When your students are working on independent assignments, begin rounds with your chosen "dates." Ask students questions about their favorite hobbies, music preferences, favorite TV shows/movies, and so on. Also share some of your own favorites, to establish your own relatability to them. You can also inquire about the extracurriculars they are involved in, since that can offer another opportunity to build rapport. You could then attend the related club or sports events in the future. As you become more familiar with your students throughout the school year, you can then ease into more personal topics, such as their future aspirations, family traditions, and favorite memories.

As you complete all of your "dates" for a class period, write down quick highlights from each conversation. (See the downloadable resource.) These details not only serve as a future reference but also as materials you can reflect on. This information also functions as an instructional resource since it offers a compilation of student interests you can organize into categories (e.g., music, culture, and learning styles) to build future lessons around. The only thing left to do now is try it out!

The Power of Professional Educators Connecting with Their Communities

Mallika Raman
Fourth–Sixth Grade Science Teacher
Chesterfield Day School, Chesterfield, MO

As a first-year professional educator moving on to year 2, I am going into the new school year confident that I am moving in the right direction with a goal in mind. I teach fourth through sixth grade science at a Montessori school in St. Louis, Missouri. I started with no curriculum from the previous teacher. I didn't know where to start. However, within a short timeframe I not only created my own curriculum but also learned to wear many hats, including the importance of thinking like an entrepreneur. Within my first year, I had the opportunity to connect with a local start-up company that allows me to use their software in my classroom with my students. Within my community, I have also been able to write curriculum for the education council of the St. Louis Aquarium. It is possible to broaden your horizons even within one school year.

Hello, Are You There? Strategies for Communicating with Families

Karen L. Kohler, EdD, Lecturer
Texas A&M University-San Antonio, San Antonio, TX

Lydia Gerzel-Short, EdD, Assistant Professor
Northern Illinois University, DeKalb, IL

Family engagement in schools can be challenging because teachers find it difficult to communicate with families. However, communicating with families is vital because when families are engaged, student achievement improves (Shumow & Schmidt, 2014). Consider enhancing family–teacher communication with the following five strategies.

1. **Change perspectives**
   Leave your assumptions at the door. If family members do not return a phone call or fail to show up for a conference, it is most likely they do not understand

the vital role they play in their child's education (Goodwin & King, 2002). Alter perspectives by:

- Getting to know your students and their backgrounds
- Valuing the differences in cultures (e.g., learn how to pronounce students' names, identify key celebrations and holidays that represent the school community [see Henderson, Mapp, Johnson, & Davies, 2007])
- Walking the school community

2. **Introduce yourself**

   By introducing yourself, you are sharing a bit of you, establishing open lines of communication with families, and creating a safe learning environment (Henderson et al., 2007). Introduce yourself by:

   - Creating an introductory postcard, like the downloadable template provided
     - Include your name, how best to connect with you, a favorite book, one other piece of semi-personal information, and a concluding thought about the upcoming school year, *before* the first day of attendance.
   - Sending a short newsletter about classroom procedures, expectations, class schedule, and/or classroom theme for the year
   - Posting your picture and a short biography on the school or class website
   - Sending a personal invitation to visit the classroom

3. **Call home**

   Make a positive call home and see what happens! Initial contact establishes rapport with families (Henderson et al., 2007). Most of the time, parents only get calls from the school when their child is sick or in trouble. Be the change. Consider these ideas for positive calls home:

   - Making improvements on a struggling subject
   - Displaying leadership in the classroom or school
   - Sharing a classroom "a-ha" moment about their child's learning (e.g., "Yulia worked well with her peers on a group presentation.")
   - Celebrating significant happenings that are culturally respectful (e.g., birthdays, holidays)

4. **Inquire first**

   We often assume that families want to be contacted by phone. However, some families may not have a working phone number or prefer other modes of communication (Goodwin & King, 2002). Something as simple as asking families about their preferred contact mode can encourage family–teacher communication. Inquiring minds consider:

   - Finding alternative times to meet or call parents (e.g., student pick-up or drop-off)
   - Creating a variety of phone-calling opportunities (e.g., calling before or after school, during teacher preparation time)
   - Using technology apps like Remind (https://www.remind.com), Google Voice (https://voice.google.com), and Seesaw (https://web.seesaw.me) that allow you to text with a different number than your own
   - Sending a family interest inventory home

5. **Keep it student centered**

   One of the best ways to engage families in open communication is by having the students reach out to their family members. Encourage students to create and send personalized invitations to attract families (Barrera & Warner, 2006). Student-centered teachers support their students by:

- Encouraging students to write a personal invitation to school events
- Having students create an email inviting families to review academic work (e.g., portfolios, presentations)
- Inviting families to a "sharing my work fair" (https://blog.ed.gov/2016/01/engaging-families-via-student-led-conferences-perspective-from-one-of-our-teaching-ambassador-fellows)
- Motivating students to post "shout-outs" to their family members in the student corner section of the class website or blog

Intentional and focused family–teacher communication promotes family engagement. Consider changing perspectives, introducing yourself, calling home, inquiring first, and focusing on student-centered communication as ways to collaborate and connect with families to provide high-quality, family–teacher relationships.

References

Barrera, J. M., & Warner, L. (2006). Involving families in school events. *Kappa Delta Pi Record*, 42(2), 72–75.

Goodwin, A. L., & King, S. H. (2002). *Culturally responsive parental involvement: Concrete understandings and basic strategies*. Washington, DC: AACTE Publications.

Henderson, A. T., Mapp, K. L., Johnson, V. R., & Davies, D. (2007). *Beyond the bake sale: The essential guide to family-school partnerships*. New York, NY: The New Press.

Shumow, L., & Schmidt, J. A. (2014). Parent engagement in science with ninth-graders and with students in higher grades. *School Community Journal*, 24(1), 17–36.

Teaming with the School Social Worker

Nancy H. Betker, LCSW
School Social Worker
Hinsdale South High School, Darien, IL

As a new teacher, you will be surrounded by teaching colleagues who can support, encourage, and challenge the growth of your skills in the classroom. Additionally, you will have access to several professionals who are considered related services. Depending on the grade levels included in your building, you may work with counselors, social workers, deans, psychologists, special education teachers, speech therapists, occupational therapists, physical therapists, nurses, and other itinerant support (e.g., vision/hearing). It is important for you to know the roles and collaboration opportunities for each of these specialists.

School social workers, depending on the state, will have a Master's in Social Work with a concentration in schools. This specialty focuses on the unique opportunities of providing social work services within the structure of a school setting. A school social worker addresses the social–emotional needs of a student, the behavioral concerns regarding the student, and any special education needs of a student who requires social work involvement.

Teachers are the window to the needs of students. You will see the student on a daily basis, resulting in a quicker and deeper understanding of their baseline personalities and any changes that you observe over time. Knowing your students and understanding the role of the school social worker will help you as you navigate support in your classroom.

A school social worker must balance the legal and moral requirements of confidentiality within the unique setting of a school that affords a team approach to supporting the student. When you meet your teammate, ask about their policy on privacy and confidentiality. Once established, you will understand what can and cannot be shared and why. Developing a trusting relationship over time will help you understand the boundaries of shared information. As a social worker in a high school for more than 30 years, I have worked hard to earn the trust of my students and the teaching staff. I am clear with the students regarding what I will and will not share, and the teachers respect that. I am at the point that I can ask a teacher to accommodate a student (more time on homework, a little TLC, increased breaks) with minimal details and the staff will follow through. I have also set up a clear boundary of not talking about students in the halls, washrooms, or lunchroom. Your students are our clients, and we need to respect them as such.

The primary role of a school social worker is to advocate for the student. Knowing information about their educational needs, social needs, behavioral challenges, and even home life are details that help us provide services to support their learning opportunities in your classroom. Precipitating factors (homelessness, hunger, family dysfunction) will impact a student. There is always a reason for behavior. If you can rationally detach from personalizing behaviors, a school social worker can help address and reshape issues that are getting in the way of student learning. This is accomplished through working with students individually, in small groups, and by providing services in your classroom. Do not hesitate to ask about our goals with a particular student and how that is related to your class material and goals. Consultation is a service that school social workers appreciate. We are a team for this student.

Not all students with a special education Individualized Education Plan (IEP) have social work services. It all depends on their eligibility and the services required to support that plan. If you have a student with an IEP, it is imperative that you understand what it says about the student, the goals they are working on, and the accommodations you may be required to incorporate in your class. Again, do not hesitate to seek out the person who understands the IEP best (special education teacher, case manager, related service provider) in order to ask any questions about your role in providing services that are legally outlined in the IEP.

School social workers are on the front lines when identifying global topics for prevention programming. Anti-bullying campaigns, disability awareness, inclusion, mindfulness, and drug prevention can all be building-wide or grade-level topics and discussions.

Crises are another frontline opportunity to work with your school social worker. The death of a student or parent, a family crisis, or a major community event are times to pull a team together to identify the best approach for support. As a teacher and mandated reporter, there will be times when you need to reach out to a child–family welfare agency regarding neglect or abuse of a student. Although you, as the teacher, need to make the call, working with the social worker will support you through the process. If the social worker is the liaison to the state or local agency, they can provide you with appropriate information in order to continue to help the student learn in your class.

Knowing community referrals and partnerships are a strength of school social workers. They can help families navigate support in the community. They can collaborate with resources that may come into the school. With signed parent permission, the social worker can gain information from other sources in order to better provide services in the school.

Understanding the role and opportunities to work with a school social worker should aid you in being a better teacher. Taking the time to develop a clear and trusting collaboration will help you, the school social worker, and ultimately the student.

I'll Be There for You

Heather Lyon, PhD, Assistant Superintendent for Curriculum, Instruction and Technology
Lewiston-Porter Central School District, Youngstown, NY

In my first year as a teacher, I cried. A lot. I was a long-term sub for half the year, teaching seventh grade. Then for the other half of the year I was a long-term sub teaching high school English. For the high school position, I worked in two different buildings and would cry in the car as I drove from one location to the other. I remember calling my parents and saying, "I don't know why I became a teacher in the first place."

In my second year, however, things changed. I was hired in a tenure-track position and had a sense of belonging that I didn't have my first year. This feeling was not because of what I was doing or where I was working, but because of who I was working with. For the first time as a teacher, I found some friends at work. Though the idea of having friends at work may sound silly, it's not.

The truth is that having someone at work you can turn to both personally and professionally can make all the difference—especially in the early years on the job. Why do the early years matter so much? There is much written about the attrition rates of teachers within the first five years. Ingersoll, Merrill, Stuckey, and Collins (2018) state that "more than 44 percent of new teachers in public and private schools leave teaching within 5 years of entry." The reasons for leaving teaching vary, of course, but going to work with someone you enjoy spending time with can be the difference between *having* to go to work and *getting* to go to work.

Interestingly, women, who have outnumbered men in the teaching profession historically, are actually entering the teaching profession at double the rate of men (Ingersoll et al., 2018). In a 2018 Gallup article, Annemarie Mann (2018) explains the importance of a workplace best friend, particularly for women. In comparison to women who strongly disagree that they have a best friend at work, women who strongly agree are:

- less likely to be actively looking or watching for job opportunities;
- more connected with their coworkers, knowing what is expected of them and trusting their integrity and ethics;

♦ more likely to rate their own, their team's, and their organization's performance more excellently;

♦ more likely to take risks that could lead to innovation;

♦ more likely to have a positive experience during the day, such as enjoying what they do, making more progress, and getting recognized for successes, and

♦ less likely to report having a negative experience during the day such as worry, stress, and feeling tired.

Though these outcomes are linked to answers from women, Gallop's research found that both men and women who have a best friend at work perform better and are more engaged.

No one told me this in my preservice education. When I sat at the lunch table in my high school long-term sub position and no one spoke to me, I felt so lonely. The belonging that I felt when I had friends gave me professional and personal joy that encouraged me to remain an educator, and now, almost 20 years later, I can't imagine doing anything else. This is my wish for you.

References

Ingersoll, R., Merrill, L., Stuckey, D., & Collins, G. (2018). Seven trends: The transformation of the teaching force – Updated October 2018. *CPRE Research Reports*.

Mann, A. (2018, January 15). *Why we need best friends at work*. Retrieved from https://www.gallup.com/workplace/236213/why-need-best-friends-work.aspx

Five Key Strategies for Conducting Effective Parent–Teacher Conferences

Pamela Kramer Ertel, EdD, Associate Professor
Middle Tennessee State University, Murfreesboro, TN

The parent–teacher conference is one of the best opportunities for teachers to develop a relationship with the parents or guardians of their students. It provides a chance for you to get to know and understand one another. These five strategies will help you make the most of the limited time you will have together. You can also use the downloadable *Parent–Teacher Conference Organizer Form* to plan your Pre-Meeting thoughts and record your Post-Meeting notes and actions.

1. **Plan ahead.**
   a. Put in writing the key points of information you want to share with the parents/guardians (McAfee, Leong, & Bodrova, 2016). Do NOT rely on your memory!
   b. Make sure you have artifacts (work samples and other evidence) to support your comments and concerns (McAfee et al., 2016). Prepare a folder for each student with your notes and work samples in an organized format.

c. Plan a tentative action plan to share with parents/guardians regarding any problems you are facing with the student (see the Parent–Teacher Conference Organization Form). Seek input from the family. Prepare possible solutions that you can discuss with them about any significant concerns or problems. You must be honest and caring to show the family how much you value their student. This is essential for establishing a positive partnership with families. Once you determine some solutions with the parents/guardians, develop a timeline for next steps along with designating responsibilities for actions.

d. Use the "Oreo Cookie Approach." Start with some good news/positive comments (the top chocolate, outside wafer). Next, share any concerns/issues (the cream filling). End on an upbeat note providing hope and encouragement to the parent/guardian (the bottom chocolate, outside wafer).

2. **Be sensitive to community and cultural diversity, as well as different family structures** (McAfee et al., 2016).

a. Do your homework and learn as much as you can about the family's background, structure, and culture.

b. Plan ideas/strategies to best support the student and family as appropriate according to their culture and needs.

c. Make sure you know and use correct names for the family members. This will be especially important for blended families in which names may be different.

3. **Communicate well** (McAfee et al., 2016).

a. You might consider sending home a questionnaire prior to the conference. You can find out what questions and concerns the parents/guardians would like you to address during the conference.

b. Avoid educational jargon and acronyms.

c. Keep your language clear and simple. You are not there to impress them with your teacher talk.

d. Be specific about the ideas you are sharing. Give examples whenever possible.

e. Use an interpreter, if necessary, to communicate with non-English-speaking families.

f. Listen well. Make sure you give the family time to share any concerns or questions (Freeman, Decker, & Decker, 2017). Seek information from them to help you get to know the student better. They know the student best and have valuable information to share.

4. **Be professional and respectful.**

a. Dress professionally.

b. Make families feel welcome. Greet them warmly.

c. Stick to your schedule. If you run out of time and have another appointment, set a time to continue your conversation with parents. By disrupting the schedule, you may be upsetting the schedule of many others simultaneously, especially those parents waiting for you. Families may have conferences scheduled with multiple teachers on the same day, especially if they have more than one student in the building.

d. Don't be rude or sarcastic.

e. Don't raise your voice (Guillaume, 2016).

f. Don't use foul language.

g. Don't speak critically about other teachers or the administration.

    h. Don't have parents sit in child-sized chairs if you are in an adult-sized chair. Keep everything on an equal level. Try to create the most comfortable, welcoming environment possible (Freeman et al., 2017).

    i. Don't sit behind your desk! That can be intimidating.

    j. Don't be critical of the parents or their parenting style (Guillaume, 2016).

    k. Don't chew gum during the conference.

    l. Be sure you don't smoke or drink alcohol prior to the meeting (it happens!).

5. **Respect confidentiality.**

    a. Don't speak about other students' behavior or academic records.

    b. If a parent shares confidential information with you, be sure to keep it confidential and don't share it with colleagues, family, or friends.

Parents/guardians can be a tremendous resource for enhancing a student's school success. The more effectively you work together as partners to do what is best for the student, the more success that student will have.

References

Freeman, N. K., Decker, C. A., & Decker, J. R. (2017). *Planning and administering early childhood programs* (11th ed.). Boston, MA: Pearson.

Guillaume, A. M. (2016). *K-12 classroom teaching: A primer for new professionals* (5th ed.). Boston, MA: Pearson.

McAfee, O., Leong, D. J., & Bodrova, E. (2016). *Assessing and guiding young children's development and learning* (6th ed.). Boston, MA: Pearson.

Planning for Successful Parent–Teacher Conferences: A Navigation Guide

Leana R. Malinowsky
Elementary Educator/Reading Specialist
Pvt. Nicholas Minue School, Carteret Public Schools, Carteret NJ

As a new teacher, hosting parent–teacher conferences will come with an array of emotions. Feeling anxious and nervous are not only acceptable but also normal. Veteran teachers often experience those emotions as well. There is also a sense of satisfaction and professionalism that educators at all levels of practice feel.

Here are some suggestions that you should consider as you begin to plan for parent–teacher conferences:

♦ **Communicate:** Conference time should *not* be your first contact with students' families. Take time to get to know families before conference time, including positive notes home, phone calls, email, and/or communication apps such as Class Dojo or Remind.

♦ **Document:** Have parents use a sign-in sheet to keep in your binder so you have a record of communication. Prepare folders with student work samples for families to see. Share celebrations, progress, and concerns. Provide access to report cards, progress reports, and other grades to aid with any questions. Have those ready to share.

♦ **Use a preplanned conference form** (see download): Include updated student data such as test scores, reading levels, and social and emotional growth. It is helpful to have two copies (one for you and one for families) to take notes on, especially if there are topics you have to address after the conference.

♦ **Plan for student attendance:** Do not forget the students! Very often students will attend conferences with families. For families with younger children who will not be participating, set up a space in your room where they can read or draw, or show a short educational film (if technology allows).

♦ **Plan for the "not-planned" parts:** Often in conversations, questions or topics will come up that take you by surprise. Speak with a veteran teacher about their experiences and consider those types of questions before conference day.

♦ **Co-teaching:** If you are in a co-teaching situation, or serve as a special education teacher, meet with your colleagues beforehand to discuss accomplishments, student concerns, and topics to discuss. Each of you should predetermine what you will discuss with the family. This avoids repetition, while highlighting necessary points.

♦ **Begin at the end:** While you have a lot of information to share with families, many will come with questions and concerns of their own. Allow families to start conferences with topics they wish to discuss. Many of the answers might already be on your premade guide sheet. Try to integrate family questions with topics you wish to discuss as often as possible, saving time in the process.

♦ **Timekeeper:** Depending on the structure of your conferences, time may be limited for each family you see. Do not feel guilty for setting a timer. Being cognizant of time helps you to effectively wrap up any needed information and last-minute questions or concerns, and end your conference without feeling you missed any information. Be willing to set an additional appointment if the family needs more time.

♦ **Ending conferences:** At the end of your conference, be sure to thank the student's family for attending. Emphasize that they are a valuable part of their child's success in school. Also reassure families that your communication will remain open and consistent. They are welcome to schedule a follow-up, if needed.

Parent–teacher conferences are an essential form of communication that both educators and families rely on to monitor student progress. For you as a new teacher, the experience might come with an array of emotions. The key is to be prepared and know that, over time, conferences will become easier. They also provide you with an opportunity to work with families to highlight student achievements and discuss ways to work collaboratively on needed skills.

Download: You can edit the sample conference form to meet the needs of your class(es) and individual students. Use the form to plan your talking points with students' families, and share with any co-teachers who might have information to add. Conference forms can also be shared electronically beforehand with parents, edited during conferences, saved for documentation, and reviewed later in the year. Parents and students are typically familiar with technology, and this advantage allows you to work on a form in real time! Keep in mind that not all families have technology at home, so be sure to offer hard copies, too.

Conferencing with Parents: What Can We Do to Help Your Child Be Successful

Nedra L. Cossa, PhD, Assistant Professor
Georgia Southern University, Savannah, GA

As a first-year teacher, one of my biggest fears was meeting and conferencing with parents. I was concerned they would blame me for their child struggling either academically or socially. As it turned out, this was not an unfounded fear. Unfortunately, I dealt with several situations like this, which only increased my anxiety about communicating and conferencing with parents. It took several years and many conferences for me to feel confident meeting with parents. With that experience in mind, I seek to share some tips to help minimize these negative experiences for you.

Parents or primary caregivers may understandably feel frustrated when their child is not succeeding. Sometimes this frustration can manifest into negative or sometimes combative behavior toward teachers. Situations such as this unfortunately put one on the defensive, having to justify yourself when a student is struggling.

With that knowledge, there are ways you can proactively prepare for conferences so that all parties are blameless. You want to build bridges, not erect walls. Because, ultimately, parents and teachers want to help their children be successful. If you can keep that in mind with even the most difficult parents, communication becomes much easier. Although not always avoidable, below are some tips to help minimize the occurrence of these situations.

Before the Conference

♦ **Be proactive.** When a parent requests a conference, give them some available times and ask them what the meeting is in reference to. If you know what the conference is about, you can prepare and be ready to discuss those concerns. You do not want to be blindsided when they sit down to meet with you.

♦ **Be transparent.** If you are requesting the conference, make sure to explain specifically why you want to meet with them. Just like you, parents do not want to be blindsided by your reasons for wanting to meet with them.

♦ **Prepare.** Gather important documents available for discussion. This may include student work samples, documentation about student behaviors, and emails you may have sent parents in the past about the topic being discussed.

♦ **Follow up.** Make sure to follow up with an email or note home confirming the day and time you are scheduled to meet.

During the Conference

♦ **Take the lead.** Regardless of who requested the meeting, set the stage. Walk to the door, greet the parents, and welcome them into the classroom. Tell them how much you appreciate them taking the time to meet with you. If you requested the conference, explain why you requested it. If it was parent-initiated, begin by explaining what you understand to be the reason they requested the conference.

♦ **Set the stage.** Explain your purpose for the meeting by providing a brief overview. For example, "I would like to speak with you about James' science paper, and then I would like to have some feedback from you about how WE can move forward to ensure that he succeeds."

♦ **Stick to the script.** Follow the outline you described. If the parent attempts to deviate or interrupt, gently remind them of that purpose you provided.

♦ **Provide documentation.** During the conference, have the documents you prepared prior to the meeting readily available for discussion. First, identify some strengths about the student's work or behavior when possible. For example, if you are discussing a writing assignment, point out how strong his organization is or how well developed her voice is in her writing. Select specific passages to demonstrate this to the parent(s). After identifying the student's strengths, share some examples of the area(s) in which s/he is struggling. Explain the kinds of errors in the work. Point out specific examples to further support your analysis. Then, explain what your expectations were for that task and why this skill/strategy is meaningful to the student's learning.

♦ **Identify supports.** Explain strategies you have used to help support the student. Provide evidence of the effectiveness of those strategies.

♦ **Seek input.** Ask for suggestions from the parent(s): "How can WE help this student be successful?" Give the parents credit. Tell them that they are the experts on their child. Share that by working together, we will identify ways to support him/her. Brainstorm other possible strategies to support cognitive or behavioral growth.

After the Conference

♦ **Thank them.** After the conference, send an email thanking them for meeting with you. Summarize the meeting's major points and plans to support the student moving forward. Create a folder to keep copies of email threads sent to parents.

♦ **Provide updates.** Continue to give regular updates on their child's progress. Parents appreciate hearing from teachers.

In summary, I hope these tips and suggestions (in the download) may help you avoid some of the negative experiences I had during my first year. Always keep in mind that parents want their child to be successful. You want your student to be successful. A proactive, positive, and collaborative approach can help reduce the likelihood of negative experiences and maximize the chances of establishing and maintaining productive and constructive relationships with parents.

The Impact of a Phone Call

Alisa M. Ross, EdD, Assistant Professor
Southern University and A & M College, Baton Rouge, LA

During my first year of teaching, I was terrified and nervous during parent–teacher conferences! I didn't know exactly what my students shared with their parents. Therefore, I was on the defensive throughout the conference. That was a HUGE mistake! My body language, tone of voice, and vocabulary reiterated my stance throughout the conference. One of the many lessons I have learned in the profession is that parents and teachers want the same thing: For their child/student to be successful!

Since "first impressions are lasting impressions," I applied this to the way I interacted with parents moving forward. The initial calls I made at the beginning of the school year were to introduce myself to the parents and to express how excited I was about the opportunity to serve as their child's teacher! In my opinion, this was the start of a positive home–school relationship.

Also, as a secondary level teacher, many of my students' parents only received a phone call if the child displayed inappropriate behavior. I decided to be an agent of change at my school. I called parents and informed them of some of the wonderful things their child was doing in my classroom. For example, if they earned an A on an assessment, I called and shared the news. This less-than-5-minute conversation was PRICELESS! Not only did the parents have something to smile about but it also helped strengthen my relationship with my students and their parents!

Chapter 10

Student Assessment and Data Literacy

Making Sense of Standardized Benchmark Assessments

Daniel M. Frederking, EdD, Technical Assistance Consultant
American Institutes for Research
Twitter: @dfrederking
LinkedIn: www.linkedin.com/in/dfrederking

Many schools today have made standardized benchmark assessments a focal point for student learning. Tests like NWEA MAP, STAR360, or i-Ready are purchased locally to monitor student progress and provide data that can be used to impact instruction. Frequently, however, new teachers come into these already-established data cultures and do not get the support they need to understand and use these assessments in their classrooms. If you feel uncomfortable digging into your students' data, you are not alone.

Schools use standardized benchmark assessments to measure student learning on a common scale. The tests are given usually three or four times during the school year and allow teachers and students to track academic growth, often through the use of tables and graphs. Most assessments will break student progress down into individual skills, providing useful information on the specific areas of need in which the teacher should address.

These benchmarks resemble a student's medical checkup, where the doctor gathers information on height, weight, blood pressure, and so on. Because this is such a common practice, doctors know what is considered normal. Medical records from around the world provide average numbers that the child can be compared to, which then provides parents with a better idea of how their child is progressing and if that is normal compared to their peers. You can use benchmark assessment results in the same way.

Standardized tests do not calculate students' scores in the same way that you might grade a classroom test. On a classroom test, for example, a student may receive a 7 out of

10 or 70%. This is called a raw score. Standardized tests, however, cannot use a simple raw score, for two reasons:

1. Students take different forms of the test, which means they see different questions and, for a standardized test, the scores need to be comparable. It would not be fair to say a student on one form who got 27 questions correct is exactly the same as a student who took a different form and got 27 questions correct. They each saw different questions, so it is not like comparing apples to apples.
2. A raw score assumes that all questions are of equal difficulty. In other words, if a student were to get an easy question correct and then a difficult question incorrect, they would be working at a 50% rate (1 out of 2). If these questions are not of equal difficulty, they should not be weighted the same.

To address these issues and provide a consistent way to report student performance, most standardized tests place their results on some sort of scale. These scaled scores provide a consistent way of reporting student performance. Each test uses their own scale so, typically, these are not comparable across tests.

Without context, these numbers will not mean anything to you or your students, which is why many tests create performance levels or utilize percentiles to explain the relevance of the number. Returning to the medical checkup metaphor, a parent might be familiar with the doctor saying things like, "Your child is in the 80th percentile for height." In simple language, this means that the specific child is as tall or taller than 80% of their peers (other children of the same age). Often, this same language is used in the standardized assessment world. Because many of these tests are administered to a large number of students all over the country, the system is able to provide comparisons that can be helpful in providing context for how the student compares to their peers. If the test says a student is performing at the 45th percentile in math, the teacher knows that 55% of the student's peers who took the test are performing at a higher level.

Tests that are able to make these comparisons are known as norm-referenced assessments, which simply means that a student's performance is compared to the performance of their peers. This is opposed to criterion-referenced tests, in which student performance is compared to a set of standards. So, for example, a criterion-referenced test might be aligned to the state standards, which state that by fourth grade, a student should have mastered skill "X." The test will assess students and then report where they are in relation to where the standards say they should be.

You can use benchmark assessment data formatively to directly impact student learning. The tests provide valuable checkpoints that you can use for goal setting. By tracking student achievement throughout the learning process, the teacher and student together can develop goals that are individualized, attainable, and directly related to the student's specific needs. You can use the Benchmark Assessment Goalsetting Worksheet as a resource for you and your students to complete collaboratively (see download).

Becoming literate in assessment data can take some time, but it is a crucial skill for raising student achievement. Understanding and utilizing benchmark assessment results can have a major impact on your students' success.

Assessment and Data Literacy

Amy Howerton, EdD, NBCT
English Division Chair and Secondary English Teacher
Oswego School District #308, Oswego, IL
Twitter: @amy_marie1201
LinkedIn: www.linkedin.com/in/amy-howerton-edd-8b497810

As you enter your first years as an educator, assessing students will be a key aspect of your role (Howerton, 2016). Understanding the expectations of assessment and its use can help make evaluative tasks less daunting as you build your assessment literacy. As defined by W. James Popham (2011), assessment literacy is "an individual's understanding of the fundamental assessment concepts and procedures deemed likely to influence educational decisions" (p. 267). Using Table 10.1, start building your own assessment literacy with the key skills needed for today's educators.

Assessment literacy standards are generally informed by the Standards for Teacher Competence in the Educational Assessment of Students (American Federation of Teachers, National Council on Measurement in Education, & National Education Association, 1990) but are better understood with two additional guidelines: The Classroom Assessment Standards (Klinger et al., 2015) and the Content Literacy Target Skills and Knowledge (Popham, 2009). Informed by these standards and guidelines, Table 10.1 also includes tips in *developing* assessments, *grading* assessments, and *using* assessments to inform instruction. A download with questions is available to guide you through developing these assessment skills.

References

American Federation of Teachers, National Council on Measurement in Education, & National Education Association. (1990). *Standards for competence in the educational assessment of students.* Retrieved from www.buros.org/standards-teacher-competence-educational-assessment-students

Howerton, A. M. (2016). *Elephant on a stepladder: An exploration of pre-service English teacher assessment literacy* (Doctoral dissertation). Retrieved from ProQuest Dissertations and Theses database (UMI No. 10240273).

Klinger, D. A., McDivitt, P. J., Howard, B. B., Rogers, W. T., Munoz, M. A., & Wylie, E. C. (2015). *Classroom assessment standards for preK-12 teachers* [Kindle edition]. Retrieved from https://www.amazon.com/Kindle-eBooks/

Popham, W. J. (2009). Assessment literacy for teachers: Faddish or fundamental? *Theory into Practice, 48*(1), 4–11. doi:10.1080/00405840802577536.

Popham, W. J. (2011). Assessment literacy overlooked: A teacher educator's confession. *The Teacher Educator, 46*(4), 265–273. doi:10.1080/08878730.2011.605048.

Table 10.1 Key Assessment and Data Literacy Skills

Assessment Skill Needed	Key Ideas from the Standards and Guidelines	What Does That Mean for Me?
Skill of **DEVELOPING** assessments	* Be respectful of diversity (English learners, students with disabilities, etc.). * Check for reliability and validity. * Choose appropriate assessment method.	Start with clarity in WHAT skill or knowledge you want to assess. It will help ground the assessment to learning standards and consider what format your assessment would best take (multiple choice, written, fill-in-the-blank, performance). Think about how you might modify or adapt the assessment for student needs. Take the assessment yourself before you offer it to students. Not only will this provide you an opportunity to create a key or use a rubric, but also it may illuminate areas of the assessment that need to be revised.
Skill of **GRADING** assessments	* Analyze assessment item(s) using a key or rubric. * Provide comments or responses. * Interpret evidence within the assessment. * Provide timely and useful feedback to students.	With clarity on WHAT you wanted to assess, grading becomes easier. Using an answer key or rubric, read and assess student responses to consider how close to the target students came. In providing comments or responses to students, be honest and encouraging. Consider what a student might need to do differently next time. When you provide feedback, students are more likely to grow in the assessed knowledge or skill. Although grading takes time, providing timely feedback is helpful before students are assessed again on the same skill.
Skill of **USING** assessments	* Collect evidence. * Use results to inform instructional planning. * Use results to share instructional outcomes.	Once you collect assessment evidence, consider how you will use it to help each student individually learn. You can also use results for your professional reflection. If most students did poorly, what was missing in their learning or your instruction? How will you reteach what was not learned? By using the assessment results and sharing data with colleagues, you can make informed decisions for shared assessments and future instruction.

Data Literacy for Teacher Teams

Adam Larsen
Assistant Superintendent
Oregon Community Unit School District 220, Oregon, IL
Twitter: @aplarsen

Teaming is an important component of the interactions that take place in the school setting. These teams take many forms: Grade levels, departments, school and building leadership teams, Response to Intervention, Multi-Tier System of Supports, Professional Learning Communities, task forces, special education teams, and many others. Each team has a specific purpose and meets according to its own rhythm and cycle, but a common thread woven through all such teams is a need for data to support the discussion. In general, the purpose of gathering people for this type of meeting is to turn data into insights and insights into actions. These actions might include moving students into or out of interventions, making adjustments to the types of services that are available, or deciding whether to reteach an entire lesson because of poor outcomes.

The pipeline by which information is delivered to the team will vary greatly, depending on the software tools in use, the skills of the administrators and assistants, the type of data being used in the meeting, and the purpose of the team. In the best of scenarios, the data are gathered, analyzed, organized, and shared well before the meeting takes place. In others, you may need to do some or all of this yourself. The key is to be as *prepared* as possible to make the discussion as *efficient* as possible. Time together is limited, and the more quickly you can make the necessary decisions, the better.

The following are a few tips for making your team meetings more efficient. These tips help you focus on the most important issues, make better use of time, and avoid confusion about what to do next.

Understand the Source

Be aware of how the datapoints were collected, including the standards assessed, the questions asked, and the methods used to score and summarize the data. If there are technical manuals or websites about the tests, rating scales, or other measures used, read and become familiar with them.

Know the Data

Scores are reported on different types of scales. Understand the differences among raw scores (simple totals), scaled scores (raw scores that have been transformed by comparing them to normative data), percentiles (the percentage of scores that fall at or below a particular score), and proprietary scales (definitions vary). It will be embarrassing (and unproductive) if a peer has to remind you that the *percent correct* and *percentile* are two different concepts. If possible, bring the test's norms tables with you to a meeting. This will help you know where a student's performance falls compared to peers. Percentiles can also be quite helpful if they are available, since it is easy to classify student performance using a heuristic such as *high* for 90 and above, *high average* for 75–89, *average* for 25–74, *low average* for 10–25, and *low* for scores below 10. You can use these even if you do not know much about the assessment itself.

Organize the Data

If the administrator or team leader can't provide well-organized data because of a lack of tools, technique, or time, do it yourself ahead of the meeting. Your goal is to remove any barriers between the data and its interpretation. Ask for raw data if you can obtain it. Use tools such as Excel or Google Sheets to bring the data together into a single place for review. The VLOOKUP() spreadsheet formula is extremely powerful for performing this task. Use color to draw attention to the highs and lows. To save time, conditional formatting spreadsheet functions can apply cell shading automatically according to specified cut scores. Use mathematical formulas such as COUNTIF() and AVERAGE() to summarize the data ahead of time so you can immediately answer questions that start with, "How many students… ." Search on YouTube for spreadsheet tutorials on topics such as data blending, heatmapping, data summarizing, and pivot charts.

Be Prepared to Take Action

Remember that the goal of the meeting is to use the data to make some kind of decision. Students will be slotted into interventions, adjustments will be made to schedules, and resources will be deployed. It helps to have your own schedule with you as well as the schedules of supporting teachers and paraprofessionals. Have a student roster for your class or grade level on hand. Be aware of all of the interventions and enrichment resources that are available for use with students who are struggling or excelling. If previous documentation exists about the services that students have been receiving, make sure it is available during the meeting. If such logs do not exist, create them before the in-person gathering. Spending minutes to document something that could have been done beforehand is a big waste of precious collaborative time.

Clarify the Purpose

This should be addressed by an administrator or team leader, but do not be afraid to ask what the purpose of a meeting is. Help establish norms such as sticking to timetables, remaining on topic, letting data inform decisions, and setting clear outcomes for the meeting. Without clear purpose, a data meeting can quickly descend into problem admiration, discussion of mere housekeeping issues, or worse.

Don't Let Data Scare You Away!

Harlee Morphis
Science Teacher
Blackman Middle School, Murfreesboro, TN

Being a new teacher is difficult, especially when coming in midyear. As I walked into my PLC group, they started talking about CFAs, data from last year, what growth they were expecting, and how they were going to select students for enrichment or remediation based on an Excel document. It was overwhelming, but I knew it would be extremely useful. I didn't know my students by name, but based on student assessment data, I was able to pinpoint students who needed enhancement and students who needed remediation.

As a biology teacher, I am used to reading data in different formats, but applying it to teaching was challenging and stressful at first. At my school we use an online testing service that supplies us with student assessment data. During my PLC time, my teammates taught me how to understand the different levels of mastery and how I could meet the needs of students who were struggling. Using data to adjust my teaching practices for groups of students has increased student success rates in my class.

Now that I have become used to reading data and applying it to my instruction, I am ahead of the game. I can identify patterns in student performance and work with the students who commonly score low ahead of time. By incorporating this into my instruction, I've already seen student improvement. This has helped my students trust me a bit more, which has been a battle since I became their teacher in January.

I've learned that data doesn't make students "just a number." Instead, it helps build a strong foundation for their future. I'm glad I had help from my team so I could realize how important this skill is to being a great teacher.

Lower Your Stress: Planning for Efficient and Effective Feedback to Students

Monica Boehle, NBCT
Social Studies Teacher, Instructional Support Coach
Community Unit School District #303, St. Charles, IL
Twitter: @mboehle1

In your first years of teaching, the summative performance assessment feels BIG. And tiring. Your students have been working on a project or other learning task. You have guided, motivated, and conferred. When the due date arrives, you cross your fingers and collect the results.

Then … the "stack" of papers or projects, whether electronic or not, becomes low on the to-do list because you need to devote energy to other tasks, even if you are excited to see the students' work. We call this the "guilt bag" that we take home every night but don't touch. You plan marathon grading sessions. Emotions start to swirl: Doubt, guilt, frustration, overwhelming paralysis. You may worry about the phrasing of your feedback because it might hurt a student's feelings. It might bother you when a student receives their paper back (that you have spent a lot of time commenting on) and throws it in the trash can.

Grading and providing feedback on the projects is an enormous cognitive load for the teacher. It requires a feedback plan that sets up the teacher's work to be growth-oriented, realistic, and targeted. The feedback plan, outlined below and on the supplemental download, works to make your feedback both efficient and effective.

Step 1: Student Reflection, Part 1

In this step, students reflect on their own completed work. This reflection includes two key components: 1) Students think about their learning and process of learning, and 2) Students highlight aspects of their work that demonstrate key skills. These will make your work more effective and efficient.

When asking students to reflect on their learning and process of learning, consider what you want to know. I often ask students what they are most proud of in the product or in the process. I also ask them where they struggled the most and how they worked to persevere. When I read the answers to these questions, I gain insight into aspects of their work that I may not have witnessed and can consider how to affirm and encourage.

Highlighting aspects of their work and self-assessing on the provided rubric is another part of the student reflection. For example, one of my learning tasks asked students to explain the evidence that they used in the essay, which they then highlight. When my students submit a video or audio project, they timestamp the rubric to indicate where those descriptors were demonstrated. These actions shift some of the cognitive load from teacher to student, the person who should be participating in this deep learning and thinking.

Step 2: Teacher-Provided Feedback

✓ Decide in advance the high-leverage skill in the product on which you will provide the most feedback as you prepare to assess the student work. We know that students struggle to prioritize feedback and cannot always distinguish between more or less significant comments. This is the important part. Don't write feedback on the other skills or parts of the product. This is not cheating. That is why you have a rubric that provides the feedback to the student on other skills.

Once you narrow down to the one or two skills that you will comment on, write evidence-based, affirmative, and constructive comments related to that one skill, rather than many short, vague comments like "good." Affirmative comments work to reinforce what the students did well, so they know what to replicate. Constructive comments draw attention to places to improve and can even be formed as a question. You can draft a few comments in advance and then fine-tune them during the feedback process. Here are a few examples:

+ Strong explanation connected to the evidence you provided. Continue to find ways to ensure that your reader knows why you included the evidence.

Δ This explanation needs a bit more depth. What could you add that helps your reader understand why that evidence is so important?

The feedback process for the teacher is focused, positive, effective, and efficient.

It becomes part of a conversation of learning between you and the student.

Step 3: Student Reflection, Part 2

After assessing the work and giving feedback, it is crucial to provide class time for
students to read, make meaning, and determine next steps based on your thoughtful
feedback. Student growth relies on using feedback as part of the learning process.

The questions you ask can vary depending upon what is important. For example, if
students will work on the skill again, they should note their next steps. If they
will not, future-oriented questions will help them visualize how they will use this
skill in other settings. You may also ask what feedback was most helpful. Their
response to this question will help you hone the effectiveness of your feedback
to better align your responses to student needs. A feedback plan will help you be
more efficient and effective while focused on student growth.

The Power of Formative Assessments: Using Classroom Assessment Techniques (CATs) to Promote Learning

Altheria Caldera, PhD, Assistant Professor
Texas A&M University at Commerce, Commerce, TX

In this era of high-stakes testing, you may have entered the teaching profession thinking
of assessment as an intimidating task dictated by state and district authorities. High-stakes
standardized assessment, often used for accountability, has major consequences for stakeholders in education, mainly students and teachers.

Think of assessment not as a mandate or unnecessary burden imposed on you, but as an
empowering tool that allows you to improve student learning. Instead of being punitive in
nature, assessment benefits students when it points them to their next steps in learning. The
most powerful assessments are *formative*. Formative assessments are "check-ins" designed
to *inform* you and your students about their learning. You can create them to use with your
own students based on the distinctive context of your classroom. On the other hand, summative assessments are often decontextualized tests created by outside entities like textbook
companies, district assessment staff, or testing services.

Unlike summative assessments that evaluate, compare, and possibly penalize students
and their teachers, formative assessments are designed to diagnose, reveal, and prepare
students for mastery of learning outcomes. A particular kind of formative assessment, used
in postsecondary classrooms but rarely seen in elementary and secondary classrooms, is
Classroom Assessment Techniques, or CATs (Angelo & Cross, 1993).

CATs are assessments that

- ◆ have low stakes (ungraded or constitutes a minor grade);
- ◆ reveal gaps in understanding and misconceptions (diagnose problems);
- ◆ remove assumptions about what students know and are able to do;

♦ can be used one-on-one, in small groups, and with the whole class (student-centered);
♦ are nonthreatening (unlike quizzes);
♦ are frequent;
♦ result in immediate feedback;
♦ make way for two-way communication between students and teachers;
♦ yield data that informs instruction;
♦ prepare students for summative assessments;
♦ are linked to learning objectives;
♦ help teachers improve learning while learning is happening; and
♦ encourage student growth.

Teachers often rely on informal assessment and feedback techniques that yield little information, neglecting the majority of students. For example, asking questions of the whole class is a common informal assessment strategy. When teachers ask questions, one or two students respond, revealing only what those two students know, not every student. Similarly, having students give a thumbs-up/thumbs-down can result in students simply guessing one or the other.

CATs are assessments *for learning* that are easy-to-use, constructive, and informative. CATs can provide detailed and specific information about student learning and can support other tasks that characterize effective teaching. In the associated document (download), I provide seven ways to use CATs in your classroom.

Reference

Angelo, T. A., & Cross, K. P. (1993). *Classroom assessment techniques: A handbook for college teachers* (2nd ed.). San Francisco, CA: Jossey-Bass.

Good Enough?

Julia Cuscaden
Second Grade EL Teacher
Madison Elementary School, Skokie, IL

Everyone's first year of teaching is tough, but mine was beyond my wildest expectations. By November, one of my students had moved to the special education classroom, but only after three months of requiring my other students to evacuate the room multiple times a day. After a total classroom management restructuring, which I felt totally unprepared for and disheartened to have to do, I finally felt as though I was somewhat confident, in control, and enjoying my students as I had hoped. But then, it was time for spring assessments. I did not think it could be possible that my students could reach their targets after all our class had been through and my inexperience in handling everything. When I saw the results, I was shocked. My students had grown. It was so fulfilling to be able to show the results of the hard work that I had seen them doing all year.

For the majority of my first year, I felt as though I was fighting a battle that could never be won. I knew that I loved my students and that I was trying my hardest, but I also felt so overwhelmed, hopeless, and as though I could never give this class what they needed and deserved. The question of being "good enough" haunted me all year. I found that asking for help when I needed it, working hard, and loving my kids even when they made it difficult to do so not only made me "good enough," but also helped me to grow into a confident, loving educator that I would not have become without this experience.

The Sticky Note Formative Assessment: Three Uses

Monica Boehle, NBCT
Social Studies Teacher, Instructional Support Coach
Community Unit School District #303, St. Charles, IL
Twitter: @mboehle1

Formative assessment is an incredibly powerful tool for teachers and students in the learning process. The effective use of formative assessments can be overwhelming for new teachers and even those with experience. It takes time to design, respond, and act upon the information that students provide. Sometimes teachers rely on student self-reports like the thumbs-up/thumbs-down, which does not provide accurate information about student progress toward the goal.

So, here is an easy and adaptable solution: The sticky note formative. Sticky notes, or index cards, are a great formative assessment tool for a few reasons. First, the size makes the information targeted and manageable for the student and the teacher. There is only so much room to write! Students feel like they can fill the note, while you know you're not collecting long responses. Second, you can use the results of the formatives in several different ways: To plan instruction, to provide feedback, and to assist student reflection.

Planning Instruction

Provide a prompt to students that relates to the learning objective, whether it's a skill or content. They write their name and response on the note. After collecting the notes, sort the student responses into three piles based on your criteria for success (see downloadable).

Stack 1: Students who have mastered the objective and are ready for enrichment.
Stack 2: Students who are right on target and are ready for the next step.
Stack 3: Students who missed a critical piece of the learning and need remediation.

The next day in class, move students into the flexible groups based on the three stacks.

Students in Group 1: Provide an enrichment opportunity for students who have already mastered the objective. This enrichment should replace, not be in addition to, the task that they would have completed if they were on the regular progression. It is also not just accelerating to the next task. How can they extend and deepen their learning?

Students in Group 2: Work on the next step of the learning progression. This group is usually the majority of students who are progressing as planned toward the learning goal.

Students in Group 3: Provide either a remediation exercise or time to work with the teacher to address the misconception from the formative. Once a student demonstrates mastery of that step, s/he moves to Group 2.

This is an easy, responsive way to differentiate for students during class time.

Targeted Feedback

A second way to use the note is to provide targeted and timely feedback to your students. After they write their formative assessment note, you then provide one affirmative and one constructive comment on the sticky note. That's it. Since the note is limited in size, the feedback will be short and quick. When you hand the notes back to students, they can immediately review the feedback and put it into practice in their learning progression.

Student Reflection

A final way to use the sticky note strategy is for student reflection. During a learning progression, ask your students to complete a sticky note several times on a skill or idea that becomes more complex, making sure to put the date and name on each note. Read and review these notes to find trends, but do not add comments. Use this information to better target your plans around the needs of the whole class for the following day. For example, find something to celebrate in their learning and a misconception that you might need to address. During this time, pass the notes back to the students, so they can add detail or revise their notes. Then recollect the notes. You can exchange the notes back and forth as many times as needed during the skill progression to aid in student reflection. The focus is on the teacher noting the trends concerning student learning and students seeing their own progress toward mastery.

At the end of the learning progression, give students all of their notes back. Have them arrange the notes in chronological order and complete a self-reflection of their progress toward the overall goal. Depending on your outcomes, you could provide many prompts to help them reflect. Here are a few:

✓ On what day did you see the most growth? What caused that growth?
✓ Describe the patterns or trends that you noticed over the course of the learning.
✓ What are your next steps for this skill or goal? How do you know?

The sticky note formative: Adaptable and effective!

Eleven Practices to Consider When Grading

Kelly Brooksher, EdD, Assistant Professor
Georgia Southern University, Savannah, GA

Grades communicate student performance and acquisition of standards. Here are 11 practices for you to consider.

Electronic Grade Books: Making Good Choices

1. **Grading system:** *Just pick one.* You typically have two types of grading systems from which to choose: Total points or weighted categories. In a total points grading system, you assign points to each assignment. You can easily calculate this grade by dividing the points earned by the points possible. Typically, your other choice is weighted categories. Here you select categories and then assign a percentage to each.

2. **Weighted categories:** *Only two categories.* If you chose to have weighted categories, it is good to have just two. This helps to keep the gradebook clean and concise. "Formative" and "Summative" are two excellent categories to use. Some may remember having a class that had multiple categories like classwork, tests, quizzes, and projects. It is important to note that if a category is never used, the percentage is spread across the others. This inflates the percentages, giving an inaccurate presentation of the data.

    You will want to choose only one grading system: Either weighted categories or total points. Mixing systems convolutes grades and may become difficult for you to understand and explain to students and parents. It is essential for you to fully understand and justify your grading system.

3. **No assignments worth 10% or more:** *That is a whole letter grade!* Most school systems use the 100-point scale (90–100 = A, 80–89 = B, etc.). If you select the weighted categories as your grading system, be careful that a graded item is not worth too much. When an assignment is worth 10% or more, a poor grade can cause a student's overall grade to drop an entire letter grade. A simple rule that you may follow is to make sure you have one more assignment than percentage points allotted to the category. This ensures that no one assignment has too great of a value.

4. **"Rule of Nine":** *Trust your mind!* This name applies to a typical 100-point grading scale. At the end of a grading period, look at your students' final grades, then apply the "Rule of Nine" (or wherever a cut-off score falls between letter grades). You simply look at any final grade that is one point away (usually ends in a nine) from the next letter grade up. Then ask yourself, "Has this student's overall performance earned them one point to move up to the next letter grade?" If so, record that letter grade.

5. **What to grade:** *You do not have to grade everything.* Allow students to practice a new concept before assigning a grade. You may need to determine which pieces of work are going into the grade book and which are not. You might choose two different ways of marking papers. Some teachers simply cut the corners off of papers that go into the

grade book. Or you might use a particular color of ink for formative and summative grades. Be sure to communicate your grading policies to students and parents.

Grading Practices: Understanding the Impact

6. **Use of zeroes:** *Be aware of the repercussions.* Recovering from a zero is extremely difficult and creates an inaccurate picture of the student's acquisition of the standards. Research also shows that zeroes impact student motivation (Cristea, 2007; McMillan, 1999; Reeves, 2004).

   Many school systems have created grading policies to circumvent the impact of the effect of zeroes. It is fundamentally important for you to understand the devastating impact zeroes have on both students' grades and motivation.

7. **Grading effort:** *Don't do it.* Although effort is important, it should be factored in separately from academic performance. As a teacher, you do not want to disadvantage students by mixing academic performance with effort as you assess. Assign a grade, then add anecdotal comments regarding effort.

8. **Grading behaviors:** *Don't do this either.* You should not add behaviors into academic grades. Examples of this include reduced points for bad behavior, tardiness, forgetting a name on the paper, and poor participation. Grading behavior also interferes with student motivation. No matter the challenge of dealing with behaviors, it should not become part of the academic grade.

9. **Grading homework:** *Here are the facts.* Best practices indicate that homework should be for practice, and not for a grade. Most students do not have equitable support at home. If graded, homework should be worth a small percentage. If homework is graded, then credit should be given for completion only. No student should fail due to low grades on homework.

10. **Grading incomplete work:** *A suggestion.* Students should be assessed by the product they produce, not the amount of time it takes to produce it. Consider grading what is submitted and record in your grade book. Have a discussion with any student who does not complete the work about their options. Then provide an opportunity for them to complete the remainder of the assignment. Apply a final grade based on the discussion.

11. **Attributes of the work:** *Just grade the content.* You need to take a moment to reflect on and understand how you feel about the visual appearance of student work. Examples of grading partialities include neatness, names, and attractiveness. Grade the content, not its appearance.

    A resource is available for your use in the download. It lists the 11 grading practices with examples and reminders to support you as you set up your electronic grade book and assess student work.

References

Cristea, J. (2007, June 28). *Are zeros fair? An analysis of grading practices* [Online forum post]. Retrieved from http://sciencefool.com/cabrini/AreZerosFair.pdf

McMillan, J. H. (1999). *The devastating effect of zeros on grades: What can be done?* Retrieved from ERIC database (ED428136).

Reeves, D. B. (2004). The case against the zero. *Phi Delta Kappan, 86*(4), 324–325. doi:10.1177/003172170408600418.

Now What? Making Instant Adjustments Based on Data

Joycelyn Forshay
Sixth Grade Social Studies Teacher
Ignite Middle School, Dallas, TX
Instagram: @ms.foshay

I participated in two separate teacher certification programs, and both told me the importance of effective questions, but neither taught me what to do with the results. In my sixth grade social studies classroom, creating, administering, and reacting to informal assessments is an arduous task. Most informal assessments I conduct are question-based and therefore word-intensive. On a campus that is majority English learners, this feels inappropriate. Social studies is not taught K–5 in this area, so students struggle using context clues.

As a new teacher, I am challenged by not knowing what to do after collecting this data from informal assessments. I aspire to instantly reteach (when needed) based on data. Once I am standing in front of students who "didn't get it," the next step is unclear. I know that I need to reteach or refresh. Diagnosing what to reteach or why students missed the assessment is where I get lost. I cannot create an effective reteach if I cannot pinpoint what students are missing in their understanding. I know that a better informal assessment would remedy this, but I don't know what a better informal assessment looks like for my content area. Because the questions used are often wordy, sometimes it feels like I am assessing students' reading comprehension skills versus their social studies content knowledge. As I continue my early years as a teacher, I compile tools for collecting informal assessment data. But still the problem persists: What do I do with this data?

Portfolios: Progress Monitoring Over Time

Davon Clarke, MA
First and Second Grade Teacher
The Children's Workshop School, New York City Department of Education,
New York, NY
Twitter: @davon_clarke
Instagram: @learningwithdc.

Portfolios can be an effective assessment tool to track your students' growth over time. A portfolio features a collection of students' work/progress over the course of a given timeframe. You can use this horizontally, tracking growth over the course of a school year, or vertically, tracking growth grade by grade from as early as pre-K to as late as 12th grade. Portfolios help paint a larger picture of a student's learning for all stakeholders involved in his/her educational experience. Through the use of student portfolios, you can track a student's progress toward learning goals as well as assess strengths and areas of growth.

Engage your students in reflective practices in order to build their metacognitive skills (deliberate reflection about their thinking/learning). One effective way to promote metacognition is for you to implement portfolios as an assessment practice in your classroom. Portfolios help students develop metacognitive skills (Braund & DeLuca, 2018). Even young learners, English learners, and students with disabilities can engage in this work. In turn, the development of metacognitive skills will help your students build critical thinking necessary for academic success.

Furthermore, if you use the portfolio assessment process in your classroom, it will help your students have an increase in internal locus of control and ownership of their learning (Ezell & Klein, 2003). If you want portfolios to be a meaningful and authentic form of assessment, you must actively involve your students in the process of selecting artifacts. One suggestion would be to hold a "portfolio day" during benchmark periods over the course of the school year. On portfolio days, students would choose a meaningful piece of work, reflect on it, and include the artifact with a written explanation of why it is important and meaningful.

As a school-wide assessment practice, we collect student portfolios to track growth from pre-K to fifth grade. Each year, students engage in collecting and reflecting on meaningful pieces of work that they would like to have included in their portfolios. In addition, teachers strategically select artifacts that will be included as well, such as end-of-unit writing projects. This helps paint a holistic view of the student and is an effective way to showcase growth. At the end of the school year, portfolios are passed on to the next teacher who will have that student. This allows the new grade level teacher to preview all students' work and begin to plan instructional supports. In doing so, holistic and individual planning becomes possible. Although this method of collecting portfolios has been implemented for many years, we are constantly thinking of ways to improve the process and build upon it.

Suggested Portfolio Process:

1. Set a goal/purpose for the portfolio.
2. Think about your method for organizing materials/artifacts.
3. Think about what to include and how to assess the collected work. (Be strategic in when you collect work and what you are collecting.)
4. Involve students in selecting work samples and reflecting on them.
5. Share portfolios during parent–teacher conferences, transition meetings, or IEP meetings.

If you choose to adopt the portfolio assessment process, there are a few things to consider. First and foremost, when portfolios are used ineffectively with no purpose or goal in mind, it often becomes a collection of too many things. Second, you should consider the amount of time that will be spent on compiling, assessing, and reflecting on your students' work. Third, think about an effective method of organization for students' artifacts and work samples. Be sure to balance what is collected and/or included (all subjects/developmental areas). Consider using other formats, such as an e-portfolio, to limit the amount of paperwork. Plan ahead and consider strategic points during the year to collect the samples. Lastly, think of ways to engage in collaboration with all stakeholders including, but not limited to, service providers, families, and other subject area teachers. Overall, make this assessment process meaningful for both you and your students.

I have one final tip for you. In today's technologically advanced society, consider the use of an electronic portfolio. I have shared with you an original portfolio cover sheet (see download). This serves as a quick overview of the artifacts included in a student's portfolio. There is an area for you to comment on the student's strengths and areas of improvement. To save time and paper, I recommend that you consider using this document as an e-portfolio cover sheet. You can upload the document to a password-protected cloud platform, such as Google Drive, that can be easily shared within your school community. Each student could have a folder dedicated to their online portfolio, where teachers include the cover sheet and pictures or scanned versions of the student's artifacts. This will allow all school professionals to have access to the student's portfolio, be able to review their work and progress, and plan necessary academic supports.

References

Braund, H., & DeLuca, C. (2018). Elementary students as active agents in their learning: An empirical study of the connections between assessment practices and student metacognition. *Australian Educational Researcher*, 45(1), 65–85. doi:10.1007/s13384-018-0265-z.

Ezell, D., & Klein, C. (2003). Impact of portfolio assessment on locus of control of students with and without disabilities. *Education and Training in Developmental Disabilities*, 38(2), 220–228.

Checks for Understanding: Maximizing Student Learning

Kimberly A. Schwartz, PhD, Literacy Coach
Hillsborough County Public Schools, Tampa FL

Marygrace Farina, EdD, Reading Specialist
Archdiocese of Chicago, Chicago, IL

Lori Sue Grieb-Severino, PhD, Literacy Coach
Hillsborough County Public Schools, Tampa FL

Arleen P. Mariotti, PhD, Adjunct Instructor
Hillsborough Community College, Tampa, FL

Checks for understanding (CFU) are activities that you, as a new teacher, should integrate into your instruction to monitor student learning. Data you gather from CFU can provide evidence about the degree of misunderstood content, which you can use to address achievement gaps. This will strengthen your ability to provide differentiated, precise (just-in-time) instruction for students (Fisher & Frey, 2014). The purpose of checking your students' understanding is to measure each individual's content knowledge in real instructional time. The data from CFU help you know "when to speed up, slow down, or reteach" as you instruct (Bogdanovich, 2014, para 6).

One commonly used approach to confirm student comprehension is questioning. Teachers ask questions like: "Everyone understand? Does this make sense? Did you get all that?" By asking these questions, what do you really learn about student proficiency? Does that mean all your students understand? Accepting answers to these superficial questions causes you to wait for data from a formative (homework) or summative (chapter test) assessment to find out what your students learned. By waiting, you lose the opportunity to adjust instruction.

CFU are a part of our larger formative assessment system (Fisher & Frey, 2014). They are different from formal tests and quizzes in that they

- rely on student self-reports of understanding,
- are informal,
- occur frequently,
- are used during instruction,
- are efficient in relaying pacing information to the teacher, and
- are not recorded in the gradebook.

As a new teacher, strive to use CFU at least three times within each lesson (Witney, 2013). You can check students' understanding following initial instruction, after guided practice, and finally at the conclusion of the lesson. Doing so provides you with evidence regarding each student's content knowledge throughout your instructional sequence.

You can choose from a variety of CFU (Fisher & Frey, 2014). Each strategy assesses whether your students reached the lesson objective(s) and their individual level of content understanding. Vary the CFU you use in your classroom as students have preferred ways of responding. For some students, kinetic responses such as fist to five may be more appropriate, while other students might better respond to technology applications, such as Padlet or Kahoot. See Table 10.2 for types of CFU and associated strategies. The download describes how you can use these various CFU with your students.

The CFU you choose should help students practice the desired skills, as well as communicate facts, ideas, and ways of thinking that are important to their learning. In daily planning, include notes about when you will pause to use these CFU. After teaching a class session, reflect on which questions were effective in obtaining evidence of student learning.

The intent of CFU is to continually monitor student understanding during instruction (Bogdanovich, 2014; Fisher & Frey, 2014; Mariotti & Schwartz, 2018). As with any instructional strategy, variety of use is important. Overuse of one format can lead to diminished student motivation and interest. Underuse may lead to poor use of instructional time because additional class periods must be spent on reteaching. Using CFU helps you to effectively deliver instruction and manage learning in a timely manner.

Table 10.2 Types of CFU and Associated Strategies

Area of Focus	Strategy
Writing	• Individualized response boards • Response cards • Interactive writing • Exit tickets • Read-write-pair-share • Quick write • Graphic organizers
Technology	• Kahoot • Padlet • Nearpod
Oral language	• Pairs discuss • Think-pair-share • Retellings
Kinetic	• Fist to five • Open/closed fist • Thumbs-up/thumbs-down • 1 finger/2 finger – true/false • Emoji cards

References

Bogdanovich, P. (2014, July 14). *The importance of checking for understanding* [Web log post]. Retrieved from https://dataworks-ed.com/blog/2014/07/the-importance-of-checking-for-understanding/

Fisher, D., & Frey, N. (2014). *Checking for understanding: Formative assessment techniques for your classroom* (2nd ed.). Alexandria, VA: ASCD.

Mariotti, A. P., & Schwartz, K. A. (2018). *Creating your instructional blueprint: A guide to effective teaching*. Independently published manuscript.

Witney, E. (2013, February 25). *How do I effectively check for understanding?* [Web log post]. Retrieved from http://blog.kipp.org/teachingstrategies/how-do-i-effectively-check-for-understanding/

Chapter 11

Work–Life Balance

First, Take Care of Your SELF

Michelle Adler, EdD, Assistant Professor
Wichita State University, Wichita, KS
Facebook: https://www.facebook.com/educationadler/?ref=bookmarks

As an educator, wife, and a mom of five boys, one of the hardest parts of my world is figuring out when my school life ends, and the rest begins. I have not always done this successfully, so my mental and physical health took the brunt of this collapse. There were years I functioned (poorly) on 4–5 hours of sleep. Months where exercise seemed impossible. Weeks with no lunch and binges late in the day. I struggled feeling well physically, mentally, and emotionally. My teaching was not as strong as a result. It is hard to keep a perky pace with students when you feel slow, sluggish, achy, and grumpy! When I started my career, no one talked about how to manage work and home while still being happy and enjoying life. As a result, I was not very good at managing it and just "got by."

Now, as a profession, we recognize that a happy human is a much stronger teacher than the one who feels defeated by 8 a.m. every day. I use a planner and mark out times for exercise and healthier habits, along with time for family and friends. When I am with my students, I can give them my best because my own needs are already met or will be. It took me too long to figure this system out for myself. Now I am a staunch advocate for helping beginning teachers like yourself find space to grow professionally while still flourishing personally. To remind you of the importance of self-care, use the acronym SELF.

S Is for <u>Setting Aside Time for Yourself</u>

Whether it is exercise, reading, meditating, enjoying music, taking a hot bath, or walking the dog, there must be time in each day for you to let your mind drift and the world melt away. Even if it is only for 20 minutes, you should mark this time on a daily calendar and honor it.

Just as professional meetings are important, personal appointments for relaxing your mind are just as significant.

E Is for <u>Engage</u>

Engage in conversations that lift you up and inspire you to do more and be better. Dedicate time to people you care about. Be present. Fully engage with them. No more multitasking. Whatever you are doing, invest in it completely. Your workdays are busy. Set manageable goals and attack them. Mark each task off when you are finished so you have a sense of accomplishment. Use a calendar and (attempt!) to plan your day so you can fully invest in each of the day's events and the people you interact with along the way. Likewise, fully invest in your downtime to start the next day recharged. Find a planner that works for you. Create spaces in your day to reflect so you can energetically reconnect.

L Is for <u>Listen</u>

Listen to those around you. Also listen to things that inspire you. Podcasts, videos, and music can provide you with positive feedback and growth. When you dedicate time to people, give them your full attention and truly listen. Set phones aside. Hold eye contact. Connect. Ask your colleagues, "What is one thing I should know about you that would help me be a better peer?" Regularly ask your students, "What is one thing I need to consider when I think about you?" Everyone has a story. Take time to listen to the stories of those around you.

F Is for <u>Friends</u>

Find your people. My mom used to say, "You can be the ripest, juiciest peach, but some people just don't like peaches." Find the people who do. Find people who push you, encourage you, share dreams with you, but also let you vent and share your heart. Jennifer Gonzalez has an excellent post entitled *Find Your Marigold: The One Essential Rule for New Teachers* (https://www.cultofpedagogy.com/marigolds/) that gives clearer meaning to the value of finding your work friends. These friendships are essential. Find them. Nurture them. Treasure them. Guard them. Let the acorns stay where they are and move toward the marigolds.

The download is a reminder you can print and clip in your planner. See it and know that it is not selfish to focus on yourSELF. Remember to recharge, engage, listen, and focus on friendships so you can give your best to your learners and your loved ones.

As educators, each day we share our life and world with our students. While exhilarating, this work can also be exhausting. We need to take time and plan ahead for how we will take care of ourselves so we can take care of those around us, including our students and our own families. Start from Day One with a plan for how you will give yourself downtime, nurture your own mind, and use that renewed sense of self to better support your colleagues and students.

Lose Yourself in Teaching: Stay in Touch with Yourself

Daria Pizzuto, PhD, World Language Teacher
Bernards Township Schools, Basking Ridge, NJ
Adjunct Professor, Department of Higher Education Leadership, Management, and Policy
Seton Hall University, South Orange, NJ
Website: www.dariapizzuto.com

The social–emotional learning framework uses core competencies to teach self- and social awareness. In education, this framework serves as a prescription to alleviate students' stress and increase well-being (Collaborative for Academic, Social, and Emotional Learning, n.d.). Teachers, on the other hand, are in charge of their own mental and physical well-being. You are required to be resilient yet vulnerable in face of difficulty. You must be supportive and creative in the classroom. You need to accept a role and engage in the school community. At the same time, you must meet or surpass an ever-growing list of professional expectations.

My first year of teaching was one of the toughest challenges I've ever experienced. Navigating the new school, building relationships with students, delivering engaging and creative lessons, realigning curriculum, nurturing relationships with parents and fellow teachers, and giving—giving everything I had to my students left me burned out. A school committee? Sign me up! A potluck or a school fundraiser? I'm there. Stay until 7 p.m. to enter grades? No problem at all. I nurtured everyone and everything but myself.

Interestingly, during that year very few people asked how I was doing. They asked about students, lessons, the school, but never how *I* was doing. Part of me is glad they didn't. It allowed me to save face and not burst into tears. But now, as a seasoned educator, I want to give that younger version of myself a big hug. What new teachers really need is support, empathy, and self-compassion.

The weekly reflection tool that I offer you is designed to help you stay in touch with yourself. When things get tough (and they will; they always do), at the end of the week give yourself this one gift: A gift of time. After taking a moment of quiet reflection, clarity and perspective can follow. As teachers, we have to hold it together in front of our students *no matter what*. We are humans. We love kids. *We have the right to feel how we feel*. When that lesson, or day, or week, or month goes wrong, allow yourself to acknowledge and process your real feelings.

Don't rush to put a positive spin on it. Use the questions in the download to gain perspective. In teaching you experience a wide range of emotions. Teaching can leave you dispirited or inspired. It can make you feel sad and frustrated, alone and angry, or happy and hopeful. There are times when you simply plateau in your craft, so you feel … average. All these feelings are normal. Putting them down on paper is a valuable self-awareness tool. I use this tool on a weekly basis. As I wrap up my work week on Friday, I take 10–15 minutes out of my day and weigh in on my thoughts. I recommend making multiple copies of the document and use one per week, like a log.

Setting time aside at the end of the week for reflection allows me to examine my week. It documents my victories and opportunities. It reminds me to be compassionate with myself and empathetic toward others. It allows me to see the big picture. It brings clarity and perspective.

So, go ahead—lose yourself in teaching. Enjoy! But remember to fill yourself first, so that you can continue giving of yourself to others.

Reference

Collaborative for Academic, Social, and Emotional Learning. (n.d.). *Core SEL competencies.* Retrieved from https://casel.org/core-competencies/

Self-Care Is Essential

Ingrid Wagner, BEd
Fourth and Fifth Grade Teacher
Cincinnati Public School District, Cincinnati, OH

In my first year of teaching I learned a lot. I experienced a lot. I took on lots of heartache, both in my work life and my personal life. Luckily, I had established strong mentoring relationships with my coworkers at school. They gave me advice, encouraged me to take personal days, and supported me through triumphs and heartaches.

Once I was able to reconnect with my fellow graduates over summer break, I became aware of how lucky I was to be part of a positive school community. I had supportive colleagues; however, many of my peers did not. Many of them were nervous to take personal days, in fear of their classroom being exposed as ineffective. Their mental health suffered because of it. While I was on the road to success in continuing my career as a classroom teacher, I found that many of my fellow graduates were no longer on that path with me. They were starting to walk down a road of burnout, as many first-year teachers do.

When you are in a helping profession like teaching, you are giving yourself to others completely and consistently. Being a teacher requires a certain level of passion to be effective. Part of that passion is caring for our students. When we see our students hurt, emotionally or physically, that takes a toll on our heart, especially when the hurt is out of our control. In teaching, we gather experiences that make permanent marks on us. Those marks build our teaching story. In order to be your best self for your students, you must take time to care for your heart, body, and soul. Self-care means taking time to heal.

Here is a list of self-care tips for you that I learned in the course of my first year of teaching:

- ♦ **Experiment.** During breaks, when you are feeling less stressed, try a variety of self-care techniques. Use that time to find a couple of strategies that you can rely on in states of high stress.
- ♦ **Schedule.** Find a time management technique that supports your needs. For example, every Sunday, I make a to-do list for each day of the upcoming week. I schedule

self-care on at least three of those days. I make a separate list of nonurgent tasks to do if I have extra time. This way I am not feeling overwhelmed. I am only scheduling as much as I can complete.

♦ **Say no.** Say no to things that will overfill your plate, such as supporting after-school extracurriculars, volunteering to head team projects, or tutoring after school. Even cleaning up after your students or searching for missing student work can be time-consuming. Hold your students accountable. Be fully present in your teaching so you can prioritize yourself during down time.

♦ **Journal.** Journal when your heart or mind needs to dump onto paper. When I journal, I focus on how I am feeling in the present and look ahead to what I want in the future. Going back to read my journal allows me to see my growth over months and years. Use some of the prompts in my download to get started.

♦ **Exercise.** The benefits are endless, especially if you are able to get out in nature.

♦ **Yoga.** I suggest "Yoga with Adriene" on YouTube. Doing at-home yoga has helped me create a mantra that I repeat after a tough day, as well as repeat to myself during moments of high stress or traumatic flashbacks.

♦ **Create a playlist.** I have a music playlist and a video playlist on YouTube titled "Teacher Tough Days." Both of these are full of songs and videos that make me smile and remind me of my passion.

♦ **Create a student log.** Keep a log of all the students who have made an impact on you. Reread this log at times when you feel like giving up.

♦ **Take a nap.** If your body needs to rest, let it.

♦ **Take a personal day.** Your classroom will survive. I promise.

♦ **Pamper your body.** Consider the benefits of a massage, bubble bath, foam roller, or a mani/pedi.

♦ **Binge.** Watch your favorite TV show or movie.

♦ **Meditate.** Occasionally, I use meditation before bed to help clear my mind and get ready for sleep. The Calm App has great supports for meditation practice. It has a variety of tools such as white noise, peaceful music, and sleep stories.

♦ **Save positive notes from your support system.** Glue them in your journal. Put them on your bulletin board. Know where to find them on a rough day.

Noooo! What Happened to My Social Life?

Jennifer Ann Flynn
Spanish Teacher
Notre Dame Academy High School, Staten Island, NY

Halfway through my first year of teaching, I was drowning in a sea of student work on a daily basis. In fact, a few years later, when I was moving into a new apartment, I found an abandoned dusty folder beneath my bed filled with one set of ungraded work from that year. I stood, amused, as I chucked the folder in the trash, reminiscing about my horrible "freshman" teaching year. But when I was actually living it, I certainly was not laughing. Back then, it felt as though I was at school seven days a week just seeing my students' names scrawled on top of all my papers, even when I took them to my couch or to a Starbucks for a change in scenery. When it started to affect my mental state as well as my social life, I knew I needed assistance to stay afloat.

Trusted colleagues became my life preservers. Teaching is about trial and error, but hearing veterans' experiences and what worked for them helps steer you in the direction that fits your teaching style. To balance teacher life with real life, one colleague passed on advice that she received when she was a new teacher in the same predicament: No grading on the weekends. It seemed an impossible feat, but once I was able to surrender to this idea in my third year of teaching, it utterly changed my ability to rejuvenate and be the equipped, energized teacher my students deserved when another Monday rolled around. Time to do whatever you want and spend with others is important to avoid burnout and the loss of your identity as your non-educator self.

Even though not all the successful strategies of your fellow colleagues will work for you, it is very healthy nonetheless to be able to talk about your first-year struggles to prevent yourself from losing confidence or abandoning the profession all together. In addition to any tactic you may try, becoming more seasoned also adds more time back into your life outside school as you become more efficient at tasks such as grading.

Finding Your Work–Life Balance

Raven Talley
Assistant Principal
Bronzeville Classical School, Chicago, IL
Facebook: http://www.facebook.com/raven.pattersontalley
Twitter: @raventalley10

How do you manage it all? This is a question new teachers ponder as they work through the first few years in the profession. How will I manage the workload? When do I have time for myself? Typical questions. I need to grocery shop, but my lesson plans are due. I need a haircut and new shoes, but I have six stacks of ungraded papers. What gives?! This is all too common for beginning teachers.

Guess what? This is very normal. My first year of teaching (many moons ago) was a blur of work tasks, student behaviors, and paperwork. Not to mention I was a newlywed with a toddler. Everyone and everything were important. Keeping myself afloat was quite a challenge in the beginning of my teaching career, but everything became manageable in time.

My first piece of advice is to understand this: *The work will always be there*. This means that as much work as you do, there will always be more. Pace yourself. If you are not energized, happy, and feeling your best self, what do you have to offer to others?

My second piece of advice to you is to organize EVERYTHING! You will need a calendar and notebook. The investment in time to organize your schedule and tasks will pay off.

Trust me. Juggling work and home life can be quite daunting, but never fear, it can be done. Think about the nonnegotiables in your personal life. What tasks must be done for basic functioning and self-care? Organize those tasks and prioritize them by frequency: Daily, weekly, monthly, and quarterly. Think about the work tasks that need to be done daily, weekly, monthly, and quarterly. Organize those tasks and prioritize them by due dates. Use the download to help organize yourself. Organization pays off.

Additionally, don't forget to enlist the help of others. Creating a village of support is super important and contributes to your happiness and longevity in the teaching profession. A few trusted individuals can help shape the course of both your professional and personal life. Create a list of the professional and personal tasks that someone else could do. When I am out of time and need groceries, I order them online. Someone does the shopping for me and delivers it to my job or home! A retired coworker serves as the transportation service for my children during the school week, to shuttle them to school and extracurricular activities. We're only human and we can only do so much.

As the year progresses, you will find that, when you've mastered one thing, another challenge presents itself. Situational challenges will surface and need to be navigated. For example, how do you respond when you see your students and parents while enjoying a much-needed cocktail at your favorite bar and grill? Don't freeze. Don't try to slip out. Be comfortable in your space during your free time. I always make it a practice to be polite and give a basic greeting and continue with my activity. My self-care and personal time are just that: Mine. Don't be ashamed or nervous to enjoy life outside of your job. If working in a small, rural community, you might want to consider moving your personal life to a neighboring town or county. Also, know and understand that it is healthy for you to do the things that make you happy.

As a new teacher, you will probably ask yourself this question: *Does work–life balance really exist?* It can, but you have to experiment with managing your tasks and time. Find out what works for you and ask other teachers how they manage their work–life balance.

A Cautionary Tale for New Teachers

Deb Coberley, EdD
Plainfield, IL

This is an authentic example of a new teacher's struggle with work–life balance. As you read, think about your own experience.

In early October, Patricia, a first-year teacher, walked into my office. The look on her face meant this was going to be a serious conversation. I stood and greeted her as she closed my door and melted into the red upholstered chair at my table. She baldly said, "If something doesn't change soon, I'm going to quit."

My mind began to race. During her first observation, Patricia had the basics down. She built positive rapport with her students. Her classroom management system worked. The lessons were engaging. She provided helpful feedback to students and parents. Her team thought she was a delightful addition. From a principal's point of view, had I missed something? How was it possible that she was ready to call it quits after a few months of working at a job she had spent four years preparing for?

As the conversation unfolded, Patricia shared the challenges that all teachers experience: Curricular expectations, home–school communication, paperwork, time management, struggling students, and so on. I asked one simple question, "What made you want to be a teacher?" She looked up at me and reiterated the vision she shared in her job interview where she spoke about the teacher who inspired her. Immediately, the desperation in her voice diminished as she reminded herself why she chose this profession.

Working Hours

During our conversation, Patricia referenced the amount of time that she was spending at work. Because she wanted to immerse herself into the community, she overextended herself on building committees and school events. As we discussed her roles and responsibilities, we were able to find ways to minimize her overall commitments. For example, we reduced her commitment to the one committee in which she was most interested. Next, we limited her to volunteering to plan one school event per semester. These changes decreased the amount of time spent before or after school. Therefore, she had more time to work on her classroom responsibilities.

We also talked about the hours she spent working at home. Patricia often worked seven days a week handling parent emails, lesson planning, and grading. Parent communication took the majority of this time. We talked about developing a communication plan that still allowed her to update students' families but set boundaries. Granted, it is hard to avoid school responsibilities at home. Be mindful of balancing the demands of work and personal life.

Support Systems

Patricia was fortunate that she recognized and utilized support systems at home and at work. She talked about her new house. She lived with her partner who was also a teacher. They found it important to take turns cooking, cleaning, shopping, and running errands. She felt they communicated well about their schedules. If one had a busy week the other one helped in the home more. Patricia also had a support system at school. She felt that she connected well with a team member and often planned lessons with her. She felt she could go to her teammates, other teachers, and administrators without fear of being judged. She was grateful that everyone got along on her team, which was not the case for her partner. As a new teacher, you will find a strong support system is crucial for establishing a work–life balance.

As we ended our conversation, Patricia still felt overwhelmed, but she was willing to try implementing the time management strategies we'd discussed. We decided to meet two weeks later to see how setting limits impacted her work–life balance.

Coping Strategies

When Patricia and I met again, she was more optimistic. She had implemented the suggestions we had previously discussed. Patricia reported that setting boundaries helped her with time management and organization. She began to utilize parent volunteers to help create bulletin boards and copy papers. Although it was a bit uncomfortable to give up some of the control, she knew it would be helpful in the long run. Patricia started to create and prioritize to-do lists. It was still hard to finish everything, but the list kept her more focused.

With the support of her partner, they began setting dedicated school hours. This allowed them to eat better because they had more time to cook. After dinner they went for walks. She admitted they usually talked about work, but it was helpful to reflect on their days. Exercise and healthy eating led to sleeping better at night. They also decided to take Friday nights and Saturdays off from work. In turn, there was more time for a social life to recharge for the following week's tasks.

At the end of this conversation, Patricia was in a better place. She still had challenges, but she had a different mindset when resolving them. You do not want to become another talented teacher lost to the demands of the job. Use the download to focus on obstacles and develop your mindset to overcome challenges with work–life balance.

Beat the Burnout

Marah Lambert
Math Teacher
Mears Middle School, Anchorage, AK

I doubted myself during student teaching. Yes, I lesson-planned, taught every day, and I connected with students. However, I thought I was doing too much work for too little of an outcome. They say that teaching is a thankless job and that we pour our hearts and souls into the profession, but who says that we have to do it all alone? Near the end of my student teaching, I realized I could step next door to the teacher who taught one of the same classes as me to share resources. This was the best realization that I had. It ultimately changed the trajectory of the beginning of my teaching career. This awesome teacher next door shared what she was going to use for her materials, and it saved me time and energy to look at what she was using to replicate or modify for my own classroom. Again, this realization did not happen until near the end of my student teaching…when I was feeling burned out.

I took this mindset of collaborating with other teachers into my first years of teaching. I found the best teacher (now great friend) to help me through this time. Because this fellow teacher taught the same classes as me and had several years of experience, she was able to share what worked and what didn't work with all the resources she had. Her reflections and advice helped me think about what I needed to do for my students. I used that information to modify her assignments or found new ones that would work better based on what she shared. I trusted and valued her insights. We also split our to-do lists when making answer keys, creating projects, or developing new forms of tests/review guides. Because we were using similar resources, we reflected daily on how the lessons went and changes we should make for the next school year. We bounced ideas off each other and shared what we truly thought.

You do not feel alone in the profession when you're able to join forces with a colleague. This is critical when you're first starting out. I strongly believe that collaborating with other teachers can help beat burnout. I'm going on my fourth year of teaching and thriving. I feel ready to take the next first-year teacher under my wing to lighten their load.

Self-Care Is the New Work–Life Balance

René Roselle, PhD, Director of Teacher Preparation and Associate Professor
Sacred Heart University, Isabelle Farrington College of Education, Fairfield, CT
Twitter: @RoselleSHU2020
Instagram: rene.roselle

As a new teacher, the best way to maintain a work–life balance is to engage in intentional self-care. The following strategies and resources will help you on your way.

Create a Caring Classroom

Create a classroom that promotes self-care for all, including you! Today we know that many students come to school having experienced trauma. Although your teacher education program might have infused trauma-based content into your curriculum, you should be aware that trauma cuts across all cultures and communities. You will find practical resources at the website Trauma Sensitive School (www.traumasensitiveschools.org). They offer two publications on teaching traumatized children and a related video series (Cole, Eisner, Gregory, & Ristuccia, 2013; Cole et al., 2005). You can also join their online community to stay informed about current practices.

In your efforts to make your classroom a more caring place, consider mindfulness. You can transform your classroom community with just a few modifications. For example, create a "peace place" where students can reset, calm down, or take a minute for themselves. The premiere organization for mindfulness in education is Mindful Schools (www.mindfulschools.org). Here you can sign up for a workshop, explore a certification program, peruse resources, or watch videos on how schools are integrating mindful practices.

Responsive Classroom (www.responsiveclassroom.org) is known for their excellent professional development and training in classroom management. The resource books are intentionally geared toward practitioners and can be used immediately in your classroom. They also have a treasure trove of resources on their YouTube channel (www.youtube.com/user/responsiveclassroom). Responsive Classroom is an elementary and middle school approach, but the best program I have found for the K–12 spectrum is Conscious Classroom Management by Smith and Dearborn (2016). When you create a classroom that is managed well, your students can be more engaged in learning.

Connect

Find people you like at work. In other words, find your squad. Feeling connected to people and having a strong sense of community helps a great deal when you have a difficult day, want to laugh, celebrate, or need a new idea. Hint: Picking positive people who have figured out how to stay optimistic and hopeful is ideal.

Retreat

Taking some time to reset yourself is critical, and it can take a lot of different forms. Is it a spa day? A kayak jaunt? Walking in the woods? Maybe you are someone who needs several days to really rejuvenate yourself. Teachers are expected to be many things to many people, and rarely do we ask teachers how they are taking care of themselves. Give yourself permission to take care of yourself. Don't wait until it is an emergency. Purposely block out time to give yourself a retreat. Don't apologize for it. Protect it.

Maintain Healthy Boundaries

Find joy in the work you do throughout your career. Teachers have been known to experience compassion fatigue and secondary trauma if their students have challenging backgrounds. Even if your students are not from difficult circumstances, you can still face burnout. In order for you to stay healthy, it's okay to place boundaries on your time or personal contact information with students and parents. Keep your personal and professional lives separate.

Stay Hopeful by Understanding and Processing Dissonance

It is easy to lose hope when, as a teacher, you hear sad student stories, disagree with decisions being made, or feel like you do not have enough resources. Snyder (2002) defines hope "as the perceived capability to derive pathways to desired goals, and motivate oneself via agency thinking to use those pathways" (p. 249). Higher hope consistently is related to better outcomes in academics, athletics, physical health, psychological adjustment, and psychotherapy. We all know high-hope and low-hope teachers. Hope and resilience can be taught. The most effective way for you to teach hope is through modeling, coaching in agency development, and assistance in identifying pathways.

I created a reflective tool called "Dissonance Processing" (see download). After identifying a situation you are struggling with, consider what you had hoped to happen (ideal), what actually happened (reality), and how you responded. Then reconsider what you would do differently if you were thinking about the situation through a hopeful lens where you have a refocused sense of insight and objectivity. Ultimately, you have the power to control your responses to situations. Frame them in the context of hopefulness.

References

Cole, S. F., Eisner, A., Gregory, M., & Ristuccia, J. (2013). *Helping traumatized children learn: Creating and advocating for trauma-sensitive schools* (Vol. 2). Boston, MA: Trauma and Learning Policy Initiative.

Cole, S. F., Greenwald O'Brien, J., Gadd, M. G., Ristuccia, J., Wallace, D. L., & Gregory, M. (2005). *Helping traumatized children learn: Supportive school environments for children traumatized by family violence* (Vol. 1). Boston, MA: Massachusetts Advocates for Children.

Smith, R., & Dearborn, G. (2016). *Conscious classroom management: Unlocking the secrets of great teaching* (2nd ed.). San Rafael, CA: Conscious Teaching.

Snyder, C. R. (2002). Hope theory: Rainbows in the mind. *Psychological Inquiry*, 13(4), 249–275. doi:10.1207/S15327965PLI1304_01.

Mindful Mood

Laura Alpaugh, MA, Professional Development School Clinical Instructor
Loyola University Maryland, Baltimore, MD
Twitter: @lauramarie_920

Introduction

How does your mood affect your day? Have you ever been in a bad mood without really being aware of what got you there? So many circumstances—from lack of sleep to poor nutritional habits to conflict in the workplace—can send you into a bad mood. This bad mood can consequently lead you to approach a situation with more negativity. Reversing a negative mood is not always easy. Your mood has an impact on your interactions with others. It is important to be mindful of your mood and the impact it has on you and your students.

Teaching is highly emotional work (Hargreaves, 1998). Emotional regulation is key to coping with the challenges you face each day in the classroom. Managing your mood and emotions may protect you from experiencing a "burnout cascade," in which stress over time can lead to poor teaching, burnout, and eventually attrition (Jennings & Greenberg, 2009, p. 492).

Emotions and Mood

Nowlis' (1963) disposition theory argues that mood is a higher-level disposition that then associates with emotions, the lower-level disposition. In short, when we are in a particular mood, we are more likely to feel certain emotions. For example, if you are experiencing an irritable mood, you will find that more things annoy you.

Compartmentalizing or even dismissing emotions can ultimately lead to feeling detached, disjointed, or separate from your daily context (Brown, 2015). Regardless of what's going on within your mind, you still have students to teach. Unprocessed feelings and emotions can sneak into the mind through triggers that can arise in daily situations in the classroom. As a new teacher, you need to be comfortable processing emotions in order to develop mood awareness and regulation.

Keeping a Pulse on Your Mood

"Mindfulness is the basic human ability to be fully present, aware of where we are and what we're doing, and not overly reactive or overwhelmed by what's going on around us" (Mindful Staff, 2014, para. 3). Developing mood mindfulness will allow you to reflect on your emotions, investigate your feelings or triggers, and support an awareness of your mood. Functioning in a personal negative space can be draining both mentally and physically, and can ultimately affect your students' ability to connect with you and thrive in your classroom. Keep a pulse on your mood using a rating system and methods of inquiry. This allows you to process and move through emotions. Ultimately you shift toward more positive thinking.

Step-by-Step Process of Mood Mindfulness

Ongoing reflection and awareness around emotional triggers can build mood mindfulness. Write a reflective journal entry each day to process your feelings. Capture your mood in as few or as many words as you need. You may not see dramatic change overnight. However, over time the process of regular reflection and mindfulness will support a clearer understanding of your triggers and a more mindful approach as you navigate situations inside and outside the classroom.

Step 1: Rate your mood.

Use the download to assign a rating to your mood morning, mid-day, and evening using a scale from one to five. One is equivalent to your lowest mood state (think feelings associated with sadness, frustration, or depression). Five is equivalent to your best mood (think feelings associated with happiness, joy, or pure contentment). Keep a record of this rating.

Step 2: Engage in inquiry.
* Question: Why am I feeling this way? This may bring up items that spark gratitude or potential negative triggers.
* Hypothesize: Reflect and record any triggers to the designated mood rating.
* Investigate: Identify past experiences or connections to the emotional triggers.
* Draw conclusions and move forward: Determine full awareness of the situation and move forward with more acceptance, awareness, and positivity.

Step 3: Repeat this exercise as many times as needed.
It is not easy to find time during a busy day to move through this exercise, but consider jotting down your rating on a notepad and reflecting during your evening downtime. Monitor progress with this exercise over time to process your emotions rather than being weighed down by them. You will begin to develop more control of your emotional responses and ultimately develop a more positive mindset.

Personal Testimony

I found journaling to be a powerful tool in supporting reflection and mindfulness. I used the mood rating and exploration of feelings personally and with my students during morning meetings. Over time, I found that I had more control of my emotional response. This realization had a positive effect on my classroom environment. My students and I developed the ability to share feelings and emotions openly and problem-solve ways to "bump up" the mood ratings throughout each day.

Self-care starts with mindset. Mood mindfulness is a powerful exercise in self-awareness and building positivity.

References

Brown, B. (2015). *Rising strong: How the ability to reset transforms the way we live, love, parent, and lead.* New York, NY: Spiegel & Grau.

Hargreaves, A. (1998). The emotional practice of teaching. *Teaching and Teacher Education, 14*(8), 835–854. doi:10.1016/S0742-051X(98)00025-0.

Jennings, P. A., & Greenberg, M. T. (2009). The prosocial classroom: Teacher social and emotional competence in relation to student and classroom outcomes. *Review of Educational Research, 79*(1), 491–525. doi:10.3102/0034654308325693.

Mindful Staff. (2014, October 8). What is mindfulness? *Mindful.* Retrieved from https://www.mindful.org/what-is-mindfulness/

Nowlis, V. (1963). The concept of mood. In S. M. Farber & R. H. L. Wilson (Eds.), *Man and civilization: Conflict and creativity* (pp. 73–89). New York, NY: McGraw-Hill.

Find the Balance That Works for You

Bethany Baer
Fourth Grade STEM Teacher
Elmer Wolf Elementary, Westminster, MD

Lesson planning consumed me in my first year of teaching. I knew what I needed to teach. I had great ideas of how to teach it, but it took me forever to create and prepare the perfect lesson. I spent hours every night coming up with lessons for the days ahead, and even more hours creating new activities, worksheets, interactive boards, and so on. To say I was exhausted would be an understatement. I was neglecting my family and the hobbies I enjoyed because of the afternoons and evenings I spent planning and preparing for future lessons. The unending cycle was draining me. I needed to find a way to balance school and my home life.

To combat this cycle, I began getting to school an hour or more earlier than students did. In the mornings, I would review my lesson plan, lay out manipulatives, copy worksheets, prepare centers, and hang anchor charts. By getting to work earlier and making the most of my in-school planning time, I was able to leave work 1 or 2 days of the week without taking my work home with me. Having a couple of nights a week where I focused on myself rejuvenated my spirit and allowed me to be a better teacher for my students. Take time for yourself, and find a planning routine that works for you!

Work–Life Balance: Getting More Hours in Your Day

Alexis Jones, PhD, Assistant Professor
Eastern Illinois University, Charleston, IL

Ask any teacher what they need to be happier or more relaxed about their job, and you will probably get one of two answers: "Money" (for supplies, books, etc.) or "time." This advice will not help with the first but could help with the second.

One of the best tips you will ever receive as a new teacher is to prioritize. However, with so many daily tasks to complete, all seem equally important at first glance. At the end of the school day, your list may seem endless. You need to clean up your classroom, grade papers, prepare for the next day, talk with a colleague, and so on. The secret is to not think about every item on your list as equally important and equally time-consuming. Some of your tasks will take 60 seconds, while others will have you stretching a 60-minute slot.

As an example, here are the tasks you have to (or would like to) accomplish before you head home. The last time your list looked like this, you struggled to get home in time for dinner.

1. Call two parents about their child's positive behavior that day. You want (or are mandated) to make these complimentary calls on a regular basis.
2. Make copies for the morning bell work, your lesson, and tomorrow's homework.
3. Set up four learning centers.
4. Respond to an email from the curriculum coordinator about upcoming professional development.
5. Write substitute plans since you have an IEP meeting in the afternoon on the next day.
6. Prepare laminated cards for your lesson.

Not all of these tasks are equally vital to complete at school. If your goal at the end of a long day is to get home in time to cook dinner, sit down with your family, or go to the gym, you may want to do only what is vital before you leave. Reserve a few tasks for later at home. For example, items 2, 3, and 6 should really be done at school. It is a good idea to do them before leaving instead of waiting until the morning. Although you might want to get *everything* done before leaving school, staying late into the evening is not wise. You need to eat a healthy dinner. You also need a good night's sleep. You also know the copy machine has a predictable tendency to break just when you need it most. Mornings are busy and unpredictable. Your revised list would look like this:

Before Leaving School	At Home
Make copies	Call parents
Set up centers	Sub plans
Laminate cards	Respond to email

Next, divide your tasks into three categories: as seen in Table 11.1.

- ◆ The task needs 5 minutes or less.
- ◆ The task needs up to 15 minutes.
- ◆ The task needs about an hour.

Table 11.1 Prioritizing Tasks

	~5 minutes	~15 minutes	~60 minutes
At school		Make copies Laminate cards	Set up centers
At home	Call parents		Write sub plans
	Respond to email		

For short tasks, squeeze them in whenever you can. They could get done during lunch without taking up your *whole* break. Tasks that take more time should be done when you are fresh. You might divide your tasks this way:

When organizing your to-do list in this way, you see that your school tasks may only take between an hour and an hour and 30 minutes. This enables you to go home, to the gym, and even cook dinner. Later, take a few minutes to call parents and respond to emails. Then you can give your sub plans your full attention.

This may look like a time-consuming way to organize your to-do list, but remember your goal is to have a *life* outside school. Use the download to organize your to-do lists.

Using Positivity and Happiness to Establish Work–Life Balance

Matthew Ohlson, PhD, Associate Professor
Director, Taylor Leadership Institute, University of North Florida, Jacksonville FL
Twitter: Matthewohlson1

A Call to Action

Teacher turnover is a chronic problem in the United States. One of the most significant reasons is the difficulty in maintaining work–life balance (Sutcher, Darling-Hammond, & Carver Thomas, 2016). Negative working conditions and constant tension between work and other life responsibilities negatively affect teacher retention (Day & Gu, 2010). In contrast, happiness in the workplace promotes success. Happy employees who reflect on their successes are more engaged and passionate about their work. Teachers should leverage happiness, joy, and celebrations of their influence on students to establish work–life balance. Teachers who embrace these qualities are less likely to leave their jobs (Hong, 2012; Simon & Johnson, 2015).

Positivity Practices

New teachers feel overwhelmed. One common complaint is their limited opportunities to realize and be recognized for the impact they have on their students. A major contributor to this problem is that teacher influence is not measured consistently throughout the school year. In response, focus on happiness to help you spotlight gains, strengths, and opportunities. Here are a few strategies for you to implement every day to realize your impact on students.

- ◆ **Parking Lot Rule**
  Each day before you leave school, think of at least one student who is better off because of you. Maybe you shared a kind word, spent extra time to help with a problem, or created an "a-ha" moment. Rather than focusing on the student who had a bad day, or overwhelming feelings caused by assessment challenges, take time to reflect on your positive acts.
- ◆ **The Positive Communicator**
  Each week send a positive email, text, or phone call to the homes of at least five students. Quite often, families hear from school only when there is a problem. Communicating these messages to families not only prompts you to recognize something positive about each student (improved performance, effort, attendance, etc.), it also allows you to reflect on the collective impact you have on them. Students who receive positive messages are likely to amplify their efforts. Their families are more likely to respond constructively when there is a problem.
- ◆ **Success Celebrations and Exit Tickets**
  Create opportunities for your students to share their greatest accomplishments for the week. You might do this with a "Celebrations" meeting, in which students share those accomplishments. They could also create an exit ticket to share with you and their families, describing their growth as a student. Be sure that you, too, participate in oral sharing and exit tickets. Through your sharing, you demonstrate to students that you have goals to accomplish. This exercise provides insight into what the students found valuable as you plan for the next week. Another benefit of sharing is showing students that you intentionally plan instruction to support their success.
- ◆ **Team Awesome**
  Using a shared bulletin board (elementary and middle school levels) or online portal (secondary level), create a forum for celebrating and spotlighting student success. Encourage your students to recognize other classmates' triumphs. When students make collective gains, spotlight that success.

The Impact

Teachers in our 11 Optimism Gap Project schools noted improved student attendance and reduced discipline referrals in their classrooms when using these Positivity Practices. Staff attendance improved by 10% because teachers wanted to come to work more often, knowing they were making a difference. Teachers felt that students became more aware of their own actions and performance through consistent celebrations and recognition of their efforts. When recognition focused on a variety of areas that went beyond standardized assessments, students were more successful.

This focus on happiness and success positively impacts work–life balance for teachers. Feeling successful makes it easier for you to take time away from work, knowing that you are having an impact. Feeling successful also counters the teacher burnout that often results when teachers focus on what went wrong and the need for improvement, and never being able to stop working because there is always more work to be done. Joy improves relationships with colleagues, students, and families. Doing so creates a network of positivity and support to help navigate the complexities of being an early career teacher.

References

Day, C., & Gu, Q. (2010). *The new lives of teachers*. London, England: Routledge.

Hong, J. Y. (2012). Why do some beginning teachers leave the school, and others stay? Understanding teacher resilience through psychological lenses. *Teachers and Teaching*, *18*(4), 417–440. doi:10.1080/13540602.2012.696044.

Simon, N. S., & Johnson, S. M. (2015). Teacher turnover in high-poverty schools: What we know and can do. *Teachers College Record*, *117*(3), 1–36.

Sutcher, L., Darling-Hammond, L., & Carver-Thomas, D. (2016). *A coming crisis in teaching? Teacher supply, demand, and shortages in the U.S.* Retrieved from Learning Policy Institute website: https://learningpolicyinstitute.org/sites/default/files/product-files/A_Coming_Crisis_in_Teaching_REPORT.pdf

Stress-Free Strategies for Sanity and Success for First-Year Teachers

Susan Trostle Brand, Professor of Early Childhood Education
School of Education, University of Rhode Island

Olga Lerner, Kindergarten Teacher
Exeter-West Greenwich School District, Rhode Island

Reflection on Olga's First Day in the Classroom

I will always remember the first day of my teaching career. My head was spinning from the moment my students arrived. My kindergarteners were like feral cats. They were clueless about what to do, and they were trying to run in so many directions at once. I had to corral them into the classroom while making sure that I had not lost any of them. Many of them were crying for their parents and wanted to go home. During the day, I had to help out with bathroom issues, jammed lockers, lost lunch boxes, and falling-down pants. I didn't even get close to starting the fun activities I had planned. In addition, parents bombarded me with emails and phone messages asking questions, voicing their concerns and requests, and informing me about their child's individual needs. On top of these, when I checked emails during lunch, I saw that I had received dozens of emails from administrators and colleagues informing me about upcoming events, testing procedures, and evaluation schedules that meant nothing to me at the time. Needless to say, the whole day felt like I was running a three-ring circus. I was overwhelmed and exhausted.

I must admit that, although the following days and months got somewhat better, the overwhelmed feeling and the physical exhaustion remained with me throughout the entire school year. In my first year of teaching, I was in constant overdrive and felt that I had signed up for more than I could handle.

As a new teacher, take time to be mindful of your overall health. Days will be long. Devoting time to communicate with families and colleagues can feel never-ending. You will be constantly planning and finding resources for your instruction. For example, you might take 90 minutes to prepare materials that will account for only 15 minutes of classroom time. With these challenges, maintaining work–life balance is critically important. The strategies below will serve you well in your professional and personal journey.

Monitor Your Health

Your health is a key component of the foundation for success and sanity in teaching. As mundane as it sounds, see your doctor for regular medical check-ups and get plenty of sleep. Avoid fast foods. Grocery shop in advance. Prepare and freeze healthy meals over the weekend to enjoy during the week.

Breathe

Throughout your busy day, regularly stop to be mindful of your emotions. Take deep breaths. Find humor in everyday exchanges. Share humor with your students. Relating simple anecdotes will break the ice, allow students to see you as human, and provide a refreshing breather for everyone.

Delegate

As a new teacher, you likely believe you need to do it *all* and do it *by yourself*. This is a myth! Remember that you have others to help and support you. Expert teachers set goals, plan ahead, and share the workload with a team of teachers and volunteers. Use Pinterest, Twitter, Facebook, and Instagram to discover innovative ideas for how other teachers collaborate.

Enlist the Support of Mentors

Identify master teachers in your building and observe the way they interact with others, plan, organize their classroom, schedule their time, and achieve the goals they have set for themselves and their students. Seek out formal and informal mentoring support.

Organize

You might obtain several large, clear storage boxes and label each with a theme. You may also develop a system to electronically organize your curricular resources. Develop labeled folders containing unit plans, assessment tools, and materials.

Re-Envision Problems

Develop the mindset that for every problem, there is a solution. Rather than wasting energy dwelling on problems, use your peer network and mentors to seek solutions. Re-envision problems as opportunities for problem-solving, growth, and creativity.

Expect a Learning Curve

Anticipate a learning curve. Realize that not everything needs to be perfect from the start. Prioritize your learning needs. Set daily and weekly goals for yourself based on what is most pressing.

Cultivate Independence

Use student-centered learning strategies and integrate media resources that give students choice. Encourage independent work. Provide small-group time for students to learn from one another. Be clear in your expectations. Make sure to clarify your instructions so that each student understands their allowable time and responsibilities. When you cultivate student independence, you provide more ownership and time for you to interact with students one on one.

Take Time for You

Limit your own screen and phone time. Exchange it with daily time set aside for leisure. Take a walk. Enroll in a yoga, exercise, or swim class. Pursue a favorite hobby. Take mini vacations. A change of scenery works wonders, both physically and emotionally.

As you gain experience and confidence as a teacher, you will no doubt add items to this basic list of de-stressors. In the meantime, plan ahead, make lists, enjoy, and focus on the positive. Network with experienced and positive colleagues. Use the download for a weekly self-reflection. (*And remember to breathe!*)

◼ Meet the Authors

Lori Abbott, NBCT, is a professional learning specialist who coordinates a mentor program for new teachers, supervises student teachers, and provides online support for candidates working toward National Board Certification.

Michelle Adler is a wife, mother of five boys, and an assistant professor at Wichita State University. In her free time, she enjoys running, reading, and attending her boys' games.

Shaunna Alcorn attended UNLV and majored in early childhood education. She teaches first grade at a Title 1 school. She recently completed a TESL certification program through Touro University.

Laura Alpaugh is a clinical instructor at Loyola University Maryland. She taught in public schools for nine years and has a total of 16 years of experience in the field.

Bethany Baer is a fourth grade STEM teacher in Carroll County, Maryland. She received her degree in elementary education from Salisbury University in 2015.

Christine Beardslee is a 20-year veteran, experienced in grades K to 4. Her awards include Who's Who Among America's Teachers, Teacher of the Year, and the 2018 NJ Exemplary Educator award.

Nancy H. Betker, LCSW, is a school social worker who works in a high school. She loves the students, families, colleagues, and wishes for less paperwork.

Marsha Black-Chen, EdD, is a LASPAU/Fulbright scholar, an educator, and senior lecturer at the Mico University College. Her research interests include nontraditional students, teacher education, and critical pedagogy.

Monica Boehle is a National Board Certified social studies teacher and instructional coach in a mid-size high school near Chicago, Illinois. Her work focuses on innovative and evidence-based instructional practices.

Nathan Bond is a professor of curriculum and instruction at Texas State University, where he teaches undergraduate and graduate courses in teacher education. His research focuses on teacher leadership and advocacy.

Beth Brabham, EdD, serves as the coordinator of Secondary ELAR/RTI/GT for Midway ISD in Waco, Texas.

Susan Trostle Brand is a professor of early childhood education. A former elementary school teacher and literacy specialist, Dr. Brand is the co-author or editor of four professional books and numerous chapters and articles.

Dr. Kelly Brooksher is an assistant professor at Georgia Southern University. Her 20 years of experience include teaching special and general education. She was an administrator at the elementary level.

Sarah Brown has been teaching first grade for four years. Sarah always knew she wanted to be a teacher, and her passion for this career continues to grow each year.

Dr. Rebecca West Burns is an award-winning associate professor in the Department of Teaching and Learning at the University of South Florida.

Altheria Caldera is an assistant professor in curriculum and instruction at Texas A&M University at Commerce. She specializes urban education, critical multicultural education, and critical pedagogy.

David Carroll teaches elementary and junior high bands in Naperville, Illinois. He received a doctor of education from Northern Illinois University in 2018 and NBPTS certification in 2006.

John Lando Carter is an assistant professor of education at Middle Tennessee State University. He teaches, researches, and presents in the areas of formative assessment, teaming, and creativity.

Joshua D. Case currently teaches science at Iselin Middle School in Woodbridge Township, New Jersey. He holds an MAT and is a National Geographic certified educator.

Anita S. Charles is a director of teacher education at Bates College. She has taught for many years across multiple grades and levels, including first grade, high school English and French, alternative education, undergraduates, and adult learners.

Candice Chiavola is a high school English teacher, mentor, and model teacher in the New York City Department of Education. She is also a doctoral candidate at Montclair State University.

Soyini Chism is a physical educator at Joliet Central High School and a doctoral student in curriculum leadership at Northern Illinois University. She can be reached at schism@jths.org.

Davon Clarke is a fifth year teacher at the Children's Workshop School in NYC. He believes in the power of building meaningful relationships with students and holding high expectations for their learning.

Dr. Mary C. Clement is a professor of education at Berry College in Georgia. She earned her doctorate from the University of Illinois at Urbana-Champaign and has published 14 books.

Julia Stearns Cloat works as a coordinator in Kaneland School District and as an adjunct professor at Northern Illinois University. She is dedicated to providing equitable and accessible learning experiences to students.

Debra Coberley lives in Plainfield, Illinois. Currently, she is an elementary principal and has also served as a classroom teacher, reading specialist, and assistant principal.

Nedra L. Cossa, PhD, is an assistant professor in elementary education at Georgia Southern University. Prior to that she was a fourth grade ELA teacher in Virginia.

Sara Curran has a passion for designing curricula that incorporates differentiation. She has enjoyed educating elementary students for the last 20 years. Sara also relishes traveling extensively with her husband.

Julia Cuscaden is a third-year teacher. She studied early childhood education at DePaul University, and is currently working toward her master's degree in reading instruction from LSU.

Hilary Dack is an assistant professor in the University of North Carolina at Charlotte's Cato College of Education. She specializes in instructional design and differentiation in K–12 general education classrooms.

Dr. Angela Danley is an associate professor of elementary education at the University of Central Missouri. She teaches undergraduate and graduate level courses and supervises aspiring teachers in their practicum.

Rocio Del Castillo is an assistant superintendent for Special Services in Huntley Community School District. She has worked in special education, bilingual, and dual language settings and is an advocate for educational equity and social justice.

George T. Dewey is a National Board Certified Teacher since 1999, high school physics teacher, Fairfax County, Virginia, Presidential Awardee for Mathematics and Science Teaching, Albert Einstein Distinguished Educator.

Dr. Marisol Diaz taught elementary school for six years. Her research investigates connections of academic achievement and classroom pedagogy. She continues to work in her community supporting teachers, parents, and students.

Beatriz Dillman is a fifth grade Sheltered English Instruction teacher. She has taught students in Developmental Bilingual Education and has worked with students as an ESL resource teacher.

Melissa Dudic is the assistant principal for teaching and learning at Maine South High School in Park Ridge, Illinois and a doctoral student in curriculum and instruction at Northern Illinois University.

Dr. Will Dwyer is a high school principal in the western suburbs of Chicago and an adjunct professor at Northern Illinois University. His research fields include principal and collective teacher efficacy.

Collin Edouard is currently a Gates Cambridge Scholar working on a master's of music in choral studies. He earned a BFA in vocal performance at the City College of New York, and an MA in music education at Teachers College, Columbia University.

Dr. Pamela Kramer Ertel has over 40 years of experience as an educator. Her current research interests as a teacher educator are classroom management and organization, student engagement, and adoption.

Marygrace Farina taught for 23 years in elementary through adult levels. She earned her EdD from Florida Southern College. Currently, she lives and works as a reading specialist in Chicago.

Jennifer Ann Flynn has been a Spanish teacher in New York City since 2007. She earned her BA in Spanish and MSEd in literacy.

Jocelyn Foshay teaches sixth grade social studies in Dallas, Texas. She earned her BA in history and education studies from Guilford College and her MED from Texas A&M Commerce.

Daniel M. Frederking has served as a high school English teacher, a state education consultant, a university lecturer, a researcher, and a technical assistance consultant with American Institutes for Research.

Megan Freeman is a teacher in Oak Park, Illinois. She received her teaching degree at the University of Wisconsin–Madison where she also certified in English as a second language.

Maryellyn Friel has been an educator for 35 years. She has spent her entire career in the field of special education and is a National Board Certified Teacher in Exceptional Needs.

Socorro Garcia-Alvarado has 17 years of experience in elementary education, as a monolingual, bilingual teacher, and administrator. currently an adjunct in the Department of Interdisciplinary Learning and Teaching at the UTSA.

Ariane N. Gauvreau is a clinical faculty member in the special education program at the University of Washington. Her research interests include personnel preparation for inclusive early childhood educators.

Dr. Lydia Gerzel-Short is an assistant professor of special education at Northern Illinois University. Her research interests include family engagement and evidence-based practices for supporting diverse learners.

Katelynn Giordano is a language arts educator in Illinois. She is passionate about student empowerment, promoting equity, and valuing teachers as professionals. You can find her work on her blog, Curriculum Coffee.

Chantelle Grace is a doctoral student and graduate teaching assistant at the University of Georgia. Her work provides support and guidance for social studies teacher candidates entering into the field.

Lori Sue Grieb-Severino has been an award-winning teacher at various grade levels for 24 years. At present, she is a literacy coach, professional development facilitator, and adjunct for Hillsborough Community College.

Lois A. Groth is an associate professor in the School of Education at George Mason University. She teaches literacy methods and facilitates in the Elementary Education Professional Development Schools Network.

Zach Hall, a second-year choral teacher, has a unique opportunity to work with fifth through twelfth grade students in three different school buildings.

Dr. Kelli Hamilton is currently a seventh grade language arts teacher. She has served as an instructional coach and classroom teacher in public schools for over 20 years.

Christal Hoch is an alumnus of Florida Gulf Coast University, in her third year of teaching. Christal's teaching experience has been at Title 1 schools in Central and SW Florida.

Tonia Holmes-Sutton, EdD, NBCT, serves as the Nevada State Director for Teach Plus, a NBPTS Board Director, and a founder of the National Board Network of Accomplished Minoritized Educators (NAME).

Katrina A. Hovey is an assistant professor at Western Oregon University. Her research focuses on preservice teacher preparation to improve outcomes for diverse learners with special academic and behavioral needs.

Amy Howerton is an English Chairperson and teacher in Oswego, IL. She earned an educational doctorate from Northern Illinois University in 2016 and National Board Certification in 2006.

Carla Huck coordinates and provides sheltered instruction training to preK–12 educators in Lee County, Florida and to preservice teachers at Florida Gulf Coast University, where she is pursuing her EdD.

Jana Hunzicker is the associate dean of the College of Education and Health Sciences and associate professor in the Department of Education, Counseling, and Leadership at Bradley University in Peoria, Illinois.

Jennifer Jaros, NBCT, earned her master's degree from the College of Notre Dame of Maryland. She taught ESL in Baltimore City Public Schools prior to serving as EL Department chair in Oak Park D97.

Brittany John is a science instructor in southern New Jersey, new to the profession. She is a Woodrow Wilson Teaching Fellow, with a master's in STEM Education from Rowan University.

Rose Johnson, MEd, serves as the middle school ELAR specialist.

Alexis Jones is an assistant professor at Eastern Illinois University. Before receiving her PhD at the University of Illinois, Dr. Jones was an elementary teacher and then a grant coordinator.

Meghan A. Kessler is a former middle and high school social studies teacher from Illinois. She is currently an assistant professor of teacher education at the University of Illinois Springfield.

Deepti Kharod, a former elementary teacher, is a faculty member at University of the Incarnate Word. She learned about ethics of care during her research at a nature-based preschool and uses these principles throughout her work.

Stephanie Kiley is a special education teacher at the Devereux Glenholme School, a therapeutic boarding school for students with emotional disabilities in Washington, Connecticut.

Dr. Karen L. Kohler is a lecturer of curriculum and instruction at Texas A&M University-San Antonio. Her research interests include family engagement, teacher preparation, and educational collaboration between teachers.

Jesse Kraft is a former National Board Certified Teacher and coach for first-year teachers. He is the 2019 Fairfax County Public School's Outstanding Principal Award recipient.

Allison Krasnow is an eighth grade math teacher in Berkeley, California. She has been recognized as a National Board Certified Teacher and a Math for America master teacher.

Dr. Deitra A. Kuester is an associate professor at Bradley University. Using multidisciplinary collaboration, her research focuses on successful inclusion of all learners with disabilities, especially in areas of autism and ADHD.

Marah Lambert is a fourth-year teacher at Mears Middle School in the Anchorage School District teaching eighth grade math (Pre-Algebra and Algebra 1) and an elective (Recreational Reading).

Adam Larsen is an assistant superintendent for Oregon Community Unit School District 220 in Oregon, Illinois. He helps district and building leaders make better use of all kinds of data to inform decision making.

Erin Laverick is the former director of an intensive English program where she taught English learners for 16 years. Currently, she teaches literature and composition at Concordia University, Ann Arbor.

Vincent T. Laverick, EdD, is an assistant professor of education and Chairperson of the Division of Education at Lourdes University. His research interests are in the scholarship of teaching and learning.

Rebecca Lehman grew up in Highland Park, Illinois, and teaches kindergarten at Madison Elementary in Skokie, Illinois. She graduated from Ohio University in 2018 with a BS in education.

Olga Lerner has been teaching kindergarten for five years. Prior to teaching, Olga worked for the Providence Children's Museum as their Early Childhood Programs Developer.

Amie Livengood, MSEd, is a middle school instructional coach in DeKalb, Illinois. She is also a National Board Certified Teacher and adjunct instructor at Northern Illinois University.

Marla J. Lohmann is an assistant professor of special education at Colorado Christian University. Her research interests include Universal Design for Learning, technology in the classroom, and Tier 1 PBIS.

Heather Lyon, PhD, is an assistant superintendent. She has been a teacher, staff developer, and administrator, but the title she likes best is student. Please follow Heather on Twitter @LyonsLetters.

Brendan McCormick has taught middle school social studies and language arts for 18 years. He recently earned an EdD in curriculum leadership from Northern Illinois University.

Leana R. Malinowsky is a full-time practicing elementary educator since 2008. She is also the associate counselor for the Delta Rho Chapter of Kappa Delta Pi.

Jace Mansfield is a fourth-year English teacher at Pekin Community High School. Some days he learns more than he teaches, and some days he teaches more than he learns!

Chelsea Marelle is a special education teacher at Simpson Elementary School in Atlanta, Georgia.

Arleen P. Mariotti was a classroom teacher, reading specialist, evaluator, professional development specialist, and college professor. Presently, she is an adjunct for Hillsborough Community College, Tampa, Florida.

Cynthia Dawn Martelli is an associate professor of Reading at Florida Gulf Coast University. Her passion involves the value of children's literature as a powerful education tool in teacher education.

Kylie Martin is a first-year teacher at Poland Regional High School in Poland, Maine. She teaches ninth grade heterogeneous and AP English Language and Composition classes.

Dr. Judy Matuszewski has worked in special and elementary education along with college and administrative experience. She is drawn to students and families who feel the most removed from our classrooms.

Anton Miglietta teaches high school history at Instituto Justice Leadership Academy, an options-based alternative school of Chicago Public Schools. This is his 14th year in the classroom.

Dr. Gary J. Miller is an assistant professor in the School of Education at the University of Texas at Tyler. He is coordinator of the master of education in educational leadership program.

Dr. Rhonda D. Miller, an assistant professor of special education at Coastal Carolina University, has experience teaching general and special education for grades K–12 and English as a second language.

Harlee Morphis is in her first year as a seventh grade science teacher in Tennessee. She received her BS degree in biology from Middle Tennessee State University.

Stephanie Morrison has been teaching kindergarten for three years. She understands that her students have more to teach her than she does to them.

Suzanna Nelson received her BS in elementary education from UNLV in 2014. She earned her MEd in curriculum and instruction in 2016. She was awarded teacher of the year by her school in 2018.

Dr. Matthew Ohlson is an associate professor in the Department of Leadership, School Counseling and Sport Management and Director of the Taylor Leadership Institute at the University of North Florida.

Dr. Jeanne Okrasinski is a professor at Eastern Illinois University. Her passion is mentoring teacher candidates to become amazing practitioners for Middle Level and EL students.

Neil O'Reilly began his teaching journey in 2017 in North Carolina, having spent 15 years in communication roles in government, politics, and academia. He teaches high school social studies.

Julie Padilla has been a social studies and literacy specialist in the Bronx for almost a decade. She continues to learn more with each day as an educator.

David Perrin began his career as an English teacher and is currently an administrator and instructional coach. He has written on education for EdWeek, The Atlantic, and other outlets.

Vicki Phelps, EdD, NBCT, has been teaching and leading gifted services for the last 20 years. She enjoys writing gifted resources, leading professional learning, and presenting at gifted conferences.

Daria Pizzuto, PhD, is a world language teacher at Bernards Township Schools and an adjunct professor at Seton Hall University. She researches teacher wellbeing and mindfulness in education.

Megan Porter is a fourth grade teacher in Tampa, Florida. Working at high needs schools throughout her career, she has been involved in the successful turnaround of an award-winning school.

Mallika Raman is a science professional educator and an adjunct professor of education at Saint Louis University. As a second-year educator, Ms. Raman has accomplished quite a bit.

Dr. Ernie Rambo, NBCT, is the programs coordinator for the Nevada National Board Professional Learning Institute. She supports National Board candidates and teacher leadership through co-facilitating virtual professional learning.

Lauralyn K. Randles is a doctoral candidate at Illinois State University. Her research and career focus primarily on school services for students with a visual impairment and multiple impairments.

Ms. Shannon Rice is a special education teacher in Jefferson, New York. Her interests include inclusive education and life skill instruction. She is a recipient of the Kappa Delta Pi Teacher of Honor Award.

Laura Roeker is a teacher and teacher educator in Madison, Wisconsin. She has taught third through sixth grade and is currently pursuing a PhD at UW-Madison in curriculum and instruction.

A former special educator, **René Roselle** won a Teaching Scholar Award while at the University of Connecticut. She is now an associate professor directing teacher preparation at Sacred Heart University.

Dr. Alisa M. Ross is an assistant professor. She has been an educator for over 17 years. She enjoys presenting at workshops and conferences and helping teachers hone their craft.

Kimberly A. Schwartz is a K–8 reading coach and has taught elementary, middle school, and college students. She is an adjunct for Saint Leo University and Hillsborough Community College.

Peggy Shannon-Baker, PhD, is an assistant professor in the Department of Curriculum, Foundations, and Reading at Georgia Southern University. Shannon-Baker's researches critical approaches to international education in teacher education programs.

Dr. Lynn Sikma is an assistant professor in the Department of Early Childhood, Elementary, Middle, Literacy, and Special Education in the Watson College of Education at the University of North Carolina Wilmington.

Aaron Sitze, a 2013 Illinois Teacher of the Year Finalist, teaches in Oregon, Illinois and leads the "changemaker pathway," a sequence of experiential courses rooted in civic engagement.

Lindsay Smith teaches multicultural and dynamic fourth graders in Oak Park, Illinois, a community located just outside Chicago. This is her 14th year in the classroom.

Alex Stampher is new to teaching adolescents. So far, she enjoys teaching high school English students as much as she enjoyed teaching college communications, composition, and English language students.

Calla Stroh has taught ELA and social studies, grades four through eight, for 11 years. She completed her master's degree in curriculum and instruction at Northern Illinois University.

Rashad J. Talley is a Chicago Public Schools veteran. He specializes in the professional development and mentorship of teachers as they pursue leadership. He emphasizes equity through student voice.

Raven Talley is a Chicago Public Schools administrator. She specializes in coaching new teachers and collaborating with educational professionals as it relates to the social emotional behaviors of young children.

Mary Frances Thomas, graduate of Knox College, has over 17 years of experience as an educator in Chicago Public Schools. She currently serves as assistant principal at an elementary school.

Katie Tice has been teaching kindergarten for four years. Katie knows each student who walks through her door has a story to tell, and all she must do is listen.

Dr. Jana Underwood is a lecturer in the College of Education at Georgia Southern University's Armstrong Campus. She is a former teacher, school and district administrator, and educational consultant.

Ingrid Wagner graduated from the University of Cincinnati with a bachelor's degree in early childhood education in April 2018. She is now a fourth and fifth grade teacher in Cincinnati.

Saroja R. Warner's Twitter profile speaks volumes – *"All about the children, maker of none, champion of every one, WestEd pays my bills, Ph.D., NBCT, Trini to de bone #edequityservant #troublemaker."*

Jennifer Wellberg works as a researcher at Duke University. She taught for the Department of Defense Education Activity. Her research focuses on early childhood development, school climate, and gifted education.

Clint Whitten is a co-lead secondary English teacher in Blacksburg, Virginia with his master's in curriculum and instruction from Virginia Tech. He sponsors several social justice clubs in his middle school.

Lynn Williams Leppich, MA (Cantab) MA, is an experienced teacher and teacher educator in northwestern Switzerland. She specializes in formative and summative assessment, differentiated instruction, and student engagement with literature.

Dr. Mary Rebecca Wells is an assistant professor in the College of Education at Georgia Southern University's Armstrong Campus.

Dustin Wright is principal of Franklin Middle School, member of principal advisory council for George Mason University Professional Development Schools, Virginia PTA Power Partner State Principal of the Year, 2018.

Jameelah R. Wright is a head teacher and assistant director at Three Stages Inc., founder of the Urban Flower Project, and a doctoral student and research assistant at Montclair State University.

Rebekah Young teaches at Woodland Middle School in North Port, Florida where she is the school's ESOL liaison. Rebekah has a reading specialist license and has taught for 15 years.